The Gender-Sensitive Univ

The Gender-Sensitive University explores the prevailing forces that pose obstacles to driving a gender-sensitive university, which include the emergence of far-right movements that seek to subvert advances towards gender equality and managerialism that promotes creeping corporatism.

This book demonstrates that awareness of gender equality and gender sensitivity are essential for pulling contemporary academia back from the brink. New forms of leadership are fundamental to reforming our institutions. The concept of a gender-sensitive university requires re-envisioning academia to meet these challenges, as does a different engagement of men and a shift towards fluidity in how gender is formulated and performed. Academia can only be truly gender sensitive if, learning from the past, it can avoid repeating the same mistakes and addressing existing and new biases. The book chapters analyse these challenges and advocate the possibilities to 'fix it forward' in all areas.

Representing ten EU countries and multiple disciplines, contributors to this volume highlight the evidence of persistent gender inequalities in academia, while advocating a blueprint for addressing them. The book will be of interest to a global readership of students, academics, researchers, practitioners, academic and political leaders and policymakers who share an interest in what it takes to establish gender-sensitive universities.

Eileen Drew coordinated the EU-Horizon 2020 Systemic Action for Gender Equality (SAGE) Project. She is a Professor in Trinity College, Dublin, and Director of the Trinity Centre for Gender Equality and Leadership.

Siobhán Canavan is a Visiting Research Associate in the Trinity Centre for Gender Equality and Leadership, Trinity College, Dublin.

Routledge Research in Gender and Society

Reframing Drag
Beyond Subversion and the Status Quo
Kayte Stokoe

Rape in the Nordic Countries
Continuity and Change
Edited by Marie Bruvik Heinskou, May-Len Skilbrei and Kari Stefansen

Refracting through Technologies
Bodies, Medical Technologies and Norms
Ericka Johnson

Young, Disabled and LGBT+
Voices, Identities and Intersections
Edited by Alex Toft and Anita Franklin

Transdisciplinary Feminist Research
Innovations in Theory, Method and Practice
Edited by Carol A. Taylor, Christina Hughes, and Jasmine B. Ulmer

Identity, Belonging, and Community in Men's Roller Derby
Dawn Fletcher

The Gender-Sensitive University
A Contradiction in Terms?
Edited by Eileen Drew and Siobhán Canavan

For more information about this series, please visit: www.routledge.com/sociology/series/SE0271

The Gender-Sensitive University

A Contradiction in Terms?

Edited by
Eileen Drew and Siobhán Canavan

Routledge
Taylor & Francis Group
LONDON AND NEW YORK

First published 2021
by Routledge
2 Park Square, Milton Park, Abingdon, Oxon OX14 4RN

and by Routledge
52 Vanderbilt Avenue, New York, NY 10017

Routledge is an imprint of the Taylor & Francis Group, an informa business

British Library Cataloguing-in-Publication Data
A catalogue record for this book is available from the British Library

Library of Congress Cataloging-in-Publication Data
Names: Drew, Eileen P., editor. | Canavan, Siobhán, editor.
Title: The gender-sensitive university : a contradiction in terms? / edited by Eileen Drew and Siobhán Canavan.
Description: Abingdon, Oxon ; New York, NY : Routledge, 2020. | Series: Routledge research in gender and society | Includes bibliographical references and index.
Identifiers: LCCN 2020012349 (print) | LCCN 2020012350 (ebook) | ISBN 9780367431174 (hardback) | ISBN 9781003001348 (ebook)
Subjects: LCSH: Sex discrimination in higher education—European Union countries. | Education, Higher—Social aspects—European Union countries. | Women in higher education—European Union countries. | Universities and colleges—European Union countries—Administration. | Universities and colleges—Faculty—Employment— Sex differences—European Union countries. | College environment—European Union countries.
Classification: LCC LC212.863.E85 G46 2020 (print) | LCC LC212.863.E85 (ebook) | DDC 378.1/982—dc23
LC record available at https://lccn.loc.gov/2020012349
LC ebook record available at https://lccn.loc.gov/2020012350

ISBN: 978-0-367-43117-4 (hbk)
ISBN: 978-0-367-53390-8 (pbk)
ISBN: 978-1-003-00134-8 (ebk)

Typeset in Times New Roman
by Apex CoVantage, LLC

"The pursuit of equality does not require the shifting
of anything from one basket to another. Equality is an
infinite resource, and there is enough of it for everyone.
On the flipside, discrimination costs the individuals that
suffer it and society as a whole dearly, in lack of personal
recognition, lack of meritocracy and loss of talent and
innovation. With the Gender Equality Strategy we are
anchoring gender equality at the core of EU policy
development. We aim to ensure that women do not have to
surmount additional hurdles to achieve what men have as
a given and are instead able to reach their full potential."

Quoted by Helena Dalli, Commissioner for Equality,
The European Commission 2020

The contents of this publication are the sole responsibility of the authors and do not necessarily reflect the opinion of the European Union.

This project received funding from the European Union's Horizon 2020 Research and Innovation Programme under grant agreement No 710534.

Contents

x   Contents

Figures

Tables

Notes on contributors

Jemimah Bailey is a Visiting Research Fellow in the Trinity Centre for Gender Equality and Leadership (TCGEL), Trinity College, Dublin, and also provides gender equality training, research and strategic services. Dr Bailey's professional interests are in gender equality and organisational change. She worked as a Postdoctoral Researcher on the FP7 FLOWS: Impact of Local Welfare Systems on Female Labour Force Participation and the EU-Horizon 2020 Systemic Action for Gender Equality (SAGE) projects.

Rita Bencivenga's research interests are in gender in higher education and ICT. After completing her PhD at the University of Paris X, Nanterre, she joined the Trinity Centre for Gender Equality and Leadership (TCGEL) at Trinity College, Dublin, as a Marie Skłodowska Curie Fellow. Her current research focuses on gender equality in higher education and ICT companies.

Jean Cahill is Head of Enterprise and Research Development, Technological University Dublin. She is a member of the university's Athena Swan SAT and represented TU Dublin on the Athena Swan National Committee Ireland. She was Project Manager for Dublin Institute of Technology's successful Athena Swan Bronze Award.

Siobhán Canavan is a Visiting Research Associate in the Trinity Centre for Gender Equality and Leadership (TCGEL), Trinity College, Dublin. She worked in the universities of Aberdeen, Robert Gordon, Abertay and Edinburgh as a lecturer in social work, sociology, women's studies, and counselling and psychotherapy. She was Head of the Counselling Service at Aberdeen University and has worked as a counsellor in private practice. Her research interests have focused on sexual violence.

Sara Clavero is a Senior Researcher at the Centre for Equality and Diversity, Technological University Dublin. With a doctorate in politics specialising in gender, her research experience is in gender politics, law and EU policies. Through the EU-Horizon 2020 Systemic Action for Gender Equality (SAGE) project, she applies her interests to the study of gender in academia.

Annie Doona is the President of Dun Laoghaire Institute of Art Design and Technology. Her research interests include women in film and gender and higher education strategy. She is a quality reviewer for EQ-Arts in Europe; Chair of the Board of Screen Ireland, a member of Women in Film and Television and the European Women Rectors Association (EWORA).

Eileen Drew is a Professor and Director of the Trinity Centre for Gender Equality and Leadership (TCGEL) at Trinity College, Dublin. Among her research interests are gender equality and the labour market, work-life balance and gender in academic leadership. For many years she has been involved in gender-related research, training and consultancy for national and EU agencies. She was the project coordinator of the EU-Horizon 2020 Systemic Action for Gender Equality (SAGE).

Julie Dunne is Head of Enterprise and Research Development, Technological University Dublin. Dr Dunne is a member of the university's Athena Swan SAT and represented TU Dublin on the Athena Swan National Committee Ireland. She was Project Manager for the Dublin Institute of Technology's Athena Swan successful Bronze Award application.

Yvonne Galligan is Professor of Comparative Politics and Director of Equality, Diversity and Inclusion in Technological University Dublin. Her research interests focus on how power and privilege intersect with gender and other identity-related inequalities in public organisations. She serves on the editorial boards of the *European Journal of Politics and Gender* and the *International Political Science Review*.

Jane Gray-Sadran is a Lecturer in English at the Institute of Political Sciences (Sciences Po), Bordeaux. Her PhD in anglophone studies focused on questions of gender and national identity in contemporary Scottish literature. She was in charge of gender equality in her institute and managed the EU-Horizon 2020 Systemic Action for Gender Equality (SAGE) Project for Sciences Po, Bordeaux.

Jadranka Gvozdanović is Chair of the LERU Thematic Group for Equality, Diversity and Inclusion and Professor of Slavic Linguistics at Heidelberg University. Her specialist interests are university structures and structural change in the realm of equal opportunities, change processes in language, information processing and social construals. She contributed to LERU papers on gender.

Jeff Hearn is Senior Professor, Gender Studies, Örebro University, Sweden; Professor of Sociology, University of Huddersfield, UK; Professor Emeritus, Hanken School of Economics, Finland; Professor Extraordinarius, University of South Africa; Fellow of Academy of Social Sciences (UK), and Honorary Doctor, social sciences, Lund University, Sweden.

Liisa Husu is a Finnish sociologist and Professor of Gender Studies at Örebro University, Sweden, and affiliated researcher at the Department of Management and Organisation at Hanken School of Economics, Finland. Her research, publications and expertise include gender in science, academia and knowledge production, especially gender dynamics and inequalities in scientific careers, organisations and policy.

Mary Kinahan is an Organisational Psychologist and Lecturer in Organisational Behaviour and Human Resource Management at Technological University Dublin. She is a member of the university's Athena SWAN SAT and EDI steering group and practice network. She is involved in gender-related research, including the EU-Horizon 2020 DIAMOND Project. Her main research interest is women and leadership.

Claire Marshall is the Equality Officer at TCD. She previously worked as Programme Manager at the Trinity Centre for Gender Equality and Leadership (TCGEL) where she project managed the EU-Horizon 2020 Systemic Action for Gender Equality (SAGE) Project. Her professional interests are in structural approaches to equality and diversity, encompassing policy, strategy and implementation.

Tony McMahon is the Director of Diversity and Inclusion at Trinity College, Dublin, with responsibility for promoting and advancing a values-based approach to diversity across the university. A key focus of his role is to guide the development and implementation of an authoritative diversity strategy. He co-authored TCD's first gender pay audit in 2016.

Tom Millar is Professor of Astrophysics at Queen's University Belfast, where he was Dean of Engineering and Physical Sciences. He chaired QUB's Athena SWAN institutional applications and co-chaired the investigation into the QUB gender pay gap. He was elected a member of the Royal Irish Academy in 2011.

Mathias Wullum Nielsen is an Associate Professor in the Department of Sociology, University of Copenhagen, and holds a PhD from Aarhus University. His research focuses on gender and social stratification in science. He undertook postdoctoral research in gendered innovations at Stanford University and is currently a part of the European Commission's Gendered Innovations 2 Expert Group.

Marion Paoletti is an Associate Professor in political science at the University of Bordeaux and Researcher at the Emile Durkheim Research Centre. She works on participatory policies and the implementation of parity in politics. She has been in charge of the gender equality policy at Bordeaux University. She recently engaged in a discussion of the effects of the #MeToo movement published in *Nouvelle revue du travail*.

Andrew Power is the Registrar and Vice President for Equality and Diversity at the Institute of Art Design and Technology in Dublin. He completed his PhD in the School of Law at Queens University, Belfast. His research interests and publications are in the area of technology and society.

Suzanne Quintin is a PhD student in sociology at the University of Rennes 2. Her main research interests include gender studies, the sociology of public action and the sociology of organisations. Her doctoral studies focus on a comparison between two territorial communities in France and Portugal to analyse gender relations in public administration and the appropriation of gender policies by public officials.

Rodrigo Rosa holds a PhD in sociology from the University Institute of Lisbon (ISCTE-IUL). He is a research fellow at ISCTE-IUL and a research member of the EU-Horizon 2020 Systemic Action for Gender Equality (SAGE) Project. His main research interests include gender perspectives, the sociology of family and work, social theory, fundamental and applied research, comparative analysis and mixed methods research design.

Laure Squarcioni is an Associate Researcher at the Emile Durkheim Research Centre, Sciences Po, Bordeaux. Dr Squarcioni joined the EU-Horizon 2020 funded Systemic Action on Gender Equality (SAGE) Project as a postdoctoral researcher. Her research focuses on gender equality and on political representation. She is currently working as a consultant on gender equality and discrimination in the work environment.

Foreword

It seems quaint to contemporary ears to be reminded that there was a time not so very long ago when the admission of women to institutes of higher education was a subject of earnest debate and considerable dispute among the intellectuals of the day. The notion of gender equality had to fight its way on to university agendas the world over. So how are we doing today? Has the battle been won or have we still work to do?

This book helps us to answer those questions. It brings together scholarly writing from across Europe reflecting a wide range of disciplines and perspectives about the timely movement for gender equality in higher education institutions. It puts down a marker for what has been achieved, most notably through EU framework programmes towards structural change. It offers examples of innovative practices and makes a strong case for shifting the emphasis from 'fixing the women' to transforming universities themselves. The centrality of feminism, in both theory and in practice, are underlined, as is the key role of committed institutions such as the European Commission, in supporting this process. Creating and taking opportunities to come together develops creative synergies, as women slowly move into their rightful place as leaders in academia. Some of the ideas and practices examined in this book would have been unthinkable 20 years ago. It is a short time for so much to change and, as a new generation of academics, students and activists take up the work, this book forms part of the developing story of trying to achieve gender balance in academia and what its potential can offer us. There are important and telling narratives of lived experience, ideas, evidence, examples, hurdles, barriers and successes.

Universities are places where gender sensitivity can and should flourish in teaching, research, management and leadership. Even more importantly they are places where it must flourish if intellectual life is to draw with any credibility from the widest wells of talent. There is good news here, for a lot of solid groundwork has been done. The concept of a gender-sensitive university is now a reality. The future holds greater possibilities for gender equality than ever before if we keep doing what many of us have done for years within the higher education sector: namely, insisting and campaigning for gender equality, challenging and overturning the embedded attitudes, perceptions, practices, procedures and prejudices which have held back not just women but communities, countries, cultures and humanity itself. I am delighted to recommend this important and necessary book. It contains something for everyone who is interested in the possibilities and potential for achieving gender sensitivity in higher education. It will help us navigate from where we are to where we need to get to.

Professor Mary McAleese,
Chancellor,
Trinity College, Dublin, Ireland

Chapter 1

An overview of gender inequality in EU universities

Rodrigo Rosa, Eileen Drew and Siobhán Canavan

Introduction

Gender equality has become an increasingly important policy requirement for academic institutions. Faced with enduring inequalities between female and male academics and administrators at all levels, university leaders have been charged with defining action strategies to ensure the effective implementation of structural measures to reduce and eliminate gender bias in their organisations. Universities play a crucial role in promoting gender equality and diversity; the last 20 years has produced a range of positive changes, through an enlarged pool of highly qualified women in academia and the wider labour market. Notwithstanding these positive developments, universities are structured around gender regimes where 'the current state of play is reflected in the macro politics of gender' (Connell 1987, 20). Gender regimes continue to impact on: who is recruited to do what work; what social divisions exist in the workplace and away from it, particularly in the domestic sphere; how emotional relations are conducted in the workplace; and how institutions relate to one another in relation to gender sensitivity. Universities are gendered since, like any other organisation, they are still defined by the fact that 'advantage and disadvantage, exploitation and control, action and emotion, meaning and identity, are patterned through and in terms of a distinction between male and female, masculine and feminine' (Acker 1990, 146).

EU policy context

Equality between women and men is one of the European Union's founding values, dating back to 1957 when the principle of equal pay for equal work became part of the Treaty of Rome. In accordance with the Treaty, the European Commission (2015) published the *Strategic Engagement for Gender Equality 2016–19*, setting out the framework for the Commission's future work towards improving gender equality. The strategic engagement focused on the following five priority areas:

1 increasing female labour market participation and equal economic independence;
2 reducing the gender pay, earnings and pension gaps and thus fighting poverty among women;

3   promoting equality between women and men in decision-making;
4   combating gender-based violence and protecting and supporting victims;
5   promoting gender equality and women's rights across the world.

The document set out objectives in each of these priority areas and identified more than 30 concrete actions, reaffirming the European Commission's commitment to gender mainstreaming through a gender equality perspective integrated into all EU policies as well as into EU funding programmes. The strategic engagement also supported the implementation of the gender equality dimension in the *Europe 2020 Strategy*. Progress is reported annually and presented in annual reports on equality between women and men (for example, European Commission 2019a).

EU policy framing and leading gender equality in research—initially STEM

The new millennium saw the emergence of a number of significant reports and policy directions from the European Commission, from key actors such as the European Technology Assessment Network (ETAN), and cross-EU policy formulation on women and science and technology specifically. The strategic objective of the European Research Area (ERA) required action to promote gender equality in science, recognising the need to promote research by, for and about women to optimise the value that they could contribute to European society (European Commission 2001).

The ETAN Report (European Commission 2000) described the continuous leakage of women at each level of the academic ladder, on which women comprised less than 10 per cent of the leaders in the 'scientific system', despite the fact that half the Science, Technology, Engineering and Mathematics (STEM) graduates were women. It pinpointed the forms of discrimination, often unconscious, against women and identified the key problems faced by women in scientific careers. The flawed operation of the peer review system was highlighted along with the low level of engagement by women in shaping scientific policy and setting the agenda in the top committees of the EU and of member states. The report advocated a sustainable improvement of women's standing in science and research, requiring a significant transformation of science and scientific institutions (European Commission 2000).

The WIRDEM (Women in Research Decision-Making) expert group report (2008) identified nomination procedures, cultural barriers and funding limitations as hindering factors in the progress of women in their academic careers. It reviewed member states' policies and existing procedures for evaluating and promoting researchers to senior positions, outlining examples of good practice at national and institutional levels and proposed recommendations for more targeted actions at the European level, arguing that European research and higher education institutions could no longer afford to exclude potential innovators.

The Helsinki Group Gender in Research and Innovation was established by the European Commission in 1999 as an advisory group to help to overcome this disadvantage of women in STEM. In 2017, the Helsinki Group was transformed into the Standing Working Group on Gender in Research and Innovation (SWG GRI) of the European Research Area and Innovation Committee (ERAC). It consists of representatives from member states, associated countries and the European Commission. The group sought to integrate a gender dimension into the mainstream of the research policy process, starting with the benchmarking of national research policies, in which the gender dimension should be integrated in all the indicators to be developed. The overall objective of the Group is to advise the Council and the European Commission on policies and initiatives on gender equality in Research and Innovation, for the benefit of scientists, research institutions, universities, businesses and society at large.

In response to these gender issues, a European Research Area (ERA) Survey pointed to actions that research organisations could take, such as recruitment and promotion measures, targets to ensure gender balance in recruitment committees, flexible career trajectories (for example, schemes after career breaks), work-life balance measures and support for leadership development (European Commission 2015). According to their survey conducted in 2014, around 36 per cent of research performing organisations had introduced Gender Equality Plans (GEPs) in 2013. The gendering of indicators on human resources in science was to be tackled in three ways: top-down (the introduction of the gender variable in the collection of data on human resources in research and development), bottom-up (organising existing data collected at national level, and developing indicators on the basis of this data), and the gendering of the benchmarking exercise. In summary:

> European research policy has been a model for 'gender mainstreaming' (consideration of gender in all aspects of policy) since 1999. . . . Some Member States were already paying attention to the issue, while others took their lead from the Commission, with more or less enthusiasm depending on their cultural and historical backgrounds. . . . Over the years, three research Framework Programmes supported activities to increase the number and role of women scientists, as well as to mainstream gender in the content of research. Despite the fact that the momentum for gender equality had been slowing down, progress towards a European Research Area 'by/for/on women' was continuing, albeit more slowly than previously. Therefore, a new policy direction was decided upon by the Commission. The new focus for activities was on the research institutions and organisations where women in science work, rather than just on the women themselves. 'Fixing the administration' became the new objective.
>
> (European Commission 2010, 12)

The stocktaking of Women in Science policy by the European Commission 1999–2009 illustrates how the European Commission 'provided the impulse, and acted as a catalyst and multiplier, shaping and coordinating the efforts' (European Commission 2010, 7).

Despite the global feminisation of the third-level student population as a striking feature of higher education over the last 40 years, women are not progressing
at the same rate as men in their academic careers. At the leadership level, women
accounted for only 24 per cent of grade A professors (professorial chairs) and
22 per cent of heads of institutions in the higher education sector across the EU
in 2017, thereby indicating the need to take action and identify good practices in
the sector to attract and promote women in research and innovation (European
Commission 2019b). The European Commission's *SHE figures 2018* reveal that
a range of gender differences and inequalities persist in research and innovation.
Whilst women were once under-represented at doctoral level, in 2018 they made
up 48 per cent of doctoral graduates in the EU-28. However, in 2018, women
accounted for just 29 per cent of doctoral graduates in engineering, manufactur-
ing and construction and only 21 per cent of those graduating from computing
(European Commission 2019b).

Striking gender inequalities persist in career advancement and participation in
academic decision-making. Despite significant progress in their level of education
relative to men in recent decades, women are increasingly under-represented as
they move up the stages of an academic career (Figure 1.1). The pool of female
graduate talents has increased, but the availability of female role models as careers
progress is still sparse, reflecting the differential in career progression by women
and men. Despite the growth in numbers of female undergraduates and postgradu-
ates, the career trajectories of men and women in academia continue to show significant inequalities. Gender trajectories take the form of a scissors-shaped trend,
which shows a significant loss of female potential after the award of doctoral
degrees. Work-life imbalance is one among the major barriers to gender equality

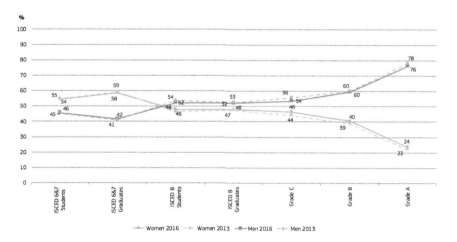

Figure 1.1 Percentage of men and women in a typical academic career, students
and academic staff (EU-28) 2013–2016

Source: SHE Figures, European Commission 2019

since it still most frequently impedes the career advancement of women in academia, 13 per cent of whom work part-time, compared with 8 per cent of male academics (European Commission 2019b). Women's representation diminishes significantly during academic careers so that the percentage of women academic staff at grade A (7.4%) is less than half of the corresponding proportion for men (16.7%). This results in: far fewer female academics in more powerful positions; a gender pay gap; gender imbalance in the composition of research teams; and a higher proportion of women, especially those in junior academic positions or other positions, relying on third-party funding, employed on precarious working contracts (European Commission 2019b). These gender differences are even more acute among students/staff in science and engineering disciplines (Figure 1.2).

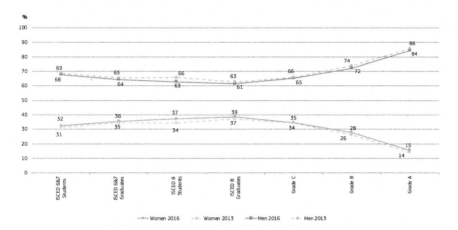

Figure 1.2 Percentage of men and women in a typical academic career in science and engineering, students and academic staff (EU-28) 2013–2016

Source: SHE Figures, European Commission 2019

Internationally, the leaky pipe metaphor (Alper 1993) has been coined to represent the progressive decrease in the presence of women in academia at each career stage and this pattern is all too evident in the SHE Scissors Diagrams (Figures 1.1 and 1.2). UPGEM (Understanding Puzzles in the Gendered European Map) noted with concern that well-qualified female scientists often leave the research system prematurely and those who stay rarely, or never, reach the top-level positions (grade A professors) or achieve distinguished careers in research and development in the same way as their male counterparts do (UPGEM 2008). The underlying causes of this phenomenon have been studied extensively across the EU with the general conclusion that contemporary academic careers, through various mechanisms, reward members of the male gender (Badaloni *et al* 2008). Policies for the recruitment, retention, promotion and leadership of researchers in EU research bodies often affect the career progression of female researchers adversely, as illustrated by the differential exit of female researchers at, or after, their doctoral studies across the EU. Moreover, when it comes to appointing skilled professionals to decision-making positions in national research and academic institutions, women are already at a disadvantage because of their smaller numbers, which in turn prevents them from participating more equitably in the highest echelons of their institutions.

US policy interventions for gender equality in STEM

The need for institutional transformation, involving organisational and cultural change within research bodies and universities was first recognised outside Europe, most visibly in US initiatives. In 1981, the US Congress adopted the National Science Foundation Authorization and Science and Technology Equal Opportunities Act. Under this law, the Director of the National Science Foundation (NSF) is required to send Congress and government officials a statistical report on the numbers of women and other minorities (*sic*) in employment and training in the science and engineering sectors every two years. Since 2001, the US National Science Foundation's pioneer ADVANCE (Increasing the Participation and Advancement of Women in Academic Science and Engineering Careers) programme has successfully encouraged major universities in the US to change their policies and procedures for recruitment, retention, tenure and promotion, in order to improve the local gender climate and the situation of women faculty in STEM disciplines (Bilimoria and Liang 2012).

The academic institutions funded through the five-year ADVANCE Institutional Transformation Awards, defined and implemented comprehensive customised action plans to address institutional structures and organisational barriers. This was undertaken through supports to women academics' career development, leadership and empowerment initiatives, work-life balance and the engagement of institutions' academic governance at the highest level. Significant results were achieved by many of the higher education institutions through the development of best practices, effective networking and dissemination strategies, and innovative transformational approaches.

These efforts provided useful examples of successful practices for the EU-funded FP7 INstitutional Transformation for Effecting Gender Equality in Research (INTEGER) partnership (2011–2015), which developed links with US institutions and practitioners involved in the ADVANCE programme (for example, the University of Michigan), and the knowledge and experience gained by them was available to the INTEGER project partners.

EU structural change-driven policy interventions in academia

In its report *Structural Change in Research Institutions*, the European Commission (2012a) argued that gender-aware management of universities and research organisations would have a positive impact on policies and practices in recruitment, promotion and retention of both women and men, ultimately benefiting the quality of the research itself. Furthermore, the report stressed that progress in integrating gender in research and innovation requires firm and sustained top-level commitment. The recommendations for different constituent institutions, aimed at universities and scientific institutions, are as follows:

1   ensure a gender dimension is integrated into the undergraduate and postgraduate curricula, across the university (particularly in engineering and science);
2   adopt an Equality Plan and include audit results (gender disaggregated statistics) in annual reports. These should include the gender pay gap, staff statistics and senior committee membership;
3   sign up to and follow a set of good practices;
4   up-skilling for career development and content of research.

Founded in 2002, the League of European Research Universities (LERU) is an association of 21 leading research-intensive universities that share the values of high-quality teaching within an environment of internationally competitive research. In 2012, LERU issued recommendations for governments, funders of research, academic publishers and, most notably, universities to address gender deficits through embarking upon actions. These sought commitment at the top and throughout the institution to gender equality; development or implementation of a gender strategy and/or action plan with the support of all divisions and levels within the university; ensuring sufficient funding for all gender equality activity to enable long term planning of gender equality activity to achieve structural change; selecting the right mix of gender-specific career development measures and gender-neutral work-life balance measures; transparency, accountability and monitoring to ensure successful implementation and improvement where needed; and promoting and supporting a gender dimension in research, taking into account the specificities of particular research fields (LERU 2012).

In the European Commission's *SHE figures 2018*, the European Commissioner for Research, Science and Innovation stated:

There is progress but it is slow. And we still have a long way to go to achieve full gender equality. . . . We cannot sit back and assume that having planted the seeds of gender equality, the positive trends will continue. . . . What we need is a complete cultural change, which requires systematic and coordinated actions, education and strong political commitment by all actors involved. . . . If we want to take scientific excellence to the next level; if we want to deliver science-based solutions to the many urgent and pressing global challenges, we need all talents in play. . . . I therefore invite you all to act as ambassadors of change to close the gender gap. Together, we will succeed.

(European Commission 2019b, 4)

Gendered research and funding

Research funding success rates in most European countries are lower for women than for male team leaders by an average of 3 per cent (European Commission 2019b). Although this gap has narrowed over time, gender differences persist. Across the EU, the gender gap (computed as men's success rate minus women's success rate) has decreased by 2.4 per cent since 2010, though men continue to have a higher success rate than women, outstripping them by 4.4 per cent in funding applications to national programmes (with 31.8 per cent male and 27.4 per cent female success rates respectively). There are, however, important national variations within the EU-28, with gender gaps ranging from 12.9 to 0.6 per cent (European Commission 2014).

Linked to the under-representation of women in funded research, female researchers remain under-represented in scientific authorship. Less than one-third (32%) of all publications named a woman as corresponding author in 2017 (European Commission 2019b). This is underlined by a relentless absence of a firm gender perspective in most research 'in the 2013–2017 period, 1.79 per cent of all research in the EU-28 included a sex or gender dimension in its research content' (European Commission 2019b, 176).

LERU identified the lack of a gender dimension in research as one of four priority areas in which universities could usefully undertake gender actions (LERU 2012). In 2015, LERU launched an advisory paper *Gendered Research and Innovation: Integrating Sex and Gender Analysis into the Research Process* (LERU 2015), showing how gendered research and innovation is an under-recognised issue, too often ignored in research design, process, content and implementation. LERU highlighted the role of social sciences and humanities (SSH) research in attending to these processes and recommended that: LERU universities lead by example; governments include a gender dimension in research policies and programmes; and that the approach taken at EU level is continued and strengthened. The importance of journals setting standards for the inclusion of information on gender in research, along with clear guidelines for authors, were also identified as positive actions (LERU 2015).

Today, university leaders face the challenge of achieving sustainable and institution-wide change towards gender equality in an age when neoliberal transformations have created a governance model for universities that prioritises economic rationality (see Chapters 2 and 11). Women have demonstrated their scholarly excellence alongside their male counterparts, yet the overt and subtle gender mechanisms identified throughout this book prevent them from making significant progress up the career ladder in an increasingly competitive academic environment, which often privileges individual success over collaborative effort. Furthermore, managerialist tools, such as the demanding measurement of scientific excellence through the 'h index', create increasing challenges to achieving gender sensitivity in academia (Paradeise *et al* 2009) (see Chapter 8).

Ending gender inequalities in academia and research: policy developments

The European Union explicitly committed to mainstreaming gender in its *Communication on women and science* (European Commission 1999) and the gender mainstreaming principle was integrated for the first time into the Fifth Framework Programme (FP5), running from 1998 to 2002. Gender equality in science was understood in terms of three dimensions: to promote research 'by, for and about women'. During the course of FP5, the European Commission required that studies produce a gender impact assessment (GIA) to monitor the way in which gender issues were being addressed (European Commission 2001; Braithwaite 2001).

It was in the context of Framework Programme 6 (FP6) (2002–2006) that gender mainstreaming was formally integrated into the EU research policy. Two main objectives were established: a target of 40 per cent women's representation on committees, groups and panels and the integration of the gender dimension in research content. Based on the results and recommendations of the FP5 Gender Impact Assessment, in FP6 the European Commission adopted guidelines for proposals to ensure better attention to the gender dimension in research. Gender monitoring studies were planned and implemented so that the results could feed into the next framework programme. Gender Action Plans were made mandatory for networks of excellence and integrated projects. In addition, under FP6, a total of 39 gender-specific projects exploring this theme were funded (European Commission 2009). Those projects analysed the factors that facilitated or inhibited the incorporation of the gender dimension in research, developed practical tools to help researchers and produced recommendations to help scientists, funding agencies, research organisations, governments and other stakeholders. The aim was to ensure that sex and gender differences were given the attention that they deserved. However, monitoring reports showed that, despite the significant contribution made in FP6, in terms of progress towards gender equality, there remained much scope for improvement. Hence, more and continued efforts were required to realise further progress towards meeting the objectives of FP6 (European Commission 2008).

A study analysing the implementation of gender mainstreaming in FP6 identified significant resistance to gender initiatives within the Directorate General for Research and Innovation. This contributed to addressing obstacles to effective implementation (Mergaert and Lombardo 2014). These included explicit and implicit, individual and institutional, resistance such as a lack of adequate capacity-building for gender mainstreaming. This in turn revealed institutional resistance by not prioritising gender mainstreaming and the fact that the voices of gender experts were not allowed any significant influence on the policy process.

In FP7 (2007–2013) the EU reinforced efforts to support gender research stressing that:

> adequate attention should be paid to gender mainstreaming, as well as to, inter alia, working conditions, transparency of recruitment processes, and

career development as regards the researchers recruited on projects and programmes funded under the actions of this programme.

(Council of the European Union 2006, 250)

Numerous projects addressing this issue were funded during FP7. One notable example was the funding of the expert group *Innovation through Gender*, convened by the European Commission in 2011. The group involved more than 60 experts from across Europe, the US and Canada. Its goal was twofold: to provide scientists and engineers with practical methods for sex and gender analysis and to develop case studies as concrete illustrations of how sex and gender analysis leads to new ideas and excellence in research. The results, initiated at Stanford University in 2009, were published in *Gendered Innovations* (Schiebinger 2013). The Gendered Innovations website is a key source for scientists seeking to integrate a gender dimension into their research. More recently, the European Commission, under the H2020 programme, decided to provide funding to the network with the aim of updating and expanding *Gendered Innovations/Innovation Through Gender* (European Commission Decision C (2019) 4575 of 2 July 2019).

Ending gender inequalities in academia has been one of the priorities of *A Reinforced European Research Area Partnership for Excellence and Growth* (ERA) (European Commission 2012b), a key objective of which was to remove barriers to recruitment, retention and career progression for female researchers, alongside addressing a better gender balance in decision-making and strengthening the gender dimension in research programmes. Member states were encouraged to correct these inequalities by creating a legal and policy environment that created incentives for institutional change in research, through Gender Equality Plans (GEPs) (European Commission 2012b, 13). Other examples of gender equality provisions are integrated into national excellence evaluation frameworks, as illustrated by Germany's Excellence Initiative (Riegraf and Weber 2017).

The implementation of national GEPs is crucial in tackling gender inequalities in academia and helps to explain variations among EU member states. In 2016, GEP implementation ranged from under 20 per cent in Slovakia and Bulgaria to 60 per cent in Ireland and over 90 per cent in Sweden, Germany and the United Kingdom (European Commission 2019b, 111). Despite this variation, the implementation of GEPs is not unrelated to progress achieved at university governance level over the last decade. Among members of the European University Association (EUA), the proportion of women rectors has increased slowly, from 9.5 per cent in 2010 to 13 per cent in 2013 and 14.3 per cent in 2019. Women account for one-quarter of the vice-rectors in 2019 (Jorgensen 2019). According to the *SHE figures 2018* (European Commission 2019b), women made up more than one-quarter (27%) of educational institution board members across the EU in 2017 and their representation among heads of institutions in the higher education sector increased slightly from 20.1 per cent in 2014 to 21.7 per cent in 2017. In contrast, data from the EUA suggest that, while barriers to women's career advancement hinder their access to the top level of the academic hierarchy, as rectors and presidents, there is more gender equality when a professorship is not a requirement for high-level management positions, such as head of international office, human resources, communication, research or quality assurance (Jorgensen 2019). More gender balanced top management leadership teams are a foundational step in achieving gender-sensitivity in higher education, since the success of any policy intervention is highly dependent on how university leaders engage in promoting gender equality (see Chapter 11).

In addition, tools for the integration of gender in research were also developed under FP7, including the *Recommendations for Integrating Gender Analysis into Research* (IGAR) tool, developed as part of the GENDER-NET project. GENDER-NET produced a set of indicators to measure the degree of integration of gender analysis into research, drawing upon the Yellow Window (a gender equality consultancy company) toolkit and training for EU gender-funded research (European Commission 2011). This widely used toolkit provides an overall introduction to gender in research and practical tools on how to make research gender sensitive, with examples of gendered contents in different disciplines, such as health, energy, nanosciences, environment, transport. Other projects funded under FP7 produced a set of guidelines and recommendations for the integration of a gender dimension of science. One example is the GenSET project, aimed at developing practical ways in which gender knowledge and gender mainstreaming expertise could be incorporated within European science institutions. In 2010, GenSET published recommendations for action on the gender dimension in science (Buitendijk *et al* 2010).

Similar tools were produced by the Gendering the Academy and Research: Combating Career Instability and Asymmetries (GARCIA) project which covered the integration of a gender-sensitive approach in teaching and research and the Effective Gender Equality in Research and the Academia (EGERA) project report on *Good Practices of Gender Sensitive Research: Guidelines and Information Sheet*, which provides background and criteria for identifying good examples of gender-sensitive research initiatives and the INstitutional Transformation for Effecting Gender Equality in Research (INTEGER) project *Tools for Action*. In the EU-Horizon 2020 programme, the gender dimension is explicitly integrated from the outset in many of the specific calls. Under this research framework initiative, the Systemic Action for Gender Equality Project (SAGE) provided the design and implementation of tailored GEPs structured around a wheel model for GEPs focusing on four quadrants: institutional governance, engendering knowledge, career progression and work-life balance (Figure 1.3).

GEPs were developed by SAGE implementing partners: University Institute of Lisbon (ISCTE-IUL), International University of Sarajevo (IUS), Kadir Has University, Istanbul (KHAS), Sciences Po Bordeaux (SciPo) and University of Brescia (UNIBS). The SAGE wheel model includes measures to achieve equality in each of the four quadrants. While identifying the causes of problems that occurred throughout the SAGE project's life and ways to avoid those problems in later project stages, SAGE partners have learned important lessons. First, it

Figure 1.3 SAGE project Gender Equality Plan (GEP) wheel model

is crucial to avoid gender binaries to address intersectional diversity. Second, actions must be data driven, designed to be gender neutral, tailored to the micro or macro environment in which they operate and strategically designed to align with the institution's core values. Third, it is important to involve men as champions/ active participants in the transformational change process. Fourth, actions need the support from top level as well as key allies, for example, Human Resources and Equality/Diversity offices, to influence gender-related policy and overcome resistance. Fifth, it is important to apply an active communication strategy, conveying information on actions and their benefits to the widest possible community of stakeholders. Sixth, while responding to the local context and specific needs, acting at institutional and school/departmental levels, making use of and/ or extending existing training and development opportunities, GEPs can prioritise unconscious bias training. Finally, it is crucial to pay attention to the unintended consequences of interventions, since a measure that seems beneficial for a portion of the target group, may not be for others. For example, during the implementation of the GEP at ISCTE-IUL, heads of departments involved in the elaboration of new class schedules needed to ensure that a redistribution of teaching hours, sensitive to the situation of parents with young children, would not adversely impact their colleagues without young children.

Conclusion

As this chapter demonstrates, the path towards gender equality in higher education has been neither simple nor linear. Creating a gender-sensitive university demands both behavioural and attitudinal change, both of which can be guided by innovative thinking, legislative frameworks and a commitment to change through data gathering, monitoring, training, leadership, networks and synergies of the most unexpected kinds. Challenging the prevailing wisdom, especially in institutions with a long history, can be lonely work, as the chapters in this book testify. The aim of this book is to put down a marker for the journey towards a gender-sensitive university to avoid this aspiration becoming a tautological dream.

A chronological outline of the emergence of gender-equality policies in higher education institutions and the drive towards the creation of a gender-sensitive academia forms the backbone of this book, in which Chapter 1 (Rosa, Drew and Canavan) has set the scene. Chapters 2 to 9 deal with the ongoing obstacles, barriers and issues that characterise gender-insensitive universities. Chapters 10 to 14 challenge the continued gendering of the social and academic order. They promote mechanisms to interrogate and address this, thereby envisioning the emergence of gender-sensitive institutions.

Chapter 2 (Rosa and Clavero) outlines the challenges of neoliberalism and precarity for achieving gender sensitivity and documents the contributions of intersectionality and feminist research. Chapter 3 (Mathias Wullum Nielsen) deals with gendered recruitment, followed by Chapter 4 (Kinahan, Dunne and Cahill), which elaborates on gendered career progression. Chapter 5 (Drew and Marshall) expands on the gendered reality of work-life balance as being more aspirational than real. Further chapters demonstrate and question the fluidity of gendered institutions leading to policy interventions that could influence their gender sensitivity. Instrumental in this process is the need to heighten awareness of sexual harassment and violence, addressed in Chapter 6 (Paoletti, Quintin, Gray-Sadran and Squarcioni) through a detailed analysis of a French campus-based case study. Chapter 7 highlights the importance of conducting gender pay gap analyses (Galligan, McMahon and Millar) in higher education institutions.

The significance of men and their masculinities, in shaping and perpetuating a fixed-gender regime in academia, is examined in Chapter 8 (Hearn), whilst the complex terrain of unconscious bias is explored and exposed in Chapter 9 (Gvozdanović and Bailey). Change management for gender equality represents a critical process in the creation of gender-sensitive institutions and is addressed in Chapter 10 (Bailey and Drew). Fundamental to this transition is the future leadership of universities. Chapter 11 (Power) places this in a wider context which embraces alternative models of leadership, better orientated to gender sensitivity. In Chapter 12 Doona explores the vital role of research funding as a driver towards achieving gender equality in academia. The potentially destructive, subtle actions and inactions that can impede the academic careers of women are addressed in Chapter 13 (Husu). Finally, Chapter 14 (Bencivenga and Drew) represents the composite learning from SAGE partners and other gender experts, whilst looking ahead to a future in which all higher education institutions are gender-sensitised and progressive in their pursuit of research innovation and excellence.

References

Acker, J. (1990) Hierarchies, jobs, bodies: A theory of gendered organizations, *Gender & Society*, 4 (2), 139–158, doi.org/10.1177/089124390004002002
Alper, J. (1993) The pipeline is leaking women all the way along, *Science*, 260, 409–411, doi.org/10.1126/science.260.5106.409
Badaloni, S., Drace, C., Gia, O., Levorato, M. and Vidotto, F. (eds) (2008) *Under-representation of women in science and technology*, Cleup, Padova.
Bilimoria, D. and Liang, X. (2012) *Gender equity in science and engineering: Advancing change in higher education*, Routledge, Abingdon, Oxon.
Braithwaite, M. (2001) *Gender mainstreaming in the European commission: Explaining the roller coaster of progress and regression*, Engender, DUP, Brussels.
Buitendijk, S., Revuelta, C. C., Corda, D., Flodström, A., Holdcroft, A., Hunter, J., James, A., Kitchen, N., Schraudner, M., Sjørup, K., Rice, C. and Tarrach, R. (2010) *Recommendations for action on the gender dimension in science*. Available at: www.genderportal. eu/sites/default/files/resource_pool/genSET_consensus_report.pdf
Connell, R. (1987) *Gender and power: Society, the person and sexual politics*, Polity Press, Cambridge.
Council of the European Union (2006) Council decision concerning the specific programme: 'Ideas' implementing the seventh framework programme of the European community for research, technological development and demonstration activities (2007 to 2013), *Official Journal of the European Union*, L400, 243–271.
European Commission (1999) *'Women and science' mobilising women to enrich European research*, European Commission, Brussels. Available at: https://ec.europa.eu/research/swafs/pdf/pub_gender_equality/g_wo_co_en.pdf
European Commission (2000) *Science policies in the European Union—promoting excellence through mainstreaming gender equality*, report from the ETAN (European Technology Assessment Network) Expert Working Group on Women and Science, European Commission, Luxembourg.
European Commission (2001) *Women and science: The gender dimension as a leverage for reforming science*, SEC(2001)771, 15 May. Available at: www.cordis.lu/improving/women/documents.htm
European Commission (2008) *Benchmarking policy measures for gender equality in science*, DG Research, EUR 23314, Capacities/Science in Society, Unit L4-Scientific culture and gender issues, European Commission, Luxembourg.

European Commission (2009) *Monitoring progress towards gender equality in the sixth framework programme synthesis report*, European Commission, Luxembourg.

European Commission (2010) *Stocktaking 10 years of 'women in science' policy by the European Commission 1999–2009*, (eds M. Marchetti and T. Raudma), ERA, Science in Society, European Commission, Luxembourg.

European Commission (2011) *Toolkit gender in EU-funded research*, European Commission, Luxembourg.

European Commission (2012a) *Structural change in research institutions: Enhancing excellence, gender equality and efficiency in research and innovation*, European Commission, Luxembourg.

European Commission (2012b) *A reinforced European research area partnership for excellence and growth*. Available at: https://ec.europa.eu/digital-single-market/en/news/reinforced-european-research-area-partnership-excellence-and-growth

European Commission (2014) *European research area- facts and figures 2014*, European Commission, Luxembourg.

European Commission (2015) *Strategic engagement for gender equality 2016–2019*, European Commission, Brussels. Available at: http://ec.europa.eu/justice/genderequality/document/files/strategic_engagement_en.pdf

European Commission (2019a) *2019 report on equality between women and men in the EU*, European Commission, Luxembourg.

European Commission (2019b) *SHE figures 2018*, European Commission, Luxembourg.

Jorgensen, T. (2019) *Gender equality in Europe's universities*. SAGE Final Event, 10 July, (unpublished), Brussels.

LERU (2012) *Women, research and universities: Excellence without gender bias*, League of European Research Universities, Leuven.

LERU (2015) *Gendered research and innovation: Integrating sex and gender analysis into the research process*, League of European Research Universities, Leuven.

Mergaert, L. and Lombardo, E. (2014) Resistance to implementing gender mainstreaming in EU research policy, in E. Weiner and H. MacRae (eds), *The persistent invisibility of gender in EU policy, European integration online papers (EIoP)*, 1 (18), 1–21, doi:10.1695/2014005

Paradeise, C., Reale, E., Bleiklie, I. and Ferlie, E. (2009) *University governance: Western European comparative perspectives*, Springer, Dordrecht.

Riegraf, B. and Weber, L. (2017) Excellence and gender equality policies in neoliberal universities. *Gender and Research*, 18 (1), 92–112, doi.org/10.13060/25706578.2017.18.1.351

Schiebinger, L. (2013) *Gendered innovations: How gender analysis contributes to research*, EU Publications Office, Luxembourg.

UPGEM (2008) *Draw the line!* UPGEM International Conference. Papers, Proceedings and Recommendations, in C. Hasse, S. Trentermoller and A. Sinding (eds), University of Aarhus, Aarhus. Available at: https://cordis.europa.eu/docs/projects/files/518/518048/116810421-6_en.pdf

WIRDEM (2008) *Mapping the maze: Getting more women to the top in research*, European Commission, Brussels. Available at: http://ec.europa.eu/research/science-society/document_library/pdf_06/mapping-the-maze-getting-more-women-to-the-top-in-research_en.pdf

Chapter 2

The challenge of neoliberalism and precarity for gender sensitivity in academia

Rodrigo Rosa and Sara Clavero

Introduction

In recent decades, academic institutions have been expected to become more gender-sensitive organisations (see Chapter 1). In a number of countries, this has already become an imperative to attract high-quality students, world-class academic staff and prestigious research funding which explicitly requires a commitment to gender equality policy implementation. However, the complex interweaving of the gendered distribution of power and division of labour, underlined by a continuing masculinist organisational culture, has been reinforced through a growing neoliberal ethos. This chapter addresses some current challenges that academic organisations face in the pursuit of gender equality in this context. It examines the gender impact of new managerialism; the emergence of a new precarious, predominantly female, academic 'underclass' of teachers and researchers; approaches to identities as diverse, fluid and interconnected, rather than fixed; and how these identities intersect with power relations in academic institutions and in feminist scholarship.

The neoliberal university

There is a growing literature investigating the impact of neoliberalism on the nature, organisation and purpose of academia and the challenges for academics working within institutions of higher education. Neoliberal policies in the public sector draw upon New Public Management (NPM), an approach developed in the United Kingdom and Australia during the 1980s as part of an effort to make the public sector more businesslike and to improve efficiency by using private sector management models (see Chapter 11). These policies, combining free market rhetoric and intensive managerial control practices, have been extensively applied in higher education organisations in a market-driven demand for growth and efficiency (Lorenz 2012). As a result, academic work has become increasingly stressful at the same time as gender inequalities have been perpetuated (Acker and Armenti 2004). The pathways towards gender equality in higher education today are at a crossroads: how to strive for a gender-sensitive university while the institutions themselves experience government funding cuts, restructuring and downsizing as a consequence of neoliberal economic trends. This dilemma underlies the literature on the gendered effects and challenges of neoliberalism in academia.

Research shows that the demands that have emerged in neoliberalised academic institutions have resulted in highly gendered outcomes, since it is female academics who experience work-life conflict more often than their male colleagues. Hence they are more likely to consider leaving academia early (see Chapter 5). Bomert and Leinfellner observed pessimistically that 'family-centred and hetero-normative values are represented within an understanding of childlessness as one of the best prerequisites for an academic career' (2017, 119). Other writers have highlighted the importance of institutional support and collective engagement, particularly for early career academics struggling to combine work and family obligations, in increasingly precarious work environments. For example, Hawkins *et al* (2014) examined how PhD students combined work and family life within complex power relations at work. The authors concluded that the task of academics 'against neoliberal academia is not merely to seek work-life balance so that the work part of the equation can continue its oppressive and exploitative function' (Hawkins *et al* 2014, 347). Lipton (2017) observed the complex and conflicting entanglements of neoliberal and gender equity discourses by focusing on women's career decisions. The study showed that while being used as statistical tools to track and quantify gender equality, policies are also 'operational tools for neoliberalising higher education, in that they "assure" quality and accountability, increasing competition and production', making women 'hyper visible and thus responsible for their own success or failure' (Lipton 2017, 487–489).

In recent years, the focus has shifted to a younger generation of academics and their responses to performativity expectations, based on the new academic ideal worker. Is it possible to work in academia without becoming a neoliberal subject? This question was explored in a study conducted by Archer which showed that, even considering that 'subjects cannot exist outside of the conditions and locations within which they are located and by which they are constituted', there are 'important moments and spaces of resistance' allowing for critique and resilience (Archer 2008, 282). Other researchers have studied gendered subjects, under prevailing male work norms, in the neoliberal university. Vayreda *et al* (2019) observed the gendered nature of the neoliberal rationale overrunning the new university; how its spaces 'provide the conditions of possibility to develop a scientific entrepreneurial self, excluding "other" scientific subjectivities and preventing possible resistances that could emerge from them' (2019, 432). The study by De Coster and Zanoni (2019) explored women's struggle to (dis)identify with the male work norm under neoliberal governance:

> Neoliberal governance functions as a double-edged sword that on the one hand constitutes an increasingly accountable academic subjectivity while on the other constrains the possibility to constitute a female subjectivity that

is open and responsive through the relations of accountability, fulfilling the gendered norms.

(De Coster and Zanoni 2019, 413)

There is an increasing scholarly interest in the conditions and barriers for combining research with a feminist approach in the neoliberal university. Some authors have reflected upon the striking resonance between neoliberalism and postfeminist sensibility, which particularly emphasises the constant surveillance, monitoring and disciplining of the self. For example, Gill contends that postfeminism urges 'the "right" kinds of dispositions for surviving in neoliberal society: aspiration, confidence, resilience and so on' (2017, 610). Meyers points out how postfeminist and neoliberal discourses 'intersect within the lives of academic women [and are] neglected as an area of study' (2013, 276). More recently, Rumens (2018) explored this connection between postfeminist and neoliberal discourses by focusing on the challenges he encountered in teaching gender equality to students in a business school. He found that 'postfeminist discourses can stifle discussion on gender equality . . . female students can vocalise a postfeminist sensibility that drains gender and feminism of its political valence' as well as inferring that it is for students themselves to overcome gender discrimination (Rumens 2018, 339). Some authors have even questioned the possibility of being an academic with feminist commitments, in the current postfeminist and neoliberal climate (Acker and Wagner 2019; Pereira 2016).

Gender equality and intersectionality

Tackling gender inequalities in academia requires dealing with the wide range of thematic areas covered in the chapters of this book and by researchers across Europe (Husu 2019; Winchester and Browning 2015; Sagaria 2007; Mason and Goulden 2004; Baylin 2003). While strategies for achieving equality in gendered institutions have become increasingly professionalised (Ikävalko and Kantola 2017), a further debate on gender equality and equity has taken place. Here, writers have criticised equality-led initiatives for lacking efficiency or failing to acknowledge the complexity of different structural, cultural and institutional factors affecting female academics (Schmidt and Cacace 2018). Until recently, institutional thinking on areas of disadvantage focused on narrow social categories such as gender binaries, LGBTQI+, race and ethnicity. The growing literature devoted to the importance of an intersectional approach seeks to widen the general discourse around equality, diversity and inclusion.

In order to explore the gendered processes of exclusion inherent in academia, a growing number of researchers favour a critical approach to gender which is not restricted to fixed dichotomies, in favour of within-gender differences, as well as incorporating an intersectional approach. This reflects the realisation that knowledge production is not only a male enterprise but also a predominantly white and economically privileged undertaking. Intersectional approaches have the potential to disrupt a number of problematic trends in sex/gender research, including binary constructions of sex (male versus female) and gender (masculine versus feminine), the treatment of sex and gender as easily separable and the disconnection of sex/gender from other significant identities. The increasing complexity of advancing gender equality in academia requires going beyond gender to interventions that develop intersectionality and critical approaches to equality (LERU 2019).

The idea that people are often disadvantaged by multiple and overlapping sources of oppression—their gender, ethnicity, class, gender identity, sexual orientation, religion, body ability and other identities—is now an accepted way of thinking about disadvantage and difference. Some women may choose to privilege gender as their identity marker; that is their choice. For most women and men, however, it is the way in which many other parts of their identity come into play alongside gender in their professional lives in academia, and their private lives away from it, that determine their intellectual ambition and agency. Intersectionality has a place in recognising and celebrating differing interwoven identities in teaching and research, in how academic institutions are designed and managed, how safe they are for those who inhabit them, how they are funded, who gets admitted to them, who the teachers and researchers are, what is taught and how, the ways in which research is framed and conducted, how and what language is used, who is in charge and how they got there.

Adopting an intersectional approach replaces assumptions about policies that will be unilaterally advantageous for all women irrespective of their other identities. Instead, the intersection of gender with these other identities is foregrounded. Intersectionality allows an examination of how, for example, women experience different obstacles to career advancement according to their race and ethnicity, body ability or age entering academia, their role as parents or as carers. For example, whilst one professorial position in four (25%) is held by a woman in the UK (European Commission 2017) the equivalent proportion for black and minority ethnic (BME) women is less than 2 per cent (Solanke 2017). An intersectional framework is able to unveil the inbuilt, interwoven inequalities and injustices in this situation as a prerequisite to finding the optimal policies for countering multiple disadvantage, rather than providing add-on policy measures that are typical of many diversity perspectives. Some recent literature has shown that standing at the intersection of different identity groups does not necessarily result in the accumulation of disadvantage. Research taking an intersectional perspective addresses the complex interconnectedness and consequences of different forms of inequality and otherness. Two studies, outlined here, show this by investigating the relationship between gender and foreignness, and gender and political identity.

Strauß and Boncori (2020) explore how gender intersects with foreignness by using the concept of the 'double-stranger' in examining the experiences of foreign female scholars working across geographic boundaries. The study demonstrates the different dynamics and temporary hierarchies between different forms of strangeness (being foreign and being a woman). Their work shows that these forms can function as categories of disadvantage or resources for resistance; they are not simply additive; and they may develop over time:

> While *being woman* appears to be a rather constant form of estrangement in othering academics within their professional environment, the *category of foreignness* is more subject to change over time, as it can improve after an initial period of adjustment to then become dormant, with the occasional threat turning into a destabilising factor for the participants' sense of belonging.
>
> (emphasis added; Strauβ and Boncori 2020, 26–27)

Drawing upon focus groups with self-identified feminist academics, Sang's recent study (2018) explores the heterogeneity of women's experiences in academia, where gender intersects with political identity and ethnic background. Findings from this study suggest a mixed pattern of experiences. Not only can intersectionality lead to an understanding of disadvantage in relation to social identities, such as gender and ethnicity, but how a political identity, such as being a feminist, can lead to the accumulation of advantage, since women may use their 'otherness' to strategically challenge and work around existing power relations. Some feminist academics argue that the intersection of gender and race restricts their ability to identify with a particular ethnic group and may result in marginalisation. For other women, being a feminist intersects with these identities, thereby creating a space for critiquing the *status quo* within their institutions (Sang 2018).

As early as 1978 the poet, academic and activist Lorde chose to define herself as black, lesbian, feminist, mother, poet and warrior, and also as a survivor of cancer. She refused to define herself, even temporarily, by any one aspect of her heterogeneous identity, whether to support a political programme or to make others feel comfortable:

> There's always someone asking you to underline one piece of yourself - whether it's *Black, woman, mother, dyke, teacher etc* - because that's the piece that they need to key in to. They want you to dismiss everything else. But once you do that, then you've lost because then you become acquired or bought by that particular essence of yourself and you've denied yourself all of the energy it takes to keep all those others in jail. Only by learning to live in harmony with all your contradictions can you keep it all afloat.
>
> (emphasis in original; Hall 2004, 31)

At its core, intersectionality creates nuanced possibilities of commonality and difference for and within all genders and it offers the opportunity to forge alliances for the work of making academic institutions more gender-sensitive.

Feminisms and women's/gender studies in the neoliberal university

There is a burgeoning literature on the impact of neoliberalism on feminisms and women's/gender studies within academia (Morley 2016; Cannella and Salazar-Perez 2012; Gill 2009). Despite a consensus among feminist scholars that the neoliberal university poses significant constraints on feminist action in academic settings, there are also studies that point to the opening up of possibilities to advance gender justice and equality, particularly through new forms of collective organising. Such opportunities and constraints are marred by tensions and contradictions that originate from the strong masculinist nature of the new neoliberal ethos permeating academic structures, procedures and work practices. In this context, the question is whether, how and to what extent can feminism succeed in challenging the neoliberal university?

The neoliberal university is characterised by the requirement of production and accessibility at all times and the use of performance indicators as measures of success, such as continuous research assessments and teaching evaluations. In this environment of neoliberal management, masculine ideologies are perpetuated and reproduced through the celebration of fierce competition, an increased (and stressful) pressure to succeed, making pastoral work invisible, devalued or displaced. There is also pre-eminence of individualist values over traditional values of academic collegiality (Acker and Wagner 2019; Ivancheva et al 2019; Lipton 2019). In addition, the neoliberal university has established new forms of precarious employment, particularly since austerity measures were introduced at the end of the 2000s. In this academic reality, feminist researchers, academics and postgraduate students constitute a new form of 'proletariat' who struggle to survive in a highly competitive and individualistic arena (Gill and Scharff 2013; Davies and O'Callaghan 2014; Nash 2013). Can this new academic environment leave any 'open space' for feminist academics to act freely and develop alternative feminist academic cultures? In addressing this question, the literature highlights two particular challenges. First, for feminist research and teaching, it is marked by the under-resourcing and/or closure of women's and gender studies degrees in many institutions. The second challenge is the possibility of feminist organising for collective action aimed at subverting the current *status quo*.

In relation to the first challenge, the emergence of gender and women's studies programmes, centres and departments, in the late 1960s and 1970s, were not adopted in all institutions and were not without criticism (Pereira 2012). The avowed commitment by feminist scholars to articulate academic inquiry and political action was invoked by critics as evidence that this work could not be taken seriously as 'proper' scholarship. The institutionalisation of gender and women's studies as a distinct research and teaching category increased its stability and professional credibility. It also gained recognition in national and international contexts, where it had already achieved some institutional autonomy and was increasingly integrated into existing disciplines (Alvanoudi 2009). However, these programmes now run the risk of disappearing from academia, since their ability to foster an environment of feminist teaching and research is hampered by the overarching neoliberal impositions of the institution and precarity in relation to staff working conditions (Bendl and Schmidt 2013).

The second challenge posits the view that the feminist struggle for gender equality in academic institutions has moved from feminist bottom-up activism to become part of the official top-down strategy for which university managers are held accountable and may be rewarded if they reach gender equality goals (see Chapter 12). In the view of Sauer and Wöhl (2008) the gender policies that were once empowering strategies of the women's movement now risk losing their critical potential to achieve social change and are becoming instruments that both steer and produce inequality. Other writers point out, however, that some of the current transformations in academia have created new possibilities for the development of forms of publicly and politically engaged academic practice (Pereira 2016). The findings of EU-Horizon 2020 supported interventions in Ireland, Austria, Italy and Turkey further demonstrate the alignment of Gender Equality Plan (GEP) actions to promote gender equality with positive outcomes:

> Top down AND bottom up support for GEPs was stressed, as was arriving at a consensus as to what could/should be done. Flowing from this was the perceived need to institutionalise gains and the development of a communications strategy (using gender sensitive language) to convey the message of gender equality needs/successes to all stakeholders.
>
> (Drew and Bencivenga 2017, 351)

Against the backdrop of broader discourses of austerity, there is now an increased emphasis on the idea that investment in academia must provide the best value for tax-payers' money by engaging with, and having effects on, communities and sectors outside the academy (Collini 2012). There are concerns that the measurement of 'impact' is primarily focused on income-generation for business and industry and direct influence on public policy (Holmwood 2001; Atwood 2010). This is confirmed by a desire to reconceptualise and reposition universities as institutions subordinated to, and shaped by, the needs of the economy and the demands of the market. This reflects an understanding of education and research that clearly clashes with key principles of feminist theory and politics (Evans 2004). Pereira's study (2016) shows, how institutional views on feminist activism have begun to shift. If feminists' political intervention is understood as something that can enhance the social, political and media visibility of their institution, it becomes reframed as valuable work that can lead to better research ratings and increased recruitment. Chapter 6 provides a detailed case study of the way in which feminist activism, in response to sexual violence on one large university campus, had this effect.

Precarity

The transformation of academic work into an individual and competitive endeavour is a consequence of pervasive neoliberal practices in higher education institutions.

These are increasingly dependent on unstable employment contracts (part time, fixed term, zero hours). Three areas of study address the intersection of precarious work and gender in this context.

One area focuses on the intersection of unpaid care work outside academia and precarious paid work within it. Drawing on 102 semi-structured in-depth interviews with female and male academics, Ivancheva et al showed that, even if male academics face precarity challenge due to labour segmentation, the relational aspect of precarity is not a major male preoccupation for them in their work narratives. For while 'both contractual and affective precarity operate coterminously for women, each poses significant limitations to a sense of security' (2019, 457). Women researchers' autobiographical experiences, aimed at rendering precarity and its ramifications more visible by exploring their lived experience, are contributing to this growing body of literature (Caretta et al 2018). This work shows how, for example, precarious working conditions and maternity combine to intensify precarity itself (Téllez 2018). Hofmann (2018) testifies to the toll of precarity contributing to the distress, financial insecurity and impossibility of planning a future, in terms of careers or personal relationships, alongside difficulties in finding secure housing. These consequences result in dependency on the goodwill of more senior academics and the accompanying sense of subservience that it can produce.

A second area is focused on studies that expose the differing status of men and women in academia who have no permanent contracts. One qualitative study explored the 'non-citizen' status of female academics who identified as precarious workers (O'Keefe and Courtois 2019). The majority were women working in social sciences and humanities (SSH), traditionally perceived as more hospitable for women, compared with science, technology, engineering and mathematics (STEM) disciplines. Among academics working in less desirable forms of precarious work 'women were especially concentrated in forms of temporary work that is hourly paid or based on pro-rata and zero hours contracts while men were more likely to be on yearly or multi-year contracts' (O'Keefe and Courtois 2019, 469). In addition, the findings suggest that 'the length of time spent performing precarious academic labour is also gendered, as women are more likely to have worked in the sector longer than their male counterparts' (O'Keefe and Courtois 2019, 469). The authors stress that often the institutional proposals to tackle gender inequality do not extend to academics in precarious employment, tending instead to focus on access to the senior ranks and leadership. Conversely, as their findings suggest, 'the "leaky pipeline" trend visible in the tenured ranks may continue' unless the ranks below are examined and anomalies addressed (O'Keefe and Courtois 2019, 469).

There is a third strand of literature that examines action research undertaken under equality initiatives. One example is a set of studies carried out as part of the European Union funded project GARCIA (Gendering the Academy and Research: Combating Career Instability and Asymmetries), a project which focused on both the top positions and early stages of academic and research careers. The study by Dubois-Shaik et al (2019) identified three types of gendered careers and experiences: first, the persistence of precarious career paths, which produces a high cumulative cost for the individuals concerned; second, continuing in ambivalent career paths, producing moderate cost; and third, striving to win in competitive career paths, which comes at specific high cost to individuals. A study by Steinþórsdóttir *et al* (2019) examined how neoliberal managerialism fosters the process of precarity in academic employment by promoting organisational practices and funding which tends to favour male-dominated STEM departments. Finally, the comparative study by Herschberg *et al* (2019) analysed how gender interferes with the construction of excellence in recruitment and selection practices for early career researchers in the STEM and SSH institutes, as well as the consequences of the gendered construction of the 'ideal candidate' for those academics with precarious work contracts (see Chapter 3).

Conclusion

This chapter highlights relevant recent studies on the neoliberalisation of academia, focusing on key issues not specifically addressed in other chapters of this book, namely, gender equality and intersectionality, feminisms, gender studies and precarity. It shows that gender equality is a particularly challenging goal in a context where the changes introduced by neoliberal management practices and the resulting demands imposed on academic staff are themselves gendered. Against this backdrop, the literature shows that postfeminist and neoliberal discourses intersect in female academic lives and women struggle to (dis)identify with the male work norm under neoliberal governance. Discourses question the attainability of a healthy work-life balance in a climate where scholarly work continues to be oppressive and exploitative; where many feminist scholars experience exhaustion and self-doubt, exacerbated by an unwillingness to collude with unchanging gendered work practices.

An understanding of the subtleties of intersectionality offers the possibility of critical approaches to traditional understandings. Examining the intersections between gender and other forms of inequality, identity and otherness is one approach. It remains a major challenge to define best practice to assess and address how all inequalities intersect in academia. Not only does the intersectionality framework show how social identities such as gender, ethnicity and family status, for example, combine to produce disadvantage, it also shows that women can use their otherness to strategically challenge and work around existing power relations.

The impact of current transformations in academic governance on possibilities for feminist mobilisation is complex. New management models impose strict requirements for enhanced productivity, which in turn significantly limit the time and energy that feminist scholars have available for social and political intervention and for community-based or advocacy research. However, those same transformations are opening up new possibilities for activism. They offer increasing institutional recognition of, and support for, feminist scholars' work with political allies and civil society organisations outside the academy. Recent studies addressing the intersection of precarious work and gender in academia show that women are especially concentrated in the most undervalued forms of precarious work in academia and that an interrogation of intersectionality throughout academia is required for a more nuanced analysis and the formulation of policies for change.

References

Acker, S. and Armenti, C. (2004) Sleepless in academia, *Gender and Education*, 16 (1), 3–24, doi:10.1080/0954025032000170309

Acker, S. and Wagner, A. (2019) Feminist scholars working around the neoliberal university, *Gender and Education*, 31 (1), 62–81, doi:10.1080/09540253.2017.1296117

Alvanoudi, A. (2009) Teaching gender in the neoliberal university, in D. Gronold, B. Hipfl and L. Pedersen (eds), *Teaching with the third wave: New feminists' explorations of teaching and institutional contexts*, ATHENA, Utrecht, 37–54. Available at: https://atgender.eu/wp-content/uploads/sites/207/2017/08/Teaching_With_The_Third_Wave.pdf

Archer, L. (2008) The new neoliberal subjects? Young/er academics' constructions of professional identity, *Journal of Education Policy*, 23 (3), 265–285, doi:10.1080/02680930701754047

Atwood, R. (2010) Impact's impact could be the stifling of new ideas, *Times Higher Education*. Available at: www.timeshighereducation.co.uk/story.asp?storycode=411487

Baylin, L. (2003) Academic careers and gender equity: Lessons learned from MIT1, *Gender, Work & Organization*, 10 (2), 137–153, doi:10.1111/1468-0432.00008

Bendl, R. and Schmidt, A. (2013) Gender mainstreaming: An assessment of its conceptual value for gender equality, *Gender, Work & Organization*, 20 (4), 364–381, doi:10.1111/j.1468-0432.2011.00584.x

Bomert, C. and Leinfellner, S. (2017) Images, ideals and constraints in times of neoliberal transformations: Reproduction and profession as conflicting or complementary spheres in academia? *European Educational Research Journal*, 16 (2–3), 106–122, doi.org/10.1177/1474904116682972

Cannella, G. and Salazar-Perez, M. (2012) Emboldened patriarchy in higher education: Feminist readings of capitalism, violence, and power, *Cultural Studies Critical Methodologies*, 12 (4), 279–286, doi.org/10.1177/1532708612446421

Caretta, M., Drozdzewski, D., Jokinen, J. and Falconer, E. (2018) 'Who can play this game?' The lived experiences of doctoral candidates and early career women in the neoliberal university, *Journal of Geography in Higher Education*, 42 (2), 261–275, doi: 10.1080/03098265.2018.1434762

Collini, S. (2012) *What are universities for?* Penguin, London.

Davies, H. and O'Callaghan, C. (2014) All in this together? Feminisms, academia, austerity, *Journal of Gender Studies*, 23 (3), 227–232, doi.org/10.1080/09589236.2014.913824

De Coster, M. and Zanoni, P. (2019) Governing through accountability: Gendered moral selves and the (im)possibilities of resistance in the neoliberal university, *Gender, Work & Organization*, 26 (4), 411–429, doi.org/10.1111/gwao.12304

Drew, E. and Bencivenga, R. (eds) (2017) Gender in Horizon 2020: The case of gender equality plans, *AG AboutGender*, 6 (12), 326–355, doi.org/10.15167/2279-5057/AG2017.6.12.488

Dubois-Shaik, F., Fusulier, B. and Vincke, C. (2019) A gendered pipeline typology in academia, in A. Murgia and B. Poggio (eds), *Gender and precarious research careers: A comparative analysis*, Routledge, London, 178–205, doi.org/10.4324/9781315201245

European Commission (2017) *Modernisation of higher education in Europe: Academic staff—2017*. Eurydice report. Education Audiovisual and Culture Executive Agency, Brussels.

Evans, M. (2004) *Killing thinking: The death of the universities*, Continuum, London.

Gill, R. (2009) Breaking the silence: The hidden injuries of neo-liberal academia, in R. Flood and R. Gill (eds), *Secrecy and silence in the research process: Feminist reflections*, Routledge, London, 228–244. Available at: http://platform-hnu.n l/wp-content/uploads/2015/05/gill-breaking-the-silence-2.pdf

Gill, R. (2017) The affective, cultural and psychic life of postfeminism: A postfeminist sensibility 10 years on, *European Journal of Cultural Studies*, 20 (6), 606–626, doi.org/10.1177/1367549417733003

Gill, R. and Scharff, C. (eds) (2013) *New femininities: Postfeminism, neoliberalism and subjectivity*, Palgrave Macmillan, Basingstoke, Hampshire, doi.org/10.1177/0959353511427291

Hall, J. (ed) (2004) *Conversations with Audre Lorde*, University Press of Mississippi, Jackson.

Hawkins, R., Manzi, M. and Ojeda, D. (2014) Lives in the making: Power, academia and the everyday, *ACME: An International Journal for Critical Geographies*, 13 (2), 328–351. Available at: www.acme-journal.org/index.php/acme/article/view/1010

Herschberg, C., Benschop, Y. and Van den Brink, M. (2019) The peril of potential: Gender practices in the recruitment and selection of early career researchers, in A. Murgia and B. Poggio (eds), *Gender and precarious research careers: A comparative analysis*, Routledge, Abingdon, Oxon, 111–142, doi.org/10.4324/9781315201245

Hofmann, S. (2018) Fragmented life: Being a precarious academic between two continents, *Revista de Dialectología y Tradiciones Populares*, 73 (1), 25–32.

Holmwood, J. (2001) Gender and critical realism: A critique of Sayer, *Sociology* 35 (4), 947–965, doi.org/10.1177/0038038501035004009

Husu, L. (2019) Gender equality in Nordic academia: Advances and challenges, in D. Vujadinović and Z. Antonijević (eds), *Rodna Ravnopravnost U Visokom Obrazovanju: Koncepti, prakse i izazovi*, Akademska knjiga, Novi Sad, 63–73.

Ikävalko, E. and Kantola, J. (2017) Feminist resistance and resistance to feminism in gender equality planning in Finland, *European Journal of Women's Studies*, 24 (3), 233–248, doi.org/10.1177/1350506817693868

Ivancheva, M., Lynch, K. and Keating, K. (2019) Precarity, gender and care in the neoliberal academy, *Gender, Work & Organization*, 26 (4), 448–462, doi.org/10.1111/gwao.12350

LERU (2019) *Equality, diversity and inclusion at universities: The power of a systemic approach*, LERU, Leuven.

Lipton, B. (2017) Measures of success: Cruel optimism and the paradox of academic women's participation in Australian higher education, *Higher Education Research & Development*, 36 (3), 486–497, doi.org/10.1080/07294360.2017.1290053

Lipton, B. (2019) Closed doors: Academic collegiality, isolation, competition and resistance in the contemporary Australian university, in M. Breeze, Y. Taylor and C. Costa (eds), *Time and space in the neoliberal university*, Palgrave Macmillan, Cham, 15–42.

Lorenz, C. (2012) If you're so smart, why are you under surveillance? Universities, neoliberalism, and new public management, *Critical Inquiry*, 38 (3), 599–629.

Mason, M. and Goulden, M. (2004) Marriage and baby blues: Redefining gender equity in the academy, *The Annals of the American Academy of Political and Social Science*, 596 (1), 86–103, doi.org/10.1177/0002716204268744

Meyers, M. (2013) The war on academic women: Reflections on postfeminism in the neoliberal academy, *Journal of Communication Inquiry*, 37 (4), 274–283, doi.org/10.1177/0196859913505619

Morley, L. (2016) Troubling intra-actions: Gender, neo-liberalism and research in the global academy, *Journal of Education Policy*, 31 (1), 28–45, doi.org/10.1080/026809 39.2015.1062919

Nash, M. (2013) Reflections on teaching gender to Australian sociology undergraduates in the neoliberal postfeminist classroom, *Journal of Sociology*, 49 (4), 411–425, doi. org/10.1177/1440783313504053

O'Keefe, T. and Courtois, A. (2019) 'Not one of the family': Gender and precarious work in the neoliberal university, *Gender, Work & Organization*, 26 (4), 463–479, doi. org/10.1111/gwao.12346

Pereira, M. do Mar (2012) 'Feminist theory is proper knowledge, but . . .': The status of feminist scholarship in the academy, *Feminist Theory*, 13 (3), 283–303, doi. org/10.1177/1464700112456005

Pereira, M. do Mar (2016) Struggling within and beyond the performative university: Articulating activism and work in an 'academia without walls', *Women's Studies International Forum*, 54, 100–110, doi.org/10.1016/j.wsif.2015.06.008

Rumens, N. (2018) Teaching gender in a postfeminist management classroom: A gay man's perspective, in Y. Taylor and K. Lahad (eds), *Feeling academic in the neoliberal university: Feminist flights, fights and failures*, Palgrave Macmillan, Cham, 321–343.

Sagaria, M. (2007) Reframing gender equality initiatives as university adaptation, in M. Sagaria (ed), *Women, universities, and change: Issues in higher education*, Palgrave Macmillan, New York, 1–6, doi:10.1057/9780230603509_1

Sang, K. (2018) Gender, ethnicity and feminism: An intersectional analysis of the lived experiences feminist academic women in UK higher education, *Journal of Gender Studies*, 27 (2), 192–206, doi.org/10.1080/09589236.2016.1199380

Sauer, B. and Wöhl, S. (2008) Governing intersectionality: A critical take on diversity politics (authors' own translation), in C. Klinger and G. Knapp (eds), *Über-Kreuzungen: Fremdheit, Ungleichheit, Differenz*, Westfalisches Dampfboot, Munster.

Schmidt, K. and Cacace, M. (2018) Setting up a dynamic framework to activate gender equality structural transformation in research organizations, *Science and Public Policy*, 46 (3), 321–338.

Solanke, I. (2017) *Black female professors in the UK*, March. Available at: www.runnyme detrust.org/uploads/BlackFemaleProfessorsMarch2017.pdf

Steinþórsdóttir, F., Einarsdóttir, Þ., Heijstra, T. Pétursdóttir, G. and Smidt, T. (2019) Gender budgeting to expose inequalities in a precarious academia—and redistribute resources to effect change, in A. Murgi and B. Poggio (eds), *Gender and precarious research careers: A comparative analysis*, Routledge, London, 83–110, doi.org/10.4324/9781315201245

Strauß, A. and Boncori, I. (2020) Foreign women in academia: Double-strangers between productivity, marginalization and resistance, *Gender, Work & Organization*, doi.org/10. 1111/gwao.12432

Téllez, V. (2018) La fortuna de la precariedad, *Revista de Dialectología y Tradiciones Populares*, 73 (1), 47–53.

Vayreda, A., Conesa, E., Revelles-Benavente, B. and Ramos, A. (2019) Subjectivation processes and gender in a neoliberal model of science in three Spanish research centres, *Gender, Work & Organization*, 26 (4), 430–447, doi.org/10.1111/gwao.12360

Winchester, H. and Browning, L. (2015) Gender equality in academia: A critical reflection, *Journal of Higher Education Policy and Management*, 37 (3), 269–228, doi.org/10.1080/ 1360080X.2015.1034427

Chapter 3

Gender in academic recruitment and selection

Mathias Wullum Nielsen

Introduction

Three social processes interact to produce gender inequalities in academic recruitment and selection: (i) institutional decoupling among hiring managers; (ii) standardisation of scientific performance assessments; and (iii) symbolic boundary work in relation to gender. All three are shaped by the organisational contexts in which they operate and act to reinforce gender inequalities in recruitment and selection. Not all of them are adequately explained by unconscious bias. Gender bias assumes many different forms in academia, including homophily (the tendency for people to seek out or be attracted to those who are similar to themselves) (Nielsen 2016). In networks of academic recruiters it may be incorporated into seemingly objective criteria for evaluating research performance (Nielsen 2017b, 2018). Systemic bias is noted in the cultural narratives of academic managers, in which ideas about women's attributes and qualities as researchers are separated from the predominant organisational image of the ideal academic (Nielsen 2017a) (see Chapter 4). This chapter outlines each of the three social processes with examples of possible 'fixes' that could help to mitigate the gender biases at play in academic recruitment and selection.

Unconscious bias is commonly noted in research and policy discussions on gender in academic recruitment and selection to explain cognitive errors made by well-intentioned decision-makers that put women and minorities at a disadvantage (Bielby 2013). Unconscious bias represents an important framework for understanding aspects of gendered academic recruitment (see Chapter 9). Due to its restricted focus on cognitive processes and snap-judgements, unconscious bias tends to individualise the problem of gender discrimination leaving aside the more complicated, sociological questions about the gendered structures, hierarchies and cultures of academia (Nielsen 2017a). Two influential studies on unconscious bias in academic hiring demonstrate this point.

In the first, Moss-Racusin *et al* (2012) asked 127 professors in US universities to rate an identical application, randomly assigned either a male or female name, for a position as laboratory manager. The evaluators, on average, rated the male applicant as more competent and hireable than the identical female candidate.

They also offered a higher starting salary and more career mentoring for the male candidate. In the second study, Williams and Ceci (2015) asked 873 US tenured staff to evaluate narrative summaries describing female and male applicants for assistant professorships. In direct conflict with the results of Moss-Racusin and colleagues, Williams and Ceci (2015) found that participants were twice as likely to prefer a female candidate over a male candidate with equivalent qualifications.

It is crucial to emphasise the differences in how the two experiments were carried out. In the Moss-Racusin study, the participants were led to believe that they were providing feedback for a real student to help his or her career development. In the Williams and Ceci study, the participants were asked to rank three candidates. They knew that the candidates were fictitious, they knew they were selecting between male and female candidates and that both a male and female candidate were described as excellent in the narrative summaries. Some critics have argued that this set-up may have triggered a social-desirability bias among the participants in the Williams and Ceci study. In a hypothetical scenario, with an equally excellent male and female candidate, the participants may have been prone to pick the female candidate in order to appear unbiased in their assessments (Williams and Smith 2015; Haynes and Sweedler 2015). Moss-Racusin *et al* (2012) overcame this problem by creating a more realistic scenario and asking each participant to rate only one subject. However, their study used ratings of hireability for lower-ranked, non-tenured positions, which may differ considerably from the considerations involved when recruiting tenured staff.

Both studies also shared another important limitation. They were too focused on what was going on 'inside the heads' of decision-makers and thereby lost sight of the organisational contexts that shape most hiring decisions in academia (Bielby 2000, 2013). To fully understand the gender dynamics at play in academic hiring, researchers need to examine the social and organisational contexts in which these gender dynamics play out. The research focus could be expanded to capture what happens *before* evaluators make their final judgements on who to hire (Nielsen 2016) and how contextual factors amplify gender bias in recruitment and selection (Correll 2017).

Decoupling in academic recruitment and selection

The first social process concerns institutional decoupling in academic recruitment and selection. As demonstrated in this section, academic managers can exploit loopholes to reduce external constraints on their hiring practices and increase managerial efficiency at department level. To borrow a term from neo-institutionalist sociology, these academic managers sometimes 'decouple' their hiring practices from formal organisational rules and procedures to make recruitment and selection 'run smoothly' (Meyer and Rowan 1977). The challenge is that this form of decoupling allows managers to make hiring decisions based on personal idiosyncrasies and social networks, with potentially negative consequences for gender equality (Reskin and McBrier 2000).

The discussion of institutional decoupling in recruitment and selection primarily draws on a case study conducted at Aarhus University in Denmark between 2013 and 2015 (Nielsen 2015a, 2016). The study was based on recruitment data from more than 1,000 associate and full professorial appointments, and interviews with 24 of the 27 department heads at the university. Aarhus University is one of Denmark's largest, with more than 40,000 students, 4,000 staff members employed on research contracts and 27 departments. At the time of the study, women comprised 15 per cent of full professors, 32 per cent of associate professors and 43 per cent of the postdocs and assistant professors at the university. In the Danish university system, department heads take on the primary responsibility for coordinating and managing the hiring of associate and full professors in coordination with the faculty deans. The role of the external assessment committees that review the applicants is limited to identifying qualified candidates.

Following a 2003 reform of the Danish university system, department heads went from being elected by their peers to being appointed by the faculty deans. They were also assigned new administrative duties including responsibilities for department budgets, strategic planning, recruitment and selection (Degn 2015). In the current university model, departments are run more like small businesses and this, arguably, places conflicting demands on department heads in recruitment and selection. The meritocratic ideal of hiring the best and the brightest while being objective, fair and transparent is sometimes at odds with an efficiency driven rationale for making recruitment and selection run 'fast, cheap and smooth'.

The ideal of the meritocracy is in the DNA of the modern university (Van den Brink and Benschop 2012; López and O'Connor 2019). In interviews with department heads at Aarhus University, many of them described their recruitment activities as based on meritocratic principles noting: '*We only look at qualifications*'; '*all of our researchers are hired on their merits*'; '*for us it's all about getting the best candidate*'. These quotes demonstrate a strong institutionalised belief in meritocracy, not only as an ideal that recruiters aspire to, but as a belief in how recruitment and selection practices actually work at their university. Social-psychological experiments suggest that deeply institutionalised meritocratic beliefs can be detrimental to gender equality. The work of Castilla and Bernard (2010) shows that performance assessments are more likely to be gender biased in organisations that explicitly pride themselves in being meritocratic. They explain their findings by arguing that 'in contexts in which people are led to feel that they are unbiased, fair, or objective, they are more likely to behave in biased ways' (Castilla and Bernard 2010, 547; see also Uhlmann and Cohen 2007).

Analysis of more than 1,000 professorial appointments at Aarhus University also demonstrates discrepancies in the adherence to meritocratic principles by department heads. In the period from 2004 to 2013, 19 per cent of new associate and full professors were hired through 'closed' procedures without advertisement, usually with only one applicant. Despite the university's efforts to align recruitment practices with the meritocratic principle of open competition, the use of closed procedures increased from 8 per cent of associate and full professorship appointments in 2004–2008 to 30 per cent in 2009–2013. This trend was not unique to Aarhus university. In the period 2011–2013, 17 per cent of full professorship and 21 per cent of associate professorship appointments in Denmark were made through closed procedures (Staahle 2014). Current research on gender dynamics in recruitment and selection suggests that such informal hiring practices are at high risk of reinforcing gender inequalities (Acker 2006; Bielby 2000; Reskin and McBrier 2000). This was also true at Aarhus University. In a statistical analysis that adjusted for scientific field, position level and number of male and female applicants per position, the likelihood of women being appointed to associate or full professorship was 79 per cent higher when appointments took place under open, publicly advertised, rather than closed procedures. The gender imbalance in 'closed hirings' was most notable at the full professor level, where women comprised 12 per cent of applicants. In contrast, women made up 23 per cent of the applicants for full professorships with 'open' recruitment. Note here that appointments under closed procedures usually have just one single applicant and represent a form of pre-selection. Similar trends have been observed for the other Danish universities. For example, the University of Copenhagen hired 10 per cent women to full professorships through closed procedures in the period 2011 to 2013 and 32 per cent through open procedures (Staahle 2014).

The analysis of recruitment data also shows that for associate and full professorships at Aarhus University a significant share attracted just a single applicant. From 2004 to 2013, 47 per cent of vacancies for full professorships and 37 per cent of vacancies for associate professorships received only one application and the proportion of appointments with only one applicant increased over time. This pattern also reflected a broader issue in Danish academia. In the period 2011–2013, 31 per cent of recruitment calls for full professorships and 17 per cent of recruitment calls for associate professorships at Danish universities had only one applicant (Staahle 2014).

While women and men at Aarhus University had approximately the same likelihood of being appointed in single applicant competitions, women may still be at a disadvantage in such scenarios, especially at the early career stages. In general, female postdocs and assistant professors at Aarhus University were far less likely than men to apply for vacancies at the associate professorship level. The relative difference between women's share of potential candidates occupying postdocs or assistant professorships and women's share of applicants for associate professorships ranged from 19 per cent to 41 per cent per year for the period 2008 to 2012.

Interviews with department heads at Aarhus University provided the opportunity to ask about the prevalent use of closed hiring procedures and single-applicant appointments allowing a deeper understanding of the sentiments underpinning the different hiring practices used and how gender bias may have shaped such practices. Several interviewees acknowledged that they had sometimes used narrow job profiles to limit the expected number of applicants for vacancies:

> 'Sometimes you can, and this is no secret, you can narrow it down in such a way that people will almost recognise . . . listen, there's probably only one or two persons in this country qualified for this position. That happens once

*in a while. It does . . . in principle it's not the right way to do it. You ought
to announce it in such a way that many are provided with an opportunity to
apply'* (department head).

(Nielsen 2016a)

Three different arguments emerged for using narrow job profiles in recruitment.
The first was related to strategic planning and the specificity of the overall tasks
and subject areas covered by a department. For example, recruiters may need to
fill a specific gap in relation to research and teaching activities. A second issue
concerned the time and costs of hiring external candidates. Hiring processes typically expand over longer time periods and increase administrative burdens at
department level. A third issue related to departmental budgets: attracting applicants from all over the world may result in a situation where the department ends
up with extra salary expenses, since it is cheaper to promote a local employee than
it is to bring in a new external candidate for a position.

Advertisements often involved a preceding identification or screening of prom-
ising local candidates:

*'I spend a lot of time figuring out which of the assistant professors and post-
docs we're going to promote for associate professorships and who to promote
for full professorships. One of our most recent professor appointments . . .
well, we had a very, very good associate professor and I've known him for
years . . . and I've wondered . . . it's actually unfair that he didn't get a
professorship . . . and he's not that young anymore. But his research is very
good. . . . In that situation, we announced the job profile narrowly, since we
had a particular interest in him. And we ended up with only two applicants'*
(department head).

(Nielsen 2016a)

In some cases, this form of pre-screening may have reduced local candidates'
interest in applying for a position, since they would be aware that the 'right person
for the job' has already been identified. A position is announced openly, but it fits
the career progression of a particular scholar and may already have a local name
on it. Unfortunately, gender bias tends to flourish in such scenarios. As demonstrated in pioneering gender research on recruitment and selection in academia
(Husu 2000; Van den Brink 2010; Van den Brink and Benschop 2012), such informal hiring scenarios depend largely on the potential candidates' reputation and
visibility to the local gatekeepers, which may put women at a disadvantage. As
noted by Husu, these are the types of hiring scenarios that where:

subtle, hardly conscious, and hidden processes [may be] at play, which have
to do with male networks, the mutual support systems of men, and the relative invisibility of women in regard to their male colleagues.

(Husu 2000, 225; see also Chapters 8 and 13)

But what is the justification for closed procedures? It was more difficult to obtain clear answers from the department heads on how and why this type of hiring practice was used. Several of them noted that external funding could result in exemptions from the university's formal hiring rules. Additionally, leaders of externally funded projects are allowed to hire temporary professorships for their projects under closed procedures. In large-scale projects, these temporary positions can be extended to permanent professorships. University managers condone such exemptions to ensure that funding agencies are willing to make further long-term investments in their institutions and disciplines. In the medical departments many positions are announced as shared clinical professorships between the university and the regional hospitals. Hospitals typically bring in most of the funding for universities and decide who to appoint as professors. In a university system that is increasingly dependent on resources from external funders, these types of exemptions, or practices of *decoupling*, represent a real threat to gender equality. In such instances, candidates tend to be recruited through formal and informal networks and research suggests that men have, on average, more extensive ties to decision-makers than women and typically engage in more gender-homophilic professional relationships (Moore 1990; McGuire 2000; Ibarra 1992).

In summary, the analysis of recruitment and selection practices at Aarhus University demonstrates how women may be at a disadvantage even before the formal assessment of applicants for associate and full professorships begins. Despite a strong belief in meritocracy among the recruiters, pre-selection is prevalent in the hiring practices and women are not always given the same opportunities to compete for the permanent research positions as their men colleagues. This problem cannot be solved solely by making managers and evaluators aware of their unconscious bias. As noted by Husu (2000), this challenge concerns the subtle gender bias embedded in academic networks and women's lower visibility to gatekeepers, compared to their male colleagues.

Standardisation

The second social process concerns standardisation in academic recruitment and selection. Specifically, this relates to the standardised bibliometric indicators that academic recruiters use to screen their local environments for talent and identify scientific excellence (see Chapter 14). This section draws upon a bibliometric study of 2,000 Danish researchers' publication activities over a three-year period (Nielsen 2017b). Bibliometric measures are advanced analytical tools used to evaluate scholarly productivity and impact. This section demonstrates how this form of standardisation, despite underlying objectives to make performance assessments more transparent and objective, can contribute to the perpetuation of gender inequalities in academic organisations. This often happens in unintended ways, through taken-for-granted organisational routines (Lamont *et al* 2014; Nielsen 2018).

The empirical example concerns the Danish Bibliometric Research Indicator (BRI) introduced in 2009 by the Danish Ministry of Science, to allocate performance-based funding to the Danish Universities. The indicator is based on a differentiated counting of scholarly publications and makes a distinction between prestigious, high quality, journals and book-publishers and normal level publication channels (Table 3.1). When researchers publish in prestigious outlets, their university will receive more indicator points and thereby more funding than when they publish via 'normal level' publication channels.

Table 3.1 The BRI classification model point system by category and level

	Level 1 (points)	Level 2 (points)
Scholarly articles in a journal	1	3
Scholarly articles in an anthology	0.5	2
Scholarly books (ISBN)	5	8

Source: Adapted from Nielsen (2017b).

It is important to note that the Danish bibliometric research indicator was developed to allocate funding for universities, not to measure the performance of individual researchers. The relative amount of university funding allocated based on the indicator is also relatively low. Nevertheless, the indicator is frequently used to measure individual performance, especially in the social sciences and humanities, where standard citation indicators are less applicable (Mouritzen and Opstrup 2020).

A bibliometric analysis based on a stratified sample of more than 2,000 Danish researchers indicated the negative gender consequences of this form of standardisation (Nielsen 2017b). The analysis compared how many indicator points women and men received for their peer-reviewed publications over a three-year period. In regression models, adjusted for scientific field and academic rank, it was observed that women, on average, received notably fewer indicator points per publication than their male colleagues. When scientific performance was measured by counting indicator points instead of counting publications, the average performance gap in favour of men increased from 14 per cent to 20 per cent. This is a relative increase of more than 40 per cent in the gender performance gap. The difference was largest in the social sciences, with a relative increase in the gender performance gap of 50 per cent. This gender bias did not appear to be driven by differences in citation rates and journal impact factors. In 2013, another bibliometric study compared the average field-normalised citation frequencies and journal impact factors of more than 3,000 male and female researchers at Aarhus University. The study showed that women and men, on average, were cited at similar rates, and that the average gender differences in field-normalised impact factor scores were minor. Another study on gender and citation impact in Denmark reached similar conclusions (Frandsen et al 2015).

A more plausible explanation for the increased performance gap caused by the Bibliometric Research Indicator concerns the gender composition of the 68 field-specific committees appointed to develop lists of prestigious and less prestigious journals and book publishers used in the indicator. These committees primarily consist of reputable researchers at the Danish Universities, of whom many are full professors. In the period covered by this research, only 24 per cent of these researchers were women. In practice, this implies that journals covering methods and topics that fall outside the interest and preferences of a relatively homogenous group of already successful male researchers, risk being undervalued by the indicator. As a result, this standardisation exercise, developed to improve the transparency and objectivity of the universities' performance assessments, ended up introducing a new form of bias into the system. As in the hiring example, this gendered disadvantage does not relate directly to the concept of unconscious bias. Instead, it serves to illustrate how gendered knowledge and status hierarchies can become encapsulated in seemingly objective criteria for evaluating research performance as a form of systemic bias (Nielsen 2017b, 2018). This finding supports Acker's (1990) argument that rationalised performance standards, modelled on the profiles and characteristics of already successful employees, are at high risk of reinforcing gendered status hierarchies.

Symbolic boundary work

The third and final social process concerns the making and maintenance of symbolic gender boundaries in academic organisations. Epstein described symbolic boundaries as:

> the lines that include and define some people, groups, and things while excluding others. They are the conceptual distinctions that people use to categorise each other, for instance, based on gender, race, class or ethnicity.
>
> (Epstein 1992, 232)

To study symbolic boundaries 'is to analyse how social actors construct groups as similar and different and how it shapes their understanding of their responsibilities toward such groups' (Lamont and Molnár 2002, 187). Lamont and Molnár (2002) define such social processes as symbolic boundary work which can be analysed by studying the cultural narratives that people draw upon to make sense of the world around them. For example, how academic managers make sense of the persistent gender imbalances in their departments. Analysing symbolic boundary work can help in understanding how academic managers rationalise gender stereotypes and how such stereotypes contribute to legitimise persistent gender inequalities in hiring and selection.

The empirical example presented here draws on a qualitative analysis of 24 interviews, conducted with department heads at Aarhus University (Nielsen 2017a). In these interviews, the department heads were asked to reflect on what they saw as the main causes of women's under-representation among associate and full professors in their respective departments. Fourteen of the 24 department heads responded by alluding to incompatibilities between the qualities and attributes of women researchers and the indispensable requisites of the local research environments. Table 3.2 summarises the prevailing characteristics of the local research environments and the so-called typical male and female attributes and behaviours emphasised by the department heads. Here, women were seen as lacking the necessary self-confidence and competitive spirit to advance in the university's individualistic and competitive work settings, characterised by insecure career paths, high publication pressures and a tough, egoistic macho-culture (see Chapters 8 and 14). Furthermore, some department heads emphasised women's need for economic security due to family responsibilities, their lack of interest in management and their lack of international mobility as primary causes of observed gender differences in academic advancement.

Table 3.2 Reflections by department heads on gender roles in the research environment

Research environments	Men's attributes	Women's attributes
Competitive environment	Alpha males	Lack of self-confidence
Individualistic organisation	Competition-driven	Shy away from competition
(focus on individual CVs)	Egoistic	Need job security
Macho culture	Science as elite sport (work > family)	More social
High publication pressure	More but less exhaustive and thorough publications	Less egoist
Science as elite sport	Societal structures:	Better at networking
Insecure career path	traditionally easier for men to pursue a career in academia	Collectivist approach
Tough world	'New type of men' (holistic/ network focus/take responsibility)	Communication competencies
Egoistic	Live (work) from hand to mouth	Family priorities
Self-centred	High-speed production	Need economic security due to family responsibilities
Making big sacrifices for research		Some shy away from management
Limitless work time norms (not a 9–5 schedule)		More exhaustive and thorough in their approach to publications
		More holistic worldview (work–life balance)
		Less mobile

Source: Adapted from Nielsen (2017a)

These statements demonstrate how symbolic gender boundaries are perpetuated in local research environments. Stereotypical assumptions about women's attributes, qualities and interests are symbolically separated from the typical characteristics of the local research environment. In other words, the women are represented as 'soft actors' in a hard world of science, in which the ideal employee is someone who is highly competitive, individualistic, having few commitments outside the workplace (see Chapter 5). Hence, the gender problem becomes a problem relating to individual women rather than the department in its institutional context. In

Table 3.2 the interviewees also emphasise positive characteristics and qualities that women researchers contribute to their departments. Accordingly, women are more exhaustive and thorough in their publication activities, more collectively oriented, less egoistical and better at communicating than men. These attributes are all critical scientific virtues in a global science system, where teamwork has become the norm (Wuchty *et al* 2007). However, in the university's individualistic and competitive research environment, they conflict with the image of the ideal employee, and become a gendered disadvantage.

In summary, analysing boundary work as a social process increases the understanding of how gender stereotypes become rationalised in local research environments. It provides insight into the actual content of the assumptions that drive unconscious bias and how specific organisational contexts shape such assumptions. As demonstrated here, some department heads mobilise cultural narratives about the different characteristics and attributes of women and men to account for academic successes and failures in their departments. Consequently, symbolic boundary work contributes to legitimising persistent gender inequalities in hiring and selection.

Promoting equality in academic recruitment and selection

What can universities do to counter the social processes that perpetuate gender inequalities in academic recruitment and selection? There are four key forms of intervention that emerge from the Danish study. Denmark is a compelling example of the importance of ensuring transparency and continuous oversight in all recruitment and selection activities. Gender bias thrives in situations where recruiters can exploit loopholes to make recruitment and selection run 'fast, cheap and smooth'. Universities need to close these loopholes with the help of administrators and gender equality taskforces. Universities should ensure, through monitoring, that appointments are made based on fair and open procedures and that recruiters are held accountable when this is not the case. Moreover, all research positions should be communicated widely nationally and internationally and university departments should be required to do long-term, transparent scheduling of job announcements. Such scheduling could help to prevent situations whereby vacancies are timed to suit the career progression of specific candidates. Finally, all position profiles should be formulated broadly and should never signal pre-selection through specific requirements.

Previous research (Dobbin and Kalev 2016; Kalev *et al* 2006; Dobbin *et al* 2015) provides important insights on the efficacy of diversity programs in promoting workplace equality. Using data from more than 800 US companies over a 30-year period, Dobbin and Kalev (2016) found that appointing diversity task forces and assigning formal responsibilities and authority to diversity managers are two of the most efficient ways to promote gender equality. Task forces and diversity managers hold managers and recruiters accountable for their activities by continuously monitoring developments in the representation of women and minorities.

Finally, a recent study by Witteman *et al* (2019) quantified the negative gender consequences of placing too much emphasis on standardised metrics of performance in academic selection processes. The study was based on data from just over 24,000 research applications to the Canadian Institutes of Health Research. These data allowed the authors to compare women's success rates in two grant programmes. One programme had an explicit review focus on the principal investigator's past performance; the other had a key focus on the quality of the actual research presented in the application. In the grant programme with an explicit focus on past performance, women's likelihood of winning a grant was 30 per cent lower than that of men. In contrast, no clear gender differences in success rates were observed when evaluators focused on the quality of the proposals. An important conclusion from this study, which is relevant for both funding agencies and academic recruiters, is that the explicit focus on past performance, based on bibliometric indices, may lead to indirect gender bias, especially at the early career stages. To avoid this, evaluators need to be instructed to focus more on the quality of the proposed research and less on the characteristics of the researcher.

Conclusion

This chapter demonstrates that creating change towards gender sensitivity requires in-depth contextualised knowledge about the institutions where change is needed. The focus on unconscious bias in policy and practice is not enough in itself. While most universities in Europe look relatively similar in the proportions of women in professorships, the social processes that perpetuate gender inequalities in research and the obstacles facing women and gender-diverse people, vary considerably across contexts and may change over time (Nielsen 2015b). Continuous research efforts to develop more fine-grained contextualised knowledge about this multi-faceted and dynamic problem are therefore crucial.

References

Acker, J. (1990) Hierarchies, jobs, bodies: A theory of gendered organizations, *Gender and Society*, 4 (2), 139–158, doi.org/10.1177/089124390004002002

Acker, J. (2006) Inequality regimes: Gender, class, and race in organizations, *Gender and Society*, 20, (4), 441–464, doi.org/10.1177/0891243206289499

Bielby, W. (2000) Minimizing workplace gender and racial bias, *Contemporary Sociology*, 29 (1), 233–256, doi.org/10.2307/2654937

Bielby, W. (2013) The challenge of effective interventions: Alternative paths to minimizing workplace gender bias, in *Organizational change*, Harvard Business School, Boston, 4–11.

Castilla, E. and Bernard, S. (2010) The paradox of meritocracy in organisations, *Administrative Science Quarterly*, 55 (4), 543–576, doi.org/10.2189/asqu.2010.55.4.543

Correll, S. (2017) SWS 2016 feminist lecture: Reducing gender biases in modern workplaces: A small wins approach to organizational change, *Gender and Society*, 31 (6), 725–750, doi.org/10.1177/0891243217738518

Degn, L. (2015) Identity constructions and sensemaking in higher education—a case study of Danish higher education department heads, *Studies in Higher Education*, 40 (7), 1179–1193, doi.org/10.1080/03075079.2014.881345

Dobbin, F. and Kalev, A. (2016) Why diversity programs fail and what works better, *Harvard Business Review*, 94 (7–8), 52–60.

Dobbin, F., Schrage, D. and Kalev, A. (2015) Rage against the iron cage: The varied effects of bureaucratic personnel reforms on diversity, *American Sociological Review*, 80 (5), 1014–1044, doi.org/10.1177/0003122415596416

Epstein, C. F. (1992) Tinkerbells and pinups: The construction and reconstruction of gender boundaries at work, in M. Lamont and M. Fournier (eds), *Cultivating differences: Symbolic boundaries and the making of inequality*, University of Chicago Press, Chicago.

Frandsen, T., Jacobsen, R., Wallin, J., Brixen, K. and Ousager, J. (2015) Gender differences in scientific performance: A bibliometric matching analysis of Danish health sciences graduates, *Journal of Informetrics*, 9 (4), 1007–1017, doi.org/10.1016/j.joi.2015.09.006

Haynes, C. and Sweedler, J. (2015) Are we there yet? Biases in hiring women faculty candidates, *Analytical Chemistry*, 87 (14), 6989, doi.org/10.1021/acs.analchem.5b02454

Husu, L. (2000) Gender discrimination in the promised land of gender equality, *Higher Education in Europe*, 25 (2), 221–228, doi.org/10.1080/713669257

Ibarra, H. (1992) Homophily and differential returns: Sex differences in network structure and access in an advertising firm, *Administrative Science Quarterly*, 37 (3), 422–447, doi.org/10.2307/2393451

Kalev, A., Dobbin, F. and Kelly, E. (2006) Best practices or best guesses? Assessing the efficacy of corporate affirmative action and diversity policies, *American Sociological Review*, 71 (4), 589–617, doi.org/10.1177/000312240607100404

Lamont, M., Beljean, S. and Clair, M. (2014) What is missing? Cultural processes and causal pathways to inequality, *Socio-Economic Review*, 12 (3), 573–608, doi.org/10.1093/ser/mwu011

Lamont, M. and Molnár, V. (2002) The study of boundaries in the social sciences, *Annual Review of Sociology*, 28 (1), 167–195, doi.org/10.1146/annurev.soc.28.110601.141107

López, E. and O'Connor, P. (2019) Micropolitics and meritocracy: Improbable bedfellows? *Educational Management Administration and Leadership*, 47 (5), 678–693, doi.org/10.1177/1741143218759090

McGuire, G. (2000) Gender, race, ethnicity, and networks: The factors affecting the status of employees' network members, *Work and Occupations*, 27 (4), 501–524, doi.org/10.1177/0730888400027004004

Meyer, J. and Rowan, B. (1977) Institutionalized organizations: Formal structure as myth and ceremony, *American Journal of Sociology*, 83 (2), 340–363, doi.org/10.1086/226550

Moore, G. (1990) Structural determinants of men's and women's personal networks, *American Sociological Review*, 55 (5), 726–735, doi.org/10.2307/2095868

Moss-Racusin, C., Dovidio, J., Brescoll, V., Graham, M. and Handelsman, J. (2012) Science faculty's subtle gender biases favor male students, *Proceedings of the National Academy of Sciences*, 109 (41), 16474–16479, doi.org/10.1073/pnas.1211286109

Mouritzen, P. and Opstrup, N. (2020) Trickling down to the individual, in P. Mouritzen and N. Opstrup (eds), *Performance management at universities*, Palgrave Macmillan, Cham, 2020, 37–56, doi.org/10.1007/978-3-030-21325-1

Nielsen, M. (2015a) Make academic job advertisements fair to all, *Nature*, 525 (7570), 427–427, doi.org/10.1038/525427a

Nielsen, M. (2015b) *New and persistent gender equality challenges in academia*, Politica, Department of Political Science, Aarhus University, Aarhus, Denmark.

Nielsen, M. (2016) Limits to meritocracy? Gender in academic recruitment and promotion processes, *Science and Public Policy*, 43 (3), 386–399, doi.org/10.1093/scipol/scv052

Nielsen, M. (2017a) Reasons for leaving the academy: A case study on the 'opt out' phenomenon among younger female researchers, *Gender, Work and Organization*, 24 (2), 134–155, doi.org/10.1111/gwao.12151

Nielsen, M. (2017b) Gender consequences of a national performance-based funding model: New pieces in an old puzzle, *Studies in Higher Education*, 42 (6), 1033–1055, doi.org/10.1080/03075079.2015.1075197

Nielsen, M. (2018) Scientific performance assessments through a gender lens, *Science and Technology Studies*, 31 (1), 2–30, doi.org/10.23987/sts.60610

Reskin, B. and McBrier, D. (2000) Why not ascription? Organizations' employment of male and female managers, *American Sociological Review*, 65 (2), 210–233, doi.org/10.2307/2657438

Staahle, B. (2014) *Videnskabeligt personale på universiteterne 2013*, Styrelsen for Videregående Uddannelser, Copenhagen, Denmark.

Uhlmann, E. and Cohen, G. (2007) 'I think it, therefore it's true': Effects of self-perceived objectivity on hiring discrimination, *Organizational Behavior and Human Decision Processes*, 104 (2), 207–223, doi.org/10.1016/j.obhdp.2007.07.001

Van den Brink, M. (2010) *Behind the scenes of science: Gender practices in the recruitment and selection of professors in the Netherlands*, Amsterdam University Press, Amsterdam.

Van den Brink, M. and Benschop, Y. (2012) Gender practices in the construction of academic excellence: Sheep with five legs, *Organization*, 19 (4), 507–524, doi.org/10.1177/1350508411414293

Williams, J. and Smith, J. (2015) The myth that academic science isn't biased against women, *The Chronicle of Higher Education*, 8 July.

Williams, W. and Ceci, S. (2015) National hiring experiments reveal 2:1 faculty preference for women on STEM tenure track, *Proceedings of the National Academy of Sciences*, 17, 5360–5365, doi.org/10.1073/pnas.1418878112

Witteman, H., Hendricks, M., Straus, S. and Tannenbaum, C. (2019) Are gender gaps due to evaluations of the applicant or the science? A natural experiment at a national funding agency, *The Lancet*, 393 (10171), 531–540, doi.org/10.1016/S0140-6736(18)32611-4

Wuchty, S., Jones, B. and Uzzi, B. (2007) The increasing dominance of teams in production of knowledge, *Science*, 316 (5827), 1036–1039, doi.org/10.1126/science.1136099

Chapter 4

In pursuit of career advancement in academia

Do gendered pathways exist?

Mary Kinahan, Julie Dunne and Jean Cahill

Introduction

Despite the worldwide increase in women's education and employment in third-level education and initiatives to decrease gender inequality, female academics remain under-represented at the senior levels of these institutions (Catalyst 2017). For example, in the US, while there is close to gender parity (52%) in low-ranking positions, female academics are still less likely to hold a tenured position (38%) and account for less than one-third (32%) of professorial posts (Catalyst 2017; National Centre for Education Statistics 2016). According to the European Commission's *SHE figures 2018*, while progress is slow throughout Europe, there is an overall improvement in women's representation among holders of PhDs and academic positions (European Commission 2019). However, female academics still remain under-represented at senior levels, with women representing 46 per cent of grade C, 40 per cent of grade B and only 24 per cent of grade A, the highest academic position (European Commission 2019). In disciplines that are considered masculine-typed or male dominated, such as science, technology, engineering and mathematics (STEM), there is an even greater gender disparity in representation at all levels, with women accounting for only 15 per cent of grade A professorial posts (European Commission 2019) (see Chapter 1). Thus, the consistent pattern is, that while there is an increasing representation of women and gender parity in lower-level positions, this does not carry through to senior posts.

This continued under-representation of female academics in senior positions in higher education institutions, especially in STEM areas, led to the creation of the Athena SWAN Charter. The Charter's original aim was to promote and support gender equality for women at all levels within higher education institutions in the UK (Equality Challenge Unit 2019). In 2015, the Athena SWAN charter was launched in Ireland (Equality Challenge Unit 2019) as part of a major national initiative by the Irish Higher Education Authority requiring Irish HEIs to commit to the principles of gender equality, as outlined in the Charter. They must also apply for an Athena SWAN award: Bronze, Silver or Gold. Bronze applications require an assessment of gender equality that identifies challenges and opportunities in the institution. The findings analysed in this chapter are based on the empirical data gathered in the Dublin Institute of Technology (now called the Technological University Dublin). Institution-wide data were collected through a staff attitudinal survey and three focus groups with senior-level academics. These results were subsequently used in the Dublin Institute of Technology's successful Bronze Athena SWAN application. Before presenting these findings, the chapter reviews the literature on career barriers faced by female academics.

Barriers to career advancement for female academics

Theories such as 'role congruity theory' of prejudice towards women leaders (Eagly and Karau 2002) and a 'lack of fit' model (Heilman 2001) emphasise that women and men are perceived differently in society and are typically associated with different characteristics and attributes. Women's perceived characteristics and attributes are stereotypically identified as warm and communal and therefore incongruent with the perceived requirements of senior positions in society. This leads to negative self-perceptions among women (Eagly and Karau 2002; Heilman 2001). The lack of fit or incongruence between the female stereotype and the perceived requirements of a senior position leads, in turn, to prejudice and discrimination (Rudman and Glick 2008).

Perceived ability and lack of mentorship and role model

The influence of this perceived lack of fit or incongruence can negatively impact women's self-perceptions, in particular, women's self-efficacy (Dickerson and Taylor 2000). Research on women's self-efficacy in academia is mixed, depending on their level and discipline, with some studies finding no gender differences in motivation and self-efficacy amongst staff (Bailey 1999). Other studies find that male academics report stronger self-efficacy, as well as more time spent on research activities and outputs (Vasil 1992). Regardless of the mixed nature of the literature, self-efficacy is considered a strong determinant of career choice and direction, with lower self-efficacy resulting in self-limiting behaviour deemed detrimental to career advancement (Dickerson and Taylor 2000). These self-limiting beliefs and behaviours may include women undervaluing their work contribution (Haynes and Heilman 2013), or lacking confidence in their ability to perform challenging roles. This, in turn, affects their beliefs about pursuing leadership or senior positions (Davis et al 2005; Dickerson and Taylor 2000; Simon and Hoyt 2012).

Lack of mentorship and positive role models are also barriers to women's advancement to senior academic positions. Typically, mentorship involves: 'a developmental relationship between two individuals, where usually the individual with more experience, provides guidance for a lesser experienced individual' (Johnson and Kaslow 2014, 273). A role model, on the other hand, is typically someone to imitate and admire. In recent years, the concept of mentorship has changed, becoming broader and more diverse. It includes group mentoring, e-mentoring and intergenerational or reverse mentoring (Karcher *et al* 2006). There is a body of literature on the topic of mentorship and role models in education and academia that lies beyond the scope of discussion for this chapter. However, in Meschitti and Lawton-Smith's (2017) work, mentoring is found to be important in addressing gender imbalance and women's exclusion from important networks (Van den Brink and Benschop 2014). Furthermore, women's exclusion from social networks can impede their ability to develop social capital which is often seen as an essential resource for a successful academic career (Angervall *et al* 2018).

Gender discrimination, promotion and pay equity

Eagly's social role theory (Wood and Eagly 2010) posits that gender stereotypes or beliefs can influence women's and men's behaviour through a combination of gender identity or self-concept and stereotypical expectations (Deaux and LaFrance 1998; Wood *et al* 1997; Wood and Eagly 2010). Stereotypes or beliefs about men's and women's attributes are located in two dimensions: agency (agentic) and communion (communal) (Bakan 1966). Characteristics more stereotypically associated with women include concern for others, affection, kindness and interpersonal sensitivity (Fiske *et al* 2002; Diekman and Eagly 2000). Agentic characteristics, more stereotypically associated with men, relate to social status and power (Conway *et al* 1996). These entail confidence, control and assertiveness (Diekman and Eagly 2000).

Eagly and Karau's (2002) work on role congruity identified two types of prejudice that correspond with women's challenge to the descriptive and prescriptive aspects of their gender stereotype. Descriptive expectations characterise the qualities that differentiate men from women (Cialdini and Trost 1998). Descriptive prejudice results from the presumed incongruence between female gender stereotype and masculine leadership role or senior position: women in communal and senior positions typically require agentic qualities (Heilman and Eagly 2008). Hence, female applicants for senior positions like professorships are more at risk of being evaluated less favourably than their male colleagues, due to the perception that they lack the required characteristics to do the job successfully (Eagly and Karau 2002; Heilman 1983; Heilman and Eagly 2008). Studies on employee selection and promotion have consistently demonstrated that in masculine-typed domains, male applicants are more likely to be hired and are perceived to succeed at specific tasks than equally qualified female applicants (Alimo-Metcalfe 1994; Davison and Burke 2000; Heilman and Haynes 2005). The suggestion is that different standards are set for men and for women, with women being set a lower minimum competency standard but a higher ability standard (Biernat and Fuegen 2001; Biernat and Kobrynowicz 1997). In a series of hiring simulations, Biernat and Fuegen (2001) found that although women were more likely than men to make the shortlist (set a lower competence standard), they were less likely to be hired for the job (set a higher ability standard). The shifting standard model argues that, due to the male stereotype and gender bias, women are evaluated to a lower standard than their male colleagues when it comes to meeting a minimum standard. However, women are evaluated to a higher standard than their male colleagues when it comes to ability to perform the job (Biernat and Fuegen 2001). These findings suggest that prejudice and the resulting negative selection and promotion expectations may contribute further to women's under-representation in senior academic positions.

In contrast, prescriptive or injunctive expectations specify the ideal behaviours for each gender, what each gender 'ought' to be like (Cialdini and Trost 1998). Perceived incongruence or lack of fit are not stable concepts, rather they are malleable, depending on the context, occupational role and candidate. So it would seem reasonable that women who seek to advance to senior positions could narrow the lack of fit between their perceived characteristics and the requirements of a senior position by adopting more agentic characteristics and behaviour. Female academics could thus avoid their perceived lack of fit for a senior academic position (Eagly and Karau 2002; Heilman 2001; Heilman and Eagly 2008). Heilman *et al* (1995) found that when women managers were depicted as successful, they were perceived to be as agentic as their male counterparts. However, despite being ascribed the same level of agency, the same women were also regarded as more hostile and less rational than their male counterparts. This demonstrates the second type of prejudice, that results from women's violation of the prescriptive aspect of their female gender stereotype. Such violations result in negative consequences such as being less liked and less influential (Butler and Geis 1990) and being perceived as less qualified than equivalent job applicants (Davison and Burke 2000). Agentic women may experience social and economic penalties for self-promotion (Rudman 1998) and for being successful in traditional male domains (Heilman *et al* 2004). Women face a double bind or lose-lose situation in that, if they fulfil the requirements of their senior position, they may violate their female gender stereotype, resulting in being perceived as competent but unlikeable. If women comply with their female gender stereotype, they could fail to fulfil the requirements of their senior position, resulting in being perceived as incompetent but likeable. Violation in either case results in negative evaluations that can negatively impact women's career progress (Eagly and Karau 2002; Heilman and Parks-Stamm 2007; Heilman *et al* 2004; Rudman and Glick 2001).

Gender disparity in service and student support responsibilities

According to Misra *et al* (2011), female academics devote more time than their male counterparts to service duties such as pastoral care, with consequently less time for research. Furthermore, many service and care duties are not considered valuable for promotion (Guarino and Borden 2017). Guarino and Borden (2017) found that female academic staff performed more service than their male colleagues and were mainly driven by internal (for example service to the university or the student body) than external service (for example service to national communities). They posit a number of explanations for the gender disparity in the allocation of these duties, including gender inequality structures that foster gender bias and discrimination, as well as promoting gender typical behaviour. This is consistent with the literature (O'Meara *et al* 2017; Pyke 2015) showing that disparities in the allocation of academic duties result from systematic gender bias, whereby women are simply asked to do more administrative, caring or 'housekeeping' work than their male colleagues and they comply with these requests (O'Meara *et al* 2017).

Another explanation for this gender disparity may be due to the consequences of lack of fit and incongruence between gender stereotype and occupational role. According to the stereotype content model (Fiske *et al* 2002), stereotypes can be rated by the level of perceived warmth and competence. As already noted, gender stereotypes can prove problematic for female academics since there is a perceived incongruence or lack of fit between the warmth or communality of female gender stereotype and the agentic or competent requirements of a senior academic position (Eagly and Karau 2002; Heilman 2001; Heilman and Eagly 2008). However women face negative consequences for not just acting in a gender atypical way, but for not acting sufficiently in a gender typical manner to counter the implied communality deficit of being a woman in a traditional male domain (Heilman and Okimoto 2007). Some studies have demonstrated that women who do not behave in a sufficiently communal way can be evaluated more negatively than their male counterparts who behave in the same way (Heilman and Chen 2005; Heilman and Eagly 2008; Heilman and Okimoto 2007; Vinkenberg *et al* 2011). Therefore women must negotiate this double bind by acting as both competent and warm in order to avoid negative consequences, such as volunteering or agreeing to more gender-typical responsibilities and service. Pyke (2015) argues that female academic staff are asked to do more service than male colleagues because they are less likely to 'say no' due to the gendered norms and expectations within academia. According to Pyke (2015) and O'Meara *et al* (2017), advising women to just 'say no' is not helpful and can actually be damaging. This is consistent with negotiating the double bind of being both competent and warm, where women can experience backlash if they violate their gender role by not acting sufficiently communal in a typical masculine role or field (Rudman and Glick 2001).

Empirical findings

In the remainder of this chapter, it is argued that women and men in academia face different career barriers and responsibilities in the workplace. Empirical findings are provided to support this. As part of the Athena SWAN project in the Dublin Institute of Technology (DIT), all members of current academic and research staff, of all genders and in all areas of the Institute, were invited to participate in a survey that was designed to explore equality of experience and of opportunity, to highlight positive actions and to raise issues that need to be tackled in the future. Survey participants comprised 385 academic and research staff (166 male, 219 female), ranging from assistant lecturer (equivalent to Grade C) to senior lecturer grade II and above (equivalent to Grade A). Due to the low number of participants not indicating their gender or identifying as nonbinary, participant confidentiality and anonymity was a concern, hence their responses were excluded from the dataset.

Data collection took place online using SurveyGizmo and branching methods based on questions such as job role in order to limit question fatigue. Participants were presented with a consent letter which included information about the survey which took approximately 15–20 minutes to complete. Focus group participants consisted of 22 academics - two groups of female senior academics and one group of male senior academics. Focus group participants were presented with a consent letter with information about the project and seeking their consent to record and transcribe the group discussion. The findings of the survey and focus groups identified a number of barriers and responsibilities that female academics face in their pursuit of career advancement

A number of career barriers were identified that were rated more highly by female, than male academics namely: lower belief in their abilities; lack of mentorship; work-life balance and greater care responsibilities; and gender discrimination, in terms of promotion and pay. More female academics (34%) than their male counterparts (16%) agreed that their gender impacted on the duties they were expected to perform with participants commenting:

> '*I think more so* [gender] *impacts on my female colleagues more. I think males are listened to more'.*
> '*In general, females are asked to do more. Men say no quicker'.*
> '*I take on more pastoral care roles than my male colleagues, I take on more admin roles too'.*

Regarding mentorship, female academic and research staff agreed that lack of mentorship was a hindrance to their careers, rating having role models and mentors more highly than their male colleagues:

> '*Not having a role model or mentor at work'.*
> '*Not knowing the right people to get ahead in my career'.*

Moreover, in the focus groups, female senior academics outlined the importance of local political connections for career development. This included developing allies with power to support and provide access to and influence opportunities within academia (O'Hagan *et al* 2016). In particular, senior female academics stressed that in their experience, younger female staff (assistant lecturers) often had weaker network links than their male colleagues and this hindered turning their talent into tangible rewards.

These survey findings show that female academic and research staff rated their experience of gender discrimination (having a boss or supervisor who is biased against people of their gender); gender disparity in pay (not being paid as much as co-workers of the opposite gender) and in promotion (people of the opposite gender receive promotions more often than people of their gender) as hindering their careers, to a greater extent than their male colleagues. More female staff disagreed that: they understood the process and criteria for promotion; the promotion process was transparent and fair; and feedback was appropriate and useful. Respondents were asked to rate the culture of their organisation in terms of gender equality in a number of key areas, on a scale of 1 = women are significantly disadvantaged to 5 = men are significantly disadvantaged (0 = don't know). Topics included promotion, salary, access to career development opportunities, access to funding, access to lab and office space, and access to administrative support (Table 4.1).

Table 4.1 Gender differences in perceived beliefs about women's disadvantage

Key areas	Women (%)	Men (%)
Promotion	36	11
Salary	20	7
Career development resources	33	13
Access to funding	16	3
Lab access	11	3
Administrative support	14	2

One of the most surprising outcomes of the survey and focus groups was the perceived gender disparity in allocation of service duties and student care responsibilities. Consistent with existing literature, the study showed that the majority of staff rated research as the most important activity for an academic career (94%) and that it was most valued by their school/department (81%). In contrast, pastoral care (6%) and administrative duties (7%) were rated as much less important in contributing to careers and in their perceived value by schools/departments. In the study, female academic staff said:

'*I appear to be given minding role more frequently than male colleagues*'.
'*I was recently asked by my manger to tidy up a lab. I am fairly certain that he would not have asked one of my male colleagues to do this*'.
'*I am expected to do a lot of the admin duties, organisational tasks and cleaning for the research group*'.
'*I tend to be allocated organisation, minute-taking administration tasks along with more pastoral care type roles*'.
'*Students in distress are passed on from male colleagues*'.
'*The view has been expressed by leadership that older, senior male academic staff cannot be expected to undertake administrative tasks to the same extent as other staff members*'.

A way forward?

From the DIT research and an examination of the literature, three main issues are apparent: a lack of formal mentorship and leadership development programmes; gender bias via structural inequalities and culture, reflected in gender discrimination in selection, promotion and pay procedures; and the lack of a transparent and fair workload allocation that recognises and takes into account extra service or caring responsibilities, such as pastoral support for students. Additionally, there are a number of processes in relation to leadership that have relevance for women who seek these roles. Alongside any leadership development programme, universities and research institutions need to implement formalised mentorship programmes that would provide support for female academic staff (Ely *et al* 2011). Furthermore, academic institutions need to address the structural inequalities and culture within their organisations, review their selection, promotion and pay procedures for gender bias (see Chapters 3, 7 and 9) and engage with all staff to maintain positive momentum for gender equality. Addressing gender bias and structural inequalities in academia calls for a review of workload models that acknowledges activities, such as administration and service work, as much as research. This study shows that female staff often undertake additional roles and activities aligned with their female gender stereotype, which are neither valued nor beneficial for their promotion prospects. A transparent and fairer workload allocation model that clearly assigns activities equitably, regardless of gender, is essential.

Conclusions

This chapter analysed a number of barriers that female academics face in their pursuit of career advancement and promotion to senior positions. Drawing upon existing literature, it is argued that, due to a perceived lack of fit and/or incongruence between the female gender stereotypes and perceived requirements of senior academic positions, female academics who wish to pursue senior academic positions are often at a greater disadvantage, compared with their male colleagues. Moreover, given the gender bias and disparities that exist within academia, female academics frequently face additional barriers such as lack of mentorship, work-life balance issues and gender discrimination in terms of promotion and pay. The empirical findings in this chapter show that female academics consistently rated barriers to their career advancement higher than their male colleagues. Furthermore, female academics are also given, or volunteer for, a disproportionate amount of support or housekeeping work that is not accorded value for promotion. This confirms the need for formal mentorship and leadership development programmes, in addition to a more transparent and fairer workload allocation model.

References

Alimo-Metcalfe, B. (1994) Gender bias in the selection and assessment of women in management, in M. Davidson and R. Burke (eds), *Women in management: Current research issues*, Paul Chapman, London, 93–109.

Angervall, P., Gustafsson, J. and Silfver, E. (2018) Academic career: On institutions, social capital and gender, *Higher Education, Research and Development*, 37 (6), 1095–1108.

Bailey, J. (1999) Academics' motivation and self-efficacy for teaching and research, *Higher Education Research and Development*, 18 (3), 343–359.

Bakan, D. (1966) *The duality of human existence: An essay on psychology and religion*, Rand McNally, Chicago.

Biernat, M. and Fuegen, K. (2001) Shifting standards and the evaluation of competence: Complexity in gender-based judgment and decision making, *Journal of Social Issues*, 57 (4), 707–724.

Biernat, M. and Kobrynowicz, D. (1997) Gender and race-based standards of competence: Lower minimum standards but higher ability standards for devalued groups, *Journal of Personality and Social Psychology*, 72 (3), 544–557.

Butler, D. and Geis, F. (1990) Nonverbal affect responses to male and female leaders: Implications for leadership evaluations, *Journal of Personality and Social Psychology*, 58 (1), 48–59.

Catalyst (2017) *Quick take: Women in academia*, 20 October. Available at: www.catalyst. org/knowledge/women-academia

Cialdini, R. and Trost, M. (1998) Social influence: Social norms, conformity and compliance, in D. Gilbert, S. Fiske and G. Lindzey (eds), *The handbook of social psychology* (Vol. 2, 4th ed.), McGraw-Hill, New York, 151–192.

Conway, M., Pizzamiglio, M. and Mount, L. (1996) Status, communality, and agency: Implications for stereotypes of gender and other groups, *Journal of Personality and Social Psychology*, 71 (1), 25–38.

Davis, P., Spencer, S. and Steele, C. (2005) Clearing the air: Identity safety moderates the effects of stereotype threat on women's leadership aspirations, *Journal of Personality and Social Psychology*, 88 (2), 276–287.

Davison, K. and Burke, M. (2000) Sex discrimination in simulated employment contexts: A meta-analytic investigation, *Journal of Vocational Behavior*, 56 (2), 225–248.

Deaux, K. and LaFrance, M. (1998) Gender, in D. Gilbert, S. Fiske and G. Lindzey (eds), *The handbook of social psychology* (Vol. 1), McGraw-Hill, Boston, MA, 788–827.

Dickerson, A. and Taylor, M. (2000) Self-limiting behaviour in women: Self-esteem and self-efficacy as predictors, *Group Organization Management*, 25 (2), 191–210.

Diekman, A. and Eagly, A. (2000) Stereotypes as dynamic constructs: Women and men of the past, present, and future, *Personality and Social Psychology Bulletin*, 26 (10), 1171–1188.

Eagly, A. and Karau, S. (2002) Role congruity theory of prejudice toward female leaders, *Psychological Review*, 109 (3), 573–598.

Ely, R., Ibarra, H. and Kolb, D. (2011) Taking gender into account: Theory and design for women's leadership development program, *Academy of Management Learning & Development*, 10 (3), 474–493.

Equality Challenge Unit (2019) *Athena swan charter*. Available at: www.ecu.ac.uk/equality-charters/athena-swan/

European Commission (2019) *SHE figures 2018*, European Commission, Luxembourg.

Fiske, S., Cuddy, A., Glick, P. and Xu, J. (2002) A model of (often mixed) stereotype content: Competence and warmth respectively follow from perceived status and competition, *Journal of Personality and Social Psychology*, 82 (6), 878–902.

Guarino, C. and Borden, V. (2017) Faculty service loads and gender: Are women taking care of the academic family? *Research in Higher Education*, 58 (6), 672–694.

Haynes, M. and Heilman, M. (2013) It had to be you (not me)! Women's attributional rationalization of their contribution to successful joint work outcomes, *Personality and Social Psychology Bulletin*, 39 (7), 956–969.

Heilman, M. (1983) Sex bias in work settings: The lack of fit model, in B. Staw and L. Cummings (eds), *Research in organizational behavior* (Vol. 5), JAI Press, Greenwich, CT, 269–298.

Heilman, M. (2001) Description and prescription: How gender stereotypes prevent women's ascent up the organizational ladder, *Journal of Social Issues*, 57 (4), 657–674.

Heilman, M., Block, C. and Martell, R. (1995) Sex stereotypes: Do they influence perceptions of managers? *Journal of Social Behavior and Personality*, 10, 237–252.

Heilman, M. and Chen, J. (2005) Same behavior, different consequences: Reactions to men's and women's altruistic citizenship behavior, *Journal of Applied Psychology*, 90 (3), 431–441.

Heilman, M. and Eagly, A. (2008) Gender stereotypes are alive, well, and busy producing workplace discrimination, *Industrial and Organizational Psychology*, 1 (4), 393–398.

Heilman, M. and Haynes, M. (2005) No credit where credit is due: Attributional rationalization of women's success in male-female teams, *Journal of Applied Psychology*, 90 (5), 905–916.

Heilman, M. and Okimoto, T. (2007) Why are women penalized for success at male tasks? Implied communality deficit, *Journal of Applied Psychology*, 92 (1), 81–92.

Heilman, M. and Parks-Stamm, E. (2007) Gender stereotypes in the workplace: Obstacles to women's career progress, in S. Correll (ed), *Social psychology of gender advances in group processes* (Vol. 24), JAI Press, Greenwich, CT, 47–77.

Heilman, M., Wallen, A., Fuchs, D. and Tamkins, M. (2004) Penalties for success: Reactions to women who succeed at male gender-typed tasks, *Journal of Applied Psychology*, 89 (3), 416–427.

Johnson, B. and Kaslow, J. (2014) *The Oxford handbook of education and training in professional psychology*, Oxford University Press, Oxford.

Karcher, M., Kuperminc, G., Portwood, S., Sipe, C. and Taylor A. (2006) Mentoring programs: A framework to inform program development, research and evaluation, *Journal of Community Psychology*, 34 (6), 709–725.

Meschitti, V. and Lawton-Smith, H. (2017) Does mentoring make a difference for women academics? Evidence from the literature and a guide for future research, *Journal of Research in Gender Studies*, 7 (1), 166–199.

Misra, J., Lundquist, J., Holmes, E. and Agiomavritis, S. (2011) *The ivory ceiling of service work*. Available at: www.aaup.org/article/ivory-ceiling-service-work#.VxllJzArI2x

National Center for Education Statistics, IPEDS Data Center (2016) *Full-time instructional staff by faculty and tenure status, academic rank, race/ethnicity and gender (Degree granting institutions)*, Fall Staff 2015 Survey. Available at: https://nces.ed.gov/

O'Hagen, C., O'Connor, P., Myers, E., Baisner, L., Apostolov, G., Topuzova, I., Saglamer, G., Mine, T. and Cağlayan, H. (2016) Perpetuating academic capitalism and maintaining gender orders through career practices in STEM in universities, *Critical Studies in Education*, 60 (2), 205–225.

O'Meara, K., Kuvaeva, A., Nyunt, G., Waugaman, C. and Jackson, R. (2017) Asked more often: Gender differences in faculty workload in research universities and the work interactions that shape them, *American Educational Research Journal*, 54 (6), 1154–1186.

Pyke, K. (2015) Faculty gender inequity and the 'just say no to service' fairy tale, in K. De Welde and A. Stepnick (eds), *Disrupting the culture of silence*, Stylus, Sterling, VA, 83–95.

Rudman, L. (1998) Self-promotion as a risk factor for women: The costs and benefits of counter stereotypical impression management, *Journal of Personality and Social Psychology*, 74 (3), 629–645.

Rudman, L. and Glick, P. (2001) Prescriptive gender stereotypes and backlash toward agentic women, *Journal of Social Issues*, 57 (4), 743–762.

Rudman, L. and Glick, P. (2008) *The social psychology of gender: How power and intimacy shape gender relations*, The Guildford Press, New York.

Simon, S. and Hoyt, C. (2012) Exploring the effect of media images on women's leadership self-perceptions and aspirations, *Group Processes & Intergroup Relations*, 16 (2), 232–245.

Van den Brink, M. and Benschop, Y. (2014) Gender in academic networking: The role of gatekeepers in professorial recruitment, *Journal of Management Studies*, 51 (3), 460–492.

Vasil, L. (1992) Self-efficacy expectations and causal attributions for achievement among male and female university faculty, *Journal of Vocational Behavior*, 41 (3), 259–269.

Vinkenberg, C., Van Engen, M., Eagly, A. and Johannesen-Schmidt, M. (2011) An exploration of stereotypical beliefs about leadership styles: Is transformational leadership a route to women's promotion? *The Leadership Quarterly*, 22 (1), 10–21.

Wood, W., Christensen, P., Hebl, M. and Rothgerber, H. (1997) Conformity to sex-typed norms, affect, and the self-concept, *Journal of Personality and Social Psychology*, 73 (3), 523–535.

Wood, W. and Eagly, A. (2010) Gender, in S. Fiske, D. Gilbert and G. Lindzey (eds), *Handbook of social psychology* (Vol. 1, 5th ed.), Oxford University Press, New York, 629–667.

Chapter 5

Work-life balance in academia
Myth or reality?

Eileen Drew and Claire Marshall

Introduction

A survey of academic and research staff in one Irish university was conducted in 2015, gathering information on: the motivations of staff in applying for university posts; their working hours, experience of flexible working and work-life balance: how they defined it and their levels of satisfaction with it. Responses were sought on family-related (maternity, paternity and parenting) leave and any issues associated with availing of it, in particular the potential impact on careers (Drew and Marshall 2017). The questionnaire design was based on surveys conducted by the Athena Survey of Science, Engineering and Technology (ASSET) across UK universities and those conducted in the University of Michigan, US.

The survey questionnaire was designed and administered online using Survey Monkey as the data collection tool and the results were downloaded into EXCEL, SPSS and WORD files for analysis. The questions sought both closed (quantitative) and open-ended (qualitative) responses. The quantitative data were analysed using the Statistical Package for the Social Sciences (SPSS). This was complemented by content analysis of the open-ended responses. Recipients (1,017 academic staff and 804 research staff) of the online survey were asked to complete all questions. Recipients were informed that each question was optional and they could withdraw from the survey at any time. Despite assurances that all information collected through the online survey would remain completely anonymous and not be traceable to any respondent, a substantial number of potential respondents exited from the survey when asked to state their school/faculty within the university. In total there were 223 respondents who completed the survey, 161 women and 62 men. Hence the response rate was 12.3 per cent which compares favourably with that of 8 per cent for the 2010 ASSET survey conducted among all STEM departments in UK universities.

In order to validate and triangulate the survey results, three faculty-level focus groups were conducted in 2018 within Trinity College Dublin (TCD). An invitation was sent to faculty staff, of all genders, in the Health Sciences (HS), Arts, Humanities and Social Sciences (AHSS) and Engineering, Mathematics and Science (EMS) faculties asking them to attend a faculty-level focus group meeting.

The invitation set out the themes that would be explored. Attendees were self-selecting and predominantly drawn from female staff. Each focus group ran for between one and two hours and the discussion was taped and transcribed, with the permission of focus group members.

Work-life balance in Trinity College Dublin

The university operates formal and informal systems of flexible working to support work-life balance for employees. Academic staff do not have prescribed contractual weekly working hours and the academic contract of employment addresses work location and working hours obligations as are reasonably necessary for the proper performance of duties and responsibilities (TCD 2020). A flexitime scheme exists for administrative and support staff providing for flexible attendance patterns outside of core hours. For all staff, the university also operates arrangements for a shorter working year and reduced working hours. A dedicated webpage for staff wellbeing was also created on the university website for flexible working and work-life balance, supporting the argument that stronger promotion of the available schemes would increase their uptake. A set of actions to improve work-life balance was designed and included in the university's successful application for renewal of its institutional Athena SWAN Bronze Award in 2018.

The definition of work-life balance used by Trinity College Dublin (TCD 2020) is 'work life balance is about seeking to maintain a balance between an individual's personal and professional life' and the following policies are referred to as assisting its achievement: maternity leave, parental leave, paternity leave and teleworking. In Ireland, maternity leave of 42 weeks (26 weeks paid and 16 weeks unpaid) is available. Paternity leave of two weeks can be taken consecutively by fathers at any time within the first 26 weeks following the birth or adoption of a child. Employers (including TCD) can top up the basic state payment of maternity and paternity benefit (Daly and Rush 2019). Unpaid parental leave of 18 weeks duration, per parent, per child, is non-transferable between parents. It may be taken up to the child's eighth birthday, in separate blocks of a minimum of six continuous weeks or on other terms, subject to their employer's agreement (Daly and Rush 2019).

Literature review

The literature on work-life balance evolved from a narrower body of research that arose in response to rising levels of female labour force participation and demands by employers for greater flexibility in more highly employee-protected EU labour markets. Since 2000 the case for work-life balance has moved the emphasis from women-led and 'family friendly' demands for shorter (part-time) working hours to encompass a range of home/teleworking, statutory entitlement for leave to reconcile work-family and other caring responsibilities, alongside demand for childcare provision and supports (Drew *et al* 2002). An implicit rationale for work-life balance has been the (as yet unrealised) expectation of 'sharing the caring' and the elimination of gender-determined roles in paid and unpaid work.

Noting the new managerialism that had permeated UK university cultures, Deem (2003) identified power relations, in terms of unequal household divisions of labour and gendered expectations of and about managers and management, as potential impediments to academic careers. While few men thought their careers had been affected by their own gender:

> women were seen as disadvantaged by gender and particularly by motherhood, while fatherhood was regarded as not harming academic careers. Gender in this sense still equates to women.
>
> (Deem 2003, 255)

Probert (2005) reiterated this finding in explaining women's under-representation at senior management levels arising from gendered choices in parenting and career roles. Kinman's (2014) work demonstrates how neoliberalism is undermining academic autonomy and working conditions in academia, referring to time-based conflict (reducing time available for non-work activities) and strain-based conflict (where the job role can have adverse consequences for individuals). This conflict is accentuated and even more difficult to counter for academic and research staff who have caring responsibilities, which are traditionally associated with women.

Lynch (2010) also pointed to the new managerial governance of universities and the pressures of marketisation as reinforcing an academic environment of 'carelessness' (having no caring responsibilities), reinforcing Acker's (1990) concept of the ideal academic as a masculine norm, against which female staff often feel that they fall short. Herschberg et al (2018) elaborated on this norm of global hegemonic masculinity as a person who is not only highly productive, career-oriented and mobile but also free from primary hands-on care responsibilities. Ivancheva et al juxtaposed the celibate travelling scholars of medieval scholastic traditions against the current:

> neoliberal demands for internationalisation and self-marketisation [that] require a new kind of monk, a truly elastic self with no boundaries in time, space, energy or emotion (Ivancheva 2019, 451).

Based on a study involving interviews with senior academic appointees in Irish universities, Gummell et al concluded that even having:

> equal opportunities policies, work-life balance programmes and campaigns to encourage women to seek promotion will have little substantive impact on women's chances of leading universities and higher education colleges when the jobs are increasingly defined as precluding those who have care-full lives outside of work.
>
> (Gummell 2009, 204)

Reinforcing this, Morley (2013) argued that the prevailing culture in academia has been of a 'care-free zone' (free of responsibilities for children and other family members) in which women encounter prejudice in an environment that compares them against the male norm and perceives female appointments as perceived risks. Morley labels universities as 'greedy organisations' in which leaders (mainly men) require 'an elastic self' to enable them to pursue increasingly corporate goals, leading to stress, lack of work-life balance and non-sustainability. Research by Huppatz *et al* highlighted the considerable tensions that academic mothers encounter in a culture of new managerialism in relation to taking maternity leave and accessing flexible work arrangements. They observed that formal or informal flexibility, facilitating self-management of workload, was a 'double-edged' arrangement in which the boundary between work and leisure was blurred and the 'quest for academic self-improvement [becomes] a vocation rather than mere employment' (Huppatz *et al* 2019, 784).

Survey results

Work-life balance, flexible working and family-related leave

The survey results showed that on average, 40 per cent of female and 46 per cent of male respondents work in excess of 50 hours per week. The gender difference was not statistically significant. To contextualise this, the EU Working Time Directive (2003/88/ED) states that each member state must ensure that every worker is entitled to a limit in their working time, which must not exceed 48 hours, including overtime. When asked if they tend to work weekends/evenings in addition to normal working hours, the vast majority of respondents (87 per cent of men and 86 per cent of women) stated that they did. If respondents worked weekends/evenings, in addition to normal working hours, they were asked about the reasons for this. These related to: excessive workloads being necessary to get the work done; to access equipment; to meet specific grant application deadlines or lectures; due to the nature of the research (for example experimental) process which could not fit into a 9–5 schedule; to compensate for flexible working (to drop or pick up children from school); and for career advancement.

Survey respondents were asked how satisfied they were with their current balance between their professional and personal life (Figure 5.1). Levels of satisfaction (satisfied/very satisfied) were not dissimilar for male (39%) and female respondents (42%). However, marginally more men (42%) than women (36%) were dissatisfied or very dissatisfied with their work-life balance. Similar satisfaction levels were noted in the 2012 survey, hence suggesting no discernible improvement.

Work-life balance was defined in very diverse terms by the women and men surveyed, ranging from being able to take time off for weekends/holidays; time to spend on other activities; access to flexible working; being able to spend time with their children; and not 'living to work'. Survey respondents were asked if they regularly worked from home. The majority of men and women respondents did, though the level was higher among male (73%) compared with female respondents (67%). One-third of the women who responded and 37 per cent of the men regularly worked evenings and/or weekends.

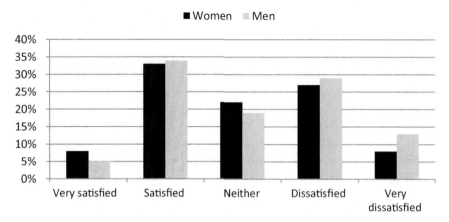

Figure 5.1 Levels of satisfaction with professional-personal life balance by gender (n = 220)

The survey established that it was women, rather than men, who opted for flexible working arrangements and who also availed of family-related leave. While 54 women had taken maternity leave, only four men had availed of paternity leave. When asked if they had experienced any difficulties in returning to work after such family-related leave, more women (28) compared to men (6) had experienced difficulties. For six women, these difficulties related to teaching: they had no cover or doubling up before taking leave. In the worst cases, mothers returned to an increased teaching load and/or were allocated new courses. Three women found that they had been removed from projects or their research group; three were faced with space or resource problems, including one who lost her desk for three months upon returning to work. Two women had to attend a job interview for a permanent post whilst on leave, which they found very stressful. Others emphasised feeling isolated, forgotten or overlooked, and they and others reported that it was difficult to catch up, particularly on their research, after three or more months on family-related leave. Mothers felt that there were no proper supports in place, including childcare, to help get them back up to their former levels of productivity. Typical of these mothers' experiences were:

> *'I did not exactly find any difficulties, but I found NO supports. You have to return to work at full speed and with the same administration and other load as everyone else. There is no consideration made of the major gap in terms of research time and research momentum which comes with maternity leave. It is not a sabbatical'.*
> *'I found myself with the heaviest timetable in the department and one of my courses had been written out of the programme. When I asked for this to be reviewed I was told it had happened because I had been absent on maternity leave. Out of sight, out of mind. Worst year of my professional life!'*

'On one occasion a research group of colleagues in my absence had under-taken to remove me from a research group as I had not inputted during mater-nity leave. . . . On return from both maternity leaves I had lost my familiar teaching and took on new subjects. This catch-up impacted on my research outputs'.

Some women returned to increases or changes to their workload:

'On returning I immediately had a full teaching load including new courses . . . and my publication rate decreased or plateaued in this time after return to work. This period is not accounted for in any promotion or grant application which usually only asks about the specific period spent on (maternity) leave without taking the knock-on consequences into account'.

'On one occasion all my teaching for the period of time that I had been on leave had been rescheduled for my return. Consequently, on my return I taught a full-years load over three and half months'.

Men also testified to the lack of adjustment and support when they were faced with parenthood:

'I only took a couple of days leave each time but was exhausted. Nothing was in place to help me with that. I just had to get on with it which I did and even-tually got used to working with a new and reduced level of sleep'.

One of the major consequences of not accommodating women as new mothers was that specific aspects of their careers suffered:

'No cover was provided for my leave except for the teaching duties . . . there was a lot of catching up to do when I came back. This is particularly hard to do at a time when you are learning to juggle family and work life in a new set up, and that baby is frequently sick'.

In extreme cases, women returned after taking maternity leave to find themselves displaced from their office or desk:

'I had no desk (my desk was given away while I was on maternity leave) for three months after I returned to work. I had to turn up every day and find a desk which was unoccupied'.

and from research groups in which they had been active:

'Research projects that may have interested me were commenced while I was away, so I was not able to be involved . . . also, it is not easy when meetings are changed at short notice or are scheduled for very early in the morning or late in the evening'.

Some women reduced the time spent on maternity leave in order to keep their research career on track:

> *'It is perhaps important to point out that few female academics actually take their full maternity leave due to the pressures of research. I came back after two weeks to hold a research meeting with PhD students. It is difficult to switch off during maternity leave . . . if I had focused solely on maternity leave then my research output would be reduced, and I would not be at my current (senior) academic grade'.*

It was not only women who were mothers who faced a non-supportive academic environment when they had caring responsibilities:

> *'My husband had cancer and I needed to be around more, so I cut to four days a week. My workload didn't reduce so I did five days in four'.*

Not surprisingly, childcare posed problems for many female respondents:

> *'It was extremely difficult to find appropriate childcare within the university (long waiting list) or outside it. There was no support within the university regarding information on childcare facilities in the local area and this became a stressful, time-consuming exercise for both of us as parents'.*
> *'I returned to work as head of my discipline with no childcare supports provided for my children. This meant additional costs and time pressures for the family. I had no assistance to support the return to work'.*

Focus group results

In order to validate and triangulate the 2015 survey findings, the issues noted were further explored in three faculty focus group sessions conducted in 2018. These focus groups concentrated on highlighting the experiences of women and men in terms of: opportunities for their career progression (including entry to senior positions); support for family-related and other leaves; availability and uptake of flexible working; and any gender differences in negotiating and achieving work-life balance. Despite issuing an open invitation to staff of all genders, it was predominantly women, in each faculty, who signed up and contributed. The abbreviated identifiers used were F/M (female/male), AHSS (Faculty of Arts, Humanities and Social Sciences), HS (Faculty of Health Sciences) and FEMS (Faculty of Engineering, Mathematics and Science).

Long hours culture

Referring to the perceived impossibility of having a life alongside an academic job, one discussant pointed to the high stress and long hours:

'I know two academics in the entire world who I would say have a good work-life balance . . . everybody else is massively overworked, frequently overwhelmed, and that's regardless of whether you're a parent, or are caring for elderly parents, which is the other big issue, and both of those responsibilities fall disproportionately on the shoulders of women at the moment, and that's societal. So, I think there's just a serious workload issue which is ever-increasing, and it's not actually sustainable'.

[AHSS] F

Focus group discussants referred to the male model that requires staff to be 'available all hours':

'We have workload allocation models, but I do think there is that . . . masculine role of . . . basically if you're to get on and do well, you need to be here 9–5 Monday to Friday, plus all the evenings, plus all the weekends'.

[HS] F

And how women fit themselves into this model:

'The workload is allocated in proportion, which is very fair, but what I've noticed over the years was, the sort of masculine model of 'be here all hours' has permeated through the females, where there are mostly females, they eat their own young almost, they're actually worse than men . . . so I think women copper-fasten the male hierarchy'.

[HS] F

'But this business of always being available . . . perish the thought that you couldn't get to a meeting on time, there's no flexibility around women having somewhere else to go besides . . . you really are under child pressure when you're a woman . . . so I do think we need a societal change, but I feel the availability is the big thing for me, that you need to be available all hours'.

[HS] F

Flexible working?

When asked if current flexible working arrangements meet the needs of staff, or need to be improved, discussants identified three different but interrelated issues. First, the potential flexibility of part-time work:

'I don't think there are any . . . what I don't understand is why there aren't more part-time roles. . . . It's not like some jobs which are quite difficult to carve up into part-time roles. Actually, in academia you can do part-time . . . it does come into that work-life balance issue, that if there were more part-time

roles, that would make it that much easier, and I think that would open up opportunities for flexibility, not just for women, but for men as well'.

[AHSS] F

Second, the difficulty of maintaining boundaries in part-time work:

'I'd say a number of people in our department, and wider, would be part-time, and I don't know if that's recognised in terms of career progression, and certainly I don't think so in terms of workload. No-one ever says 'You're a 0.5, so let's give you half the amount of teaching hours and half the amount of . . . it never works like that. I think people maybe forget that you're part-time and have the same expectations of you as a full-time person'.

[HS] F

Third, the extent to which part-time working is not recognised positively in career progression:

'Yes, you're in part-time hours and pay. Well not part-time hours, because you're working more [than part-time hours]. *Maybe it's not acknowledged enough that while it's great that you're given flexibility in terms of maybe suiting your family, I don't know if it's acknowledged in terms of career progression, or in terms of workload'.*

[HS] F

While some female discussants enjoyed the practical benefits of flexibility, in terms of autonomy:

'I was coming from a professional background into academia, I love the flexibility. I love that I can go home and do something, and take my kids to the dentist, and then do two hours at night . . . it suits me. I also love the autonomy, it's part and parcel of the same thing. And I think there are things within Trinity that they are very good at. So, I took a short period of parental leave to top up maternity leave, and that was no problem'.

[AHSS] F

Others referred to the *quid pro quo* (favouring employers) and the precarious nature of part-time employment:

'I think for me, talking very personally, the decision that I have made is not to work full-time, and not to pursue the full-time thing, because I want to balance it with my other commitments in life. And so to me the cost of that is that I am in this kind of precarious non-permanent situation. But the benefit of that is that I have absolute autonomy and flexibility, and that's the bargain I've made, if you like'.

[AHSS] F

Gendered division of family care

Some discussants noted how their research inevitably suffered with consecutive periods of maternity leave:

'You could be doing excellent teaching in the time between maternity leaves . . . you might be very creative, very innovative, and doing great things for the students, but because you're not doing any research . . . it would be . . . extremely hard to have continuous research if you have one or two or three maternity leaves. So, it's almost like you're putting your entire career on hold for the time that you want to have children . . . how would you do that [be research active] *if you were someone who wanted to have a couple of children, how would it be possible to maintain that and to also be able to progress?'*

[HS] F

Challenges relating to the pace of research were also identified:

'Research, depending on the type of space you're working in, can move very quickly, so even six months out of this place can put you behind and you're trying to play catch-up'.

[HS] F

One participant commented that taking time out contributed to the over-representation of men in senior positions:

'Some women that are very career-focused have to make a choice . . . it's almost like you're being punished for it. There's an amount of maternity leave you're required to take, there's a little bit of paternity for men, but they're not required to take any . . . you're out of the workforce for a certain amount of time, like it or lump it, whereas there's never a situation for men where they are absent from the workforce as a requirement. There's just a huge break in continuity for women'.

[HS] F

Suggestions for positive child-friendly facilities at conferences, networking events and places where research discussions take place were explored:

'One thing that a few conferences are starting to do, but there's no provision for it in any funding applications or anything, is bringing your children along to conferences, and childcare at conferences, because that's the thing . . . it's not just six months of maternity leave during which I can't travel, there's pregnancy during which I can't travel the last three months of, and then there's the breastfeeding phase, or a young child that can get sick at any point, during which I can't travel. That's conferences, that's networking,

that's proposals. Some conferences are starting to provide childcare on site, but there's something that Trinity could do, like a "bring your child to conference travel fund"'.

[FEMS] F

The societal issue of gender roles and expectations was raised in different ways corresponding to societal inequalities in the allocation of caring:

'the concept of co-parenting is not yet established in Ireland and would require that family work is shared more equitably, reflecting the more interchangeable gender roles now evident in the labour market'.

(Drew and Watters 2014, 4)

First, the demands of the daily transition from professional to domestic life:

'I think really a lot of it has to do with the fact that women are still primary caregivers at home'.
'Yes, I think it's a wider systemic issue. If you are literally thinking "I have three small kids, I pick them up from crèche, I make their dinner, I do their homework with them, my partner gets home at 8 o'clock' or whatever", and you have the option of going for a senior position, you're probably thinking "How am I going to do that, because I do all that at home, and possibly a lot more. How am I going to do that as well as my job"'.

[HS] F

Second, work practices which extend the professional working day:

'We've had in our school, supervision at 8am and 7.30am in recent times, underpinned by superwomen. I couldn't do that, it would be very, very difficult. Another thing about children too is, you're actually working when you go home. So, you've a whole day's work to do when you go home in the evening time usually as well'.

[HS] F

Third, expectations generated by the behaviour of other (super) women:

'About the superwomen, it really does put extra pressure on other women, because you feel like you should be able to achieve that. If one woman can achieve that, why can't you? . . . A lot of the time women are actually carers for parents as well, and it happens more so than for men, so you could have your kids at home and be a carer for a parent, and all those things that in a lot of circumstances, and I won't say always, but a lot of men don't have to consider'.

[HS] F

The daily reality of life for women in academia with dependent children was graphically described by one participant:

> 'When it's that busy time in your life, all you can do is just work and family, there's no time for you. I've been trying for years to try and do a yoga class or something like that, and I just don't have time. So, it's either work or family, and then just flake out, fall asleep on the couch, you're so tired. I suppose it's a choice as well, we work and we have family, whatever, but I don't see that you really do have a good work-life balance, because just there just aren't enough hours in the day, and I'm not going to get up and do a class at 5 or 6 in the morning, I'm going to sleep while I can. I don't know what the answer to that is, because you have to do your work hours. Maybe men need to step up a little bit more to give you time off, I don't know, but that's my experience'.
>
> [HS] F

Finally, there was a recognition of one aspect of shared parenting as a positive way forward:

> 'This is not purely a female versus male issue, it's a primary caretaker issue, which in society we know how it breaks down, but . . . I'm in a very fortunate situation where my husband is almost caring more than I am, I'm more relaxed than he is. But I was reading the report before coming in, and it said about how few men take paternity leave'.
>
> [FEMS] F

Paternity leave

Participants debated how current gender roles, in which caring is the primary responsibility of women, could be addressed, whether voluntarily:

> 'Could men have maternity leave . . . the way in some countries they split the maternity leave? I really think that society as a whole won't understand as long as we're the only ones who experience it. Whereas, if men had three or four months maternity leave and women had four or five months, like they do in some other countries, where women have slightly more but men still have a big chunk'.
>
> [HS] F

Or as mandatory:

> 'One thing that institutions can do, is expect the new father to take paternity leave. It should be almost suggested to them. I know it's something crazy to say, but it should be. When they start from the very beginning getting really

involved, then there's more hope of them picking up that burden later on in the life of the child. I suppose the only way of helping women deal with this problem is when the men pick up and start doing more'.

[FEMS] F

The advantages to parents, if there is an expectation that both are involved in parenting, was clearly identified:

'I certainly believe that a very long maternity leave means that for the first six months of your child, you become the expert because you are full-time with them. . . . I just wish there could be an expectation [of] parents that it should be three months . . . of the dad taking over so that they become the expert'.

[FEMS] F

Light at the end of the tunnel?

Finally, there was a recognition of the different demands of caring for young children during a period when expectations in the workplace are high, with consequences for personal development and wellbeing:

'I'm back running now with a few friends and that's fantastic, and that's my little bit of time out now, but before that I was really thinking "this is my life at the moment. All I do is work, or else family, there's no me time. What about me?" But I feel like my children are getting a little bit older now so it's a little bit easier, but like I said I'm not sure what the solution to that is. I'm reading a book at the moment that's called "The Gift of Time" ' so I'm going to see if it will generate more hours in the day or something [laughs]. Time is at a premium when you've got multiple demands'.

[HS] F

Conclusion

The findings in this chapter underline those of Currie and Eveline's (2011) study in which flexibility in working hours and working from home have facilitated work-life balance but as 'a double-edged sword' since the expectations and demands of academic and research work clearly permeate into other spheres of life. The chapter supports the existing literature in demonstrating that expectations of family care and domestic responsibilities remain greater sources of work-life conflict for female scholars and reiterate that:

Societal attitudes and employers' behaviour need to alter to ensure that (a) men (as well as women) can also avail of leaves; (b) taking leave is socially acceptable and (c) it will not adversely affect parents' career prospects.

(Drew and Watters 2014, 17)

Despite the perception of freedom to juggle with working hours and place of work, male and female respondents surveyed worked well in excess of 40 hours in an average week, often spilling over into weekends and evenings, through working from home. Evidence from the survey and focus groups demonstrate that it is women, rather than men, who opt for flexible working arrangements and take leave for family-related care. Hence it was women who experienced difficulties returning to their posts, after leave, in which many were required to 'double up' their teaching before and after availing of leave. Some mothers emphasised feeling isolated or overlooked and described how difficult it was to catch up, particularly on their research, after taking leave. Mothers felt that there were no proper supports in place, including childcare, to help get them back up to the level they were at previously, in teaching and particularly with their research. The chapter concludes that work-life balance among staff is more aspirational than real with many staff testifying to academic work overload encroaching on their non-working time.

References

Acker, J. (1990) Hierarchies, jobs, bodies: A theory of gendered organizations, *Gender and Society*, 4, 139–158, doi.org/10.1177/089124390004002002

Currie, J. and Eveline, J. (2011) E-Technology and work-life balance for academics with young children, *Higher Education*, 62 (4), 533–550, doi:10.1007/s10734-010-9404-9

Daly, M. and Rush, M. (2019) Ireland country note, in A. Koslowski, S. Blum, I. Dobrotić, A. Macht and P. Moss (eds), *International review of leave policies and research*. Available at: www.leavenetwork.org/lp_and_r_reports

Deem, R. (2003) Gender, organizational cultures and the practices of manager—academics in UK universities, *Gender, Work & Organization*, 10 (2), 239–259, doi.org/10.1111/1468-0432.t01-1-00013

Drew, E., Humphreys, P. and Murphy, C. (2002) *Off the treadmill: Achieving work/life balance*, National Framework Committee for Family Friendly Policies, Dublin, 140. Available at: www.academia.edu/1504121/Off_the_Treadmill_Achieving_Work_Life_Balance

Drew, E. and Marshall, C. (2017) *Mind the gap! Gender (in)equality in Trinity College Dublin*, Trinity Centre for Gender Equality and Leadership, Trinity College, Dublin. Available at: www.tcd.ie/tcgel/assets/pdf/INTEGER%20TCGEL%20Report%202017%20FINAL.pdf

Drew, E. and Watters, A. (2014) 'We're not much use, but good for logistics': An exploratory study of parenting leaves in Ireland, *Journal of International and Comparative Social Policy*, 31 (3), 245–264, doi.org/10.1080/21699763.2014.964286

Grummell, B., Devine, D. and Lynch, K. (2009) The care-less manager: Gender, care and new managerialism in higher education, *Gender and Education*, 21 (2), 191–208, doi.org/10.1080/09540250802392273

Herschberg, C., Benschop, Y. and van den Brink, M. (2018) Precarious postdocs: A comparative study on recruitment and selection of early-career researchers, *Scandinavian Journal of Management*, 34, 303–310, doi.org/10.1016/j.scaman.2018.10.001

Huppatz, K., Sang, K. and Napier, J. (2019) 'If you put pressure on yourself to produce then that's your responsibility': Mothers' experiences of maternity leave and flexible work in the neoliberal university, *Gender, Work & Organisation*, 26, 772–788.

Ivancheva, M., Lynch, K. and Keating, K. (2019) Precarity, gender and care in the neoliberal academy, *Gender, Work & Organisation*, 26, 448–462, doi.org/10.1111/gwao.12314

Kinman, G. (2014) Doing more with less? Work and wellbeing in academics, *Somatechnics*, 4 (2), 219–235.

Lynch, K. (2010) *Carelessness: A hidden doxa of higher education*, CHEER/ESRC seminar series imagining the university of the future, Seminar 2: What are the disqualified discourses in the knowledge society? Centre for Higher Education and Equity Research (CHEER), University of Sussex. Available at: www.sussex.ac.uk/education/cheer/events/esrcseminars/seminar2

Morley, L. (2013) *Women and higher education leadership: Absences and aspirations*, Stimulus Paper, Leadership Foundation for Higher Education, London. Available at: www.ses.unam.mx/curso2015/pdf/23oct-Morley.pdf

Probert, B. (2005) 'I just couldn't fit it in': Gender and unequal outcomes in academic careers, *Gender, Work & Organisation*, 12 (1), 50–72, doi.org/10.1111/j.1468-0432.2005.00262.x

Trinity College Dublin (TCD) (2020) *Human resources work-life balance policy*. Available at: www.tcd.ie/hr/staff-wellbeing/work-life-balance.php

Chapter 6

Sexual violence on campus
Objectification, awareness-raising and response

Marion Paoletti, Suzanne Quintin,
Jane Gray-Sadran and Laure Squarcioni

Context

The Bordeaux campus, in the south-west of France, covers an area of several hundred hectares and its buildings are located on different sites around Greater Bordeaux. This study focuses on one specific part of the campus, the surface area of which is shared by the neighbouring towns of Pessac, Talence and Gradignan (PTG), located 15 kilometres from the centre of Bordeaux. The campus is home to several university faculties and Grandes Ecoles: the University of Bordeaux; Bordeaux Montaigne University; Sciences Po Bordeaux; Bordeaux Institut National Polytechnique (a group of engineering schools) and Bordeaux Sciences Agro (Institute of Agricultural Sciences).

Approximately 50,000 people study or work on this vast 235-hectare campus. For the purpose of this chapter, the PTG campus is divided into two zones: zone 1, where the faculties and schools in social and human sciences are located; and zone 2, where the science, technology, engineering and mathematics (STEM) faculties and schools are found. More than 60 per cent of students and staff who attend zone 1 are women while in zone 2 men comprise 60 per cent of students and staff from the University of Bordeaux. The campus was built between 1961 and 1970, to accommodate the growing number of students, following the expansion of higher education in that decade. Its architectural and urban design is typical of the period with long buildings, surrounded by car parks, parks and woodland, far from Bordeaux's city centre and poorly integrated into the adjoining towns. The construction of the campus followed the functionalist ideal of a place specifically dedicated to study and work (Dubet and Sembel 1994). Shops and a cinema were included in the initial plans but were subsequently cancelled by the Ministry of Higher Education. The campus was built under political pressure as there was a need to relocate the students and minimise the cost, based on the idea of a 'pure' study campus: 'green, clean and calm' (Dubet and Sembel 1994, 226). This idea has guided the campus development for years and created an isolated place, linked to Bordeaux city centre by the tram line. This runs through the campus and began operating in 2007, one year after the campus construction was completed. There are three tram stops, one of which has posed a number of safety problems.

Since 2008, the entire Bordeaux campus has undergone a vast renovation programme by *Operation Campus*, a development project that falls within the remit
of the University of Bordeaux and is jointly financed by the state, the Nouvelle-
Aquitaine Regional Council and the urban community of Bordeaux Métropole.
The renovation of zones 1 and 2 of the PTG campus began in 2014 and will
end in 2022. It is in this context that the gender equality officers, of the different
universities and schools located on the PTG campus, brought to the fore the question of recurring reported incidents of sexual aggression, predominantly against
young women. These incidents are an unfortunate reality on campus, requiring
analysis and solutions that needed to be taken into account in the renovation project, to prevent future assaults. Gender equality officers and colleagues were fully
committed to their responsibilities at the University of Bordeaux and Sciences
Po Bordeaux. This chapter outlines the process of awareness-raising leading to
the proposals submitted for the integration of gender equality into the different
planning stages of the renovation of the campus, with lessons learned from this
experience. The chapter raises the more general question of how to address the
phenomenon of sexual violence on campus. It also illustrates how a concerted
prevention campaign against sexual violence can be built and maintained, despite
resistance.

Even though there has already been extensive research on the question of sexual violence endured by young women (VIRAGE, ESSIMU), there are, to date,
few studies focussing on sexual violence experienced by female students on campus (Day 1994). PTG campus is a public space with a layout of buildings that
is perceived to be conducive to the presence of potential sexual predators. This
perception is supported by a general feeling of anxiety, fuelled by students' shared
stories about their exposure to and experience of sexual violence. There are three
halls of residence on the PTG campus and the majority of residents are female
students. For women, in particular, going from one place to another on the PTG
campus has precipitated feelings of anxiety, especially after dark and at night.
The relationship between the built environment and women's fear of assault has
contributed to the constitution of fear as a social reality (Koskelka and Pain 2000;
Lieber 2008).

Methodology

The perception of insecurity, related to reported incidents of sexual violence on
the PTG campus, was raised with the planners and decision-makers through two
research interventions, an online survey and the implementation of safety audits
involving walks through the campus to determine areas of perceived insecurity or
danger. The methodology of the safety audit was conducted in two stages, in two
different contexts. In 2017, the question of sexual violence on the campus was
raised by the gender equality officers. In 2019, when a new series of safety audits
was organised, in the area around one of the tram stops where there had been
reported incidents of rape and sexual aggression, the specific context of insecurity

at that time led to the university administration having to face student action in a crisis situation.

The close coordination between the gender equality officers of the different schools and universities on the campus was a determining factor in persuading the planners and decision-makers to take the issue of sexual violence seriously. The political behaviour of students in relation to feminist issues including sexual violence was also highlighted, alongside the challenges that institutions have encountered when engaging the participation of feminist student groups in discussion of these issues.

Researching sexual violence on campus

Gathering solid, reliable data on sexual violence on campus was essential to the analysis of what is a diffuse phenomenon, a problem that existed but had never been quantified. Such data are particularly useful for raising awareness among students and staff and also of interest to researchers in the wider academic context.

In the first instance, an online survey was carried out by questionnaire, designed by the gender equality officers with the support of *Opération Campus*, and distributed by email to the entire university community of the PTG campus. The questionnaire included thirty, mainly closed questions with opportunities to make open-ended comments. The aim was to identify the scale and type of sexual aggression experienced by respondents, where it took place on campus and the perceptions of personal safety by staff and students on campus. Data collection took place between April and June 2017 and 4,920 people responded, the majority of whom were students and women: 70 per cent of respondents were students and 28 per cent were staff, 62 per cent of respondents were women, 36 per cent were men. Less than 2 per cent identified as 'other'.

Experience on campus was perceived very differently according to the time of day. Half of respondents stated that they were not comfortable on campus after dark and, unsurprisingly, a request for improved street lighting was frequently expressed in responses. However, this request does not accord with the sustainable development policies of the local authorities, who switch off public streetlights at 1am, and on campus 30 minutes after the arrival of the last tram at 12.30am on weekdays (1.30am on weekends). This is in order to save energy and avoid disturbing animal and insect life. This questions the extent to which the local government's environmental policies conflict with the needs expressed by students and staff in relation to personal safety in public spaces.

Compared to men, women were twice as anxious about their safety (60 per cent versus 30%) and this feeling had consequences for the routes taken from one place to another. Two-thirds of all respondents stated that they avoided certain dimly lit areas, half did not come on campus outside office or class hours and one-third declared that they avoided walking alone on campus. The sports fields, along with car parks, were the areas that were most avoided, especially by women. One-quarter of respondents had heard of cases of sexual aggression on campus.

Knowledge of these cases mainly stemmed from conversation and rumours but also from certain schools that systematically informed staff and students when an incident had occurred.

In order to establish an inventory of the forms of aggression experienced, the following question was asked: 'Have you ever experienced one or more of the following situations on the PTG campus?' and a list of situations was presented. More than one response was possible. Nearly three-quarters of respondents (74 per cent, or 3,558 respondents) declared that they had never had to face such situations. In contrast, 26 per cent, or 1,260 respondents, stated that they had experienced one or several of the situations mentioned in Table 6.1.

Table 6.1 Reported incidents on the PTG campus (n = 4,819)

Nature of incident	Number	Percentage
Chatted up insistently	780	16
Followed over a long distance	468	10
Insulted	442	9
Confronted by an exhibitionist	246	5
Undergone unwanted physical contact	235	5
Victim of sexual aggression	12	0.2
Victim of rape, or attempted rape	5	0.1
None of these situations	3,558	74

Note: The total percentage adds up to more than 100 per cent due to the fact that several choices were possible.

Among the 1,260 people who declared they had experienced sexual aggression, only 36 specified that they knew the attacker. The experience 'chatted up insistently', which can be identified as a form of sexual harassment, was chosen most frequently (780 people) and took place mainly between 5pm and 9pm. 'Followed over a long distance' was cited by 468 people. This phenomenon was said to increase as the day progressed and was at its worst after 9pm. This affected people living on campus twice as much as those who did not. These results were reinforced by the oral testimonies collected during the awareness-raising meetings prior to the safety audits. Female students living in the halls of residence on campus explained that they felt particularly exposed to being followed home after lectures, especially in the evening, and as a result felt uneasy and worried about being attacked. A total of 246 respondents declared that they had already come across an exhibitionist on campus.

Even though the survey provided a much clearer picture of sexual aggression on campus, identifying precise locations proved to be less clear since the incidents occurred over the entire area of the campus and were not concentrated in specific zones. However, the survey did shed light on the universities' lack of knowledge of the problem, since the victims declared that they rarely turned to the prevention services of their university for help (only 62 people reported the incidents to their university) (Table 6.2).

Table 6.2 Responses to incidents (n = 1,210)

Response	Number	Per cent (%)
I spoke about it to my friends and family	622	51
I spoke about it to a doctor/nurse/psychologist	14	1
I reported the incident to the prevention services of my university school	62	5
I reported the incident to the police	51	4
I did not speak about it	497	41
Other	66	5

The survey, which constituted the first stage of the awareness-raising and quantification of the problem, enabled an assessment of incidents of which universities were unaware. One of the reasons for this lay in the large number of public stakeholders in charge of security on campus: universities, schools, the city council, local authorities, the students' welfare office, inter-university services responsible for street lighting, security and the planners. None of these had any systematic mechanisms for recording such incidents or for sharing knowledge concerning them. The results of the online survey confirmed, for the first time, that aggressive acts were a recurring problem on a campus, where services were used by a majority of female students (60%). This in itself justified the need for the problem to be taken seriously.

The online survey concluded with an open-ended question: 'Do you have anything you would like to add (recommendations, testimonies and so on)?' The 520 respondents who took the time to answer this question provided personal testimonies, expressed their feelings about the problem, criticised the universities' services or made recommendations. The majority of these responses fell into four categories:

1   adapt to the situation (by avoiding certain areas, taking the car, avoiding the campus at night, moving out, learning self-defence techniques);
2   raise awareness (poster campaigns, informing all students);
3   crack down on the problem (by imposing disciplinary sanctions, reporting the offence, taking legal action);
4   make improvements to security installations (railings, gates) or to places where people can meet socially. Improved street lighting was quoted as a top priority.

Identifying campus problem zones

The next phase of the initiative focused on the safety audits as a pre-requisite to demarcating safe, inclusive, gender-neutral spaces. The audits were undertaken in two phases, in two very different contexts: in 2017–2018 and again in 2019. They consisted of organising group walks in a specific area or neighbourhood, by day and night, with the purpose of identifying the physical and social characteristics that contributed to making the location(s) a safe or unsafe place. This method was based on two assumptions: that women were more likely to experience a greater feeling of insecurity in their use of public spaces than in private; and also that women could identify the factors that lead to aggression. Safety walks are a useful tool, especially if they take place at the beginning of an urban development project, to evaluate the safety of a particular geographical place and to raise awareness of potential problem areas. The safety audit concept was developed in 1989 in Toronto by the Metropolitan Action Committee on Violence against Women and Children (Andrew *et al* 2013) to evaluate the degree of comfort and security that women experience in urban public spaces. Since then, the concept has been used to develop an inclusive urban design project. From a woman's perspective, safety audits are generally undertaken only by women, so that they feel free to express themselves about their fears in a safe environment.

Within the context of the PTG campus renovation, the gender equality officers jointly proposed conducting safety audits. *Opération Campus* fully supported their request to benefit from their expertise. The methodology for the safety audit was developed from 'A Places Egales' led by a sociologist, Dominique Poggi. It is described as a 'simple yet rigorous' design to analyse the social causes as well as the problems in urban design that lead to insecurity and avoidance strategies. Its stated aim is to make 'recommendations in favour of more inclusive public spaces' (https://aplacesegales.wordpress.com) by mobilising women who are trained as experts to work on the different stages of the safety audit. Given the level of interest expressed by male students and academic colleagues, it was decided that men could be invited to participate in one of the walks.

The first stage involved raising awareness among stakeholders and the public. In March 2017, a steering committee was established to address the issue of sexual violence on campus. Its members included the directors or vice-chancellors of each of the schools and universities, local politicians and *Opération Campus*. A public meeting was organised and the 30 or so people who attended provided insights into the problems experienced by female students. These included: groups of male youths loitering on campus shouting sexist remarks and insults; female students being followed back to the halls of residence; and the presence of exhibitionists or prowlers. These testimonies illustrated the different ways in which female students experienced one important aspect of residential life on the campus.

The following month, a mapping session was organised to determine two routes for the walks in zone 1. The aim was to analyse plans of the campus grounds in order to establish the routes. Discussions explored questions such as: 'How do I feel in this particular part of the campus?'; 'Do I feel safe there during the day? At night?'; 'Where do people tend to hang around and what do they do there?' Specific areas were identified on the plans. This was done simply by placing different-coloured stickers on the maps to locate both the problematic places and the zones that everyone agreed were safe. Two walks were then identified for the safety audit, each one lasting up to two hours, including stops along the way. These walks took place between May and October 2017, one by day and another by night. A final walk, with the managers of *Opération Campus* and media, focused on raising their awareness and communicating recommendations. More than 20 people participated on each walk. They were attributed specific roles and everyone was given the opportunity to express themselves. The group observed their surroundings, described how they felt, analysed street signs, considered visibility, street lighting and the availability of public transport. The general state of the grounds and the buildings was also noted as was the frequency of use of specific areas. There was a final group discussion to identify proposals which derived from observations made during the walks.

A summary report and recommendations were published and presented to *Opération Campus*. The report was officially presented at public meetings on campus and at meetings with decision-makers, including local councillors and civil servants, the director of *Opération Campus*, student welfare services and university board members. The results were also communicated to students and staff at a meeting in December 2017 during which a female police commander from the Direction of Public Security, French Ministry of the Interior, gave advice on safety and precautionary measures to adopt in public spaces. Whilst this kind of meeting was seen as useful by the majority of those present, it was also met with criticism by some female students who felt that it was not only the responsibility of women to protect themselves, but equally the responsibility of the authorities to make sure the campus was a safe place for all students.

The main priorities were for signposts (the names and locations of the different buildings and services, distances, information to help people find their way around campus), which were deemed non-existent or inaccurate. Numerous pathways needed to be improved with better lighting. Sports facilities were not designed to encourage gender diversity and the pathways leading to sports halls or pitches also needed improved street lighting. Sheltered bicycle parking stands, where some aggressive acts had taken place, needed renovation. There was also a lack of places where students could meet socially. Many embankment slopes needed to be removed and branches of trees pruned to improve visibility. A further suggestion was that tram-stops and halls of residence should be named after famous or important women since all were currently named after men.

These recommendations were taken into account by *Opération Campus* and integrated into the future renovation programme. The safety audits, together with the online survey contributed to heightening awareness of aggression on campus and mobilising the university community to respond positively to the problem. Perpetrators were seldom prosecuted because victims tend not to report assaults to the universities or the police. The phenomenon had therefore remained largely hidden and ignored, but thanks to the safety audits, this was no longer the case. However, it was not certain that these walks encouraged the decision-makers on campus to coordinate their responses to the question of sexual violence. What did encourage them was when a large group of female students gathered in 2018 to express their anger, following further incidents of sexual aggression. It was in the context of this crisis that the gender equality officers organised another safety audit in January 2019. This time it took place in zone 2, particularly around a tram stop named *Doyen Brus* that subsequently became a symbol for publicising sexual violence on campus. Making physical changes to improve campus safety is a long process that is inevitably programmed over several years. The work undertaken to raise awareness and propose solutions was not enough to prevent acts of aggression. However, it did lead to greater transparency in terms of communicating the problem, at the risk of stirring emotions conducive to student mobilisation.

Dealing with emotion and student protest against sexual violence on campus: a new series of walks

The recurrence of sexual aggression on the PTG campus and, more specifically, the complaint registered following the rape of a female student on 26 November 2018 close to the Doyen Brus tram stop, heightened feelings of insecurity, especially among women, on campus. For the first time, the vice-chancellor of the University of Bordeaux, with the support of the vice-chancellors and directors of the other universities and schools, chose to inform the campus community about this case of rape. This was done by email, and the message also included advice for students and staff, so that they would be in a better position to protect themselves from any future assault. This information, which was widely relayed on social networks, caused a strong emotional reaction. Students took to social networks in protest. This happened within the context of #MeToo, a movement that symbolises a new wave of feminism (Bertrand 2018). By 13 December 2018, the students had created a private, women-only Facebook page called *Les Campusciennes* (*The Campus Women*), which quickly attracted more than 3,000 members. Their aim was to set up a support and discussion platform among female students so that victims could share their experience of aggression and find information about the prevention of sexual and sexist violence (Albenga and Dagorn 2019). Their exchanges on the Facebook group page highlighted the frequency of aggressive acts and the feeling of anxiety among many women on the PTG campus.

The email sent by the universities and schools was fiercely criticised for its advice-giving. *Les Campusciennes* deemed it guilt-inducing for women. In the wake of the #MeToo movement, the aim of the protests, which were more outspoken than before, was to develop a narrative of women's experience of insecurity in public spaces, act collectively against sexual and sexist violence and position themselves as the main group that decision-makers would liaise with. Supported by several feminist associations and student unions, they organised a set of *noisy* collective actions (Boussaguet 2009), with the aim of publicising the issue and gathering more support. In addition to Facebook discussion groups, they organised meetings, conferences and workshops and launched a petition that had a particularly strong impact. Entitled '*For a Real Battle Against Sexual Aggression on the Bordeaux Campus*', this petition, launched in December 2018, addressed to the vice-chancellors of Bordeaux Montaigne University and the University of Bordeaux, rapidly gained 15,000 signatures. In only a few days, *Les Campusciennes* had become a media sensation. Numerous national and regional newspapers followed the story.

On the evening of 19 December 2018, the group *Nous toutes 33 Etudiantes* organised a protest march from Bordeaux Montaigne University to the *Doyen Brus* tram stop. Several hundred students attended the march, equipped with torches, fairy lights and candles to symbolically 'bring back the light on campus', according to the *Nous Toutes 33* press release. The participants of this march expressed their anger through slogans such as 'A well-lit pathway = a rape prevented', 'Stop the carnage, bring back the light', 'I said no, we must warn against aggression' and 'Rape is never the victim's fault'. Their main demands for improved street lighting were similar to the recommendations made during the safety audits of 2017.

The vice-chancellor of the University of Bordeaux responded by bringing together the different groups and individuals to find an immediate response to the crisis and formalise coordination of security on campus. These included *Bordeaux Métropole*, the town councils, inter-university services, the higher education institutions and *Opération Campus*. The first meeting, in January 2019, set out an emergency plan for the first two quarters of 2019: the installation of a CCTV camera and the presence of a dog-handler between 8pm and 2am at the tram stop, as well as the general reinforcement of security measures. In the months that followed, the renovation of street lighting and the setting up of the new security commission was undertaken. In the longer term, the creation of an official pathway to replace an unofficial, unlit 300 metre shortcut that students regularly took from the tram stop to the halls of residence was confirmed. In January 2019, in reaction to the media coverage of the events, the vice-chancellors and directors of the universities and schools sent out a second message to the campus community to respond to the students' criticism that there was a rape culture and a climate of fear on campus and to communicate the prevention initiatives that had already been taken or were underway. At the same time, the gender equality officers organised a second series of safety audits, focused on the problem area around the *Doyen Brus* tram station (zone 2), an area that had not been explored in 2017. Female students and staff spoke of precautions taken to make sure they were never alone on this part of the campus. Students alighted at this stop to walk back to their halls of residence or to the private student flats close by. However, they did not use the official pathways, but instead took shortcuts through fields or woodland which were neither signposted nor lit. The second series of walks was undertaken using the same method as before and, although they led to recommendations for improvement to that area, very few students took advantage of the walks to assert their demands. However, given the previous student protests, interest was expressed by journalists at the first of these walks, which took place at the end of January 2019.

It is worth placing the assertive actions of the students within the wider context of protest in contemporary France. Research has shown that French citizens tend to view their institutions with mistrust (Grossmann and Sauger 2017; Rosanvallon 2002). Young people, in particular those who are politically engaged, tend to reject their institutions more strongly than others (Muxel 2010). In the current context, which is marked by a feeling of scepticism and an expression of political radicalisation, institutions like universities are struggling to encourage participation or an interest in their projects. Based on the experience of gender equality officers there is a perception that students in the social sciences tend to be particularly critical of higher education institutions, even more so when they have been trained in gender studies. The context of a new, worldwide reaction against sexual violence was also significant. Additionally, throughout December 2018 and January 2019 the *Gilets Jaunes* (*Yellow Vests*), a street protest movement against economic inequality, was at its height. A meeting between a delegation of *Gilets Jaunes* and the students mobilised around the question of sexual violence on campus took place in December 2018. These contextual elements may partly explain why there was such a weak student mobilisation around the new walks, perceived as a top-down offer from the academic institution, even though protests related to sexual violence on campus had reached an unprecedented scale (Neveu 2011).

The two safety walks, one organised by day and the other by night around the *Doyen Brus* tram stop, on a route that was planned during the mapping session, led to a series of new recommendations. There was a lack of visibility on this part of the campus due to insufficient street lighting and a total absence of lights in certain areas. Darkness, trees, hilly grounds, dark corners and building sites all limited the possibility for people both to see and be seen. A second issue was the difficulty participants had in finding their way about. Several signs indicated the wrong direction and the majority of pathways had no signs whatsoever. In addition, the participants complained about the absence of a means of calling for help in case of aggression (alarm signals, emergency call stations or phone numbers). A third observation highlighted the lack of services or facilities where students could meet socially: there were no cafés, sports or leisure facilities or picnic tables that could make that part of the campus a more user-friendly place.

The most sensitive area was the unofficial pathway leading from the tram stop to the halls of residence. At the beginning of autumn 2019, Bordeaux Métropole carried out a study to examine the specific problem related to this pathway, and the security commission is currently preparing to set up the emergency plan established in January 2019. The problem of sexual violence on the campus seems to have been taken seriously, even though it runs the risk of being placed within the more general category of 'security issues'. The gender equality officers continue their awareness campaigns and workshops on the theme of sexual and sexist violence through exhibitions, debates and conferences to ensure the functioning of the sexual harassment monitoring units set up in their respective universities. The campus security services were also trained to deal with sexist and sexual violence by the gender equality officer of the University of Bordeaux and the police.

Conclusion

Estimated at a cost of €600 million, the vast planning operation carried out by *Opération Campus*, due for completion in 2022, has already begun to have a noticeable and positive effect on the PTG campus environment. The atmosphere is more convivial and the planning currently underway in zones 1 and 2 has taken account of the recommendations made during the safety audits. *Opération Campus* financed and fully supported this project. In doing so, it contributed to raising awareness about sexual and sexist violence throughout the entire campus community. The safety audit has proved extremely useful for collecting information to make recommendations for improvements to the campus. Combined with quantitative data analysis it helped put the problem of sexual violence on the decision-makers' table. Based on the Bordeaux experience, the Universities of Rennes and Paris Dauphine have since organised safety walks on their campuses.

Actions by feminist groups certainly contributed to accelerating the responses from different stakeholders on PTG campus, something that the first safety audit in 2017 had not succeeded in doing. In this way, their actions were certainly effective. Their initiatives have since become more radical. For example, on 8 March 2019 (International Women's Day) and at the start of the academic year, slogans painted on the walls of Bordeaux Montaigne University and Sciences Po Bordeaux denounced the alleged tolerance of institutions towards sexual harassment by teachers ('Yes! Teachers can also be rapists'). The practice of 'naming and shaming' has also been used. Pressure on institutions to deal with sexual violence has not diminished. On the contrary, it has increased with the help of social networks and in a wider context of political radicalisation across France. Consequently, in addition to the efforts made by the French Ministry of Higher Education, Research and Innovation and the European Union, student protest movements, as well as institutional mobilisation driven by the gender equality officers, have all contributed to pushing the problem of sexual violence higher onto the agenda of university leaders.

References

Albenga, V. and Dagorn, J. (2019) Après #MeToo: Réappropriation de la sororité et résistances pratiques d'étudiantes françaises, *Mouvements*, 3 (99), 75–84, doi:10.3917/mouv.099.0075
Andrew, C., Canuto, M. and Travers, K. (2013) Le défi d'être, à la fois, local et mondial: Femmes et Villes International, *Économie et solidarités*, 43 (1–2), 55–69, doi:10.7202/1033275a
Bertrand, D. (2018) L'essor du féminisme en ligne. Symptôme de l'émergence d'une quatrième vague féministe? *Réseaux*, 208–209 (2), 232–257.
Boussaguet, L. (2009) Les 'faiseuses' d'agenda. Les militantes féministes et l'émergence des abus sexuels sur mineurs en Europe, *Revue française de science politique*, 59 (2), 221–246, doi:10.3917/rfsp.592.0221

Day, K. (1994) Conceptualising women's fear of sexual assault on campus: A review of causes and recommendations for change, *Environment and Behaviour*, 26 (6), 742–765, doi:10.1177/0013916594266002

Dubet, F. and Sembel, N. (1994) Les étudiants, le campus et la ville. Le cas de Bordeaux, *Les Annales de la recherche urbaine*, 62–63, 225–234, doi:10.3406/aru.1994.1798

Grossman, E. and Sauger, N. (2017) *Pourquoi détestons-nous autant nos politiques?* Presses de Sciences Po, Paris.

Koskela, H. and Pain, R. (2000) Revisiting fear and place: Women's fear of attack and the built environment, *Geoforum*, 31 (2), 269–280, doi:10.1016/S0016-7185(99)00033-0

Lieber, M. (2008) *Genre, violences et espaces publics. La vulnérabilité des femmes en question*, Presses de Sciences Po, Paris.

Muxel, A. (2010) *Avoir 20 ans en politique*, Editions du Seuil, Paris.

Neveu, C. (2011) Démocratie participative et mouvements sociaux: Entre domestication et ensauvagement? *Participations*, 1, 186–209, doi:10.3917/parti.001.0186

Rosanvallon, P. (2002) *La contre-démocratie. La politique à l'âge de la défiance*, Editions du Seuil, Paris.

Chapter 7

Gender pay gap reporting

Lessons from Queen's University, Belfast and Trinity College, Dublin

Yvonne Galligan, Tony McMahon and Tom Millar

Introduction

The gender pay gap is a key indicator of gender equality in employment. In the last decade, reducing this gap has been a focus of the United Kingdom (UK) government as part of a broader agenda for enhancing equality. In Ireland, there has been a significant focus on gender equality in higher education as a strategic priority of government since 2016. In response, higher education institutions have informally initiated gender pay auditing. This chapter discusses the initiatives taken by Queen's University Belfast (QUB) in Northern Ireland, UK and Trinity College Dublin (TCD) in Ireland to address the gender pay gap. The introduction sets out the wider policy environment on gender pay in the UK and Ireland. It then turns to the higher education environment more generally, and examines the academic staff structure in each university, along with mapping their formal and discretionary pay arrangements. The data collection process and tailored measures to address the gender pay gap revealed by the data, are outlined. The chapter concludes by discussing the shared and individual challenges encountered by TCD and QUB and draws general lessons from their experiences.

The United Kingdom's public policy on the gender pay gap

The UK Equality Act 2010 provides the legal basis for gender pay reporting by private and voluntary sector employers in England, Scotland and Wales, excluding Northern Ireland. The UK government sought to obtain voluntary compliance among employers in order to 'minimise the regulatory burden on business' (Secretary of State for Education 2015, 30), supported by the 2011 policy paper *Think, Act, Report*. The paper provided a step-by-step framework to assist companies with more than 150 employees to address gender equality, take corrective action in recruitment, retention, promotion and pay and report on the effects of their actions and outcomes. Annual reporting on the initiative revealed that it prompted attention by the drivers of gender inequality in the workplace and yielded information on a wide range of actions taken by individual companies to redress gender imbalances (Government Equalities Office 2015).

Although embedded in the UK government's equality strategy (HM Government 2010), voluntary compliance was not widely observed by employers. Thus, the government brought Section 78 into effect on 22 August 2016, making it obligatory to address the 19 per cent gender pay gap in UK employment. The regulation provided that from 6 April 2017 employers with over 250 employees were required to report annually on their gender pay gap and gender bonus gap. Section 78 stipulated the collection of data on mean and median hourly pay across four quartile pay bands. This information was to be made available on the employer's website for three years as well as uploaded onto a government website. The gender pay gap reporting applied to England and provisions to give it effect were passed by the devolved governments in Scotland and Wales. Regulation orders to bring Section 78 into effect in Northern Ireland were not passed. Table 7.1 illustrates the gradual reduction of the gender pay gap from 22 per cent in 2009 to 17.3 per cent in 2019.

Table 7.1 Gender pay gap for median gross hourly earnings (excluding overtime), UK 2009–2019 (%)

Year	All	Full time	Part time
2009	22.0	12.2	−2.5
2010	19.8	10.1	−4.3
2011	20.2	10.5	−5.1
2012	19.6	9.5	−5.5
2013	19.8	10.0	−5.9
2014	19.2	9.6	−5.5
2015	19.3	9.6	−6.8
2016	18.2	9.4	−6.1
2017	18.4	9.1	−6.3
2018	17.8	8.6	−4.9
2019	17.3	8.9	−3.1

Source: UK Office for National Statistics 2019, *Gender Pay Gap*

Ireland's public policy on the gender pay gap

In 2017, the Irish *National Strategy for Women and Girls* identified the gender pay gap as one item in a package of measures designed to support women in the workplace (Department of Justice and Equality 2017). This statement followed a commitment in the 2016 *Programme for Government* to empower women through measures such as addressing pay inequalities and encouraging companies of 50 employees and more to conduct wage surveys (Government of Ireland 2016).

Attention to the gender pay gap was not confined to domestic politics but extended to external organisations. In 2017, the United Nations Commission on the Elimination of Discrimination Against Women (CEDAW) noted that it was 'particularly concerned at . . . the gender wage gap, partly because women work part-time owing to family responsibilities' and it urged the Irish government to 'take concrete measures to reduce the gender wage gap by enforcing the principle of equal pay for work of equal value and intensifying the use of wage surveys' (UN Committee on the Elimination of Discrimination Against Women 2017, 11). This strong direction from a United Nations equality body complemented the efforts of the European Commission (2014) which identified tackling the gender pay gap as one of the five thematic priority areas for gender equality for 2016–2019. In 2018, the gender wage gap in Ireland was 13.9 per cent, compared to an average 16.2 per cent gap across the EU (Figure 7.1).

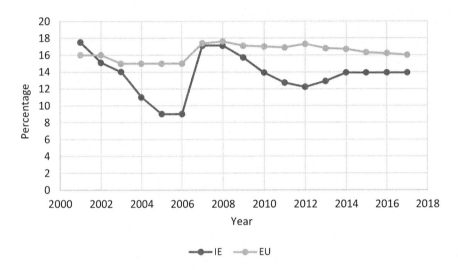

Figure 7.1 Percentage gender pay gap for mean gross earnings, Ireland and EU 2001–2017

Higher education and gender pay

The UK context

Since 2010, higher education institutions in the UK have regularly conducted equal pay reviews which included a gender pay gap analysis between grades. Length of service, workforce composition and pay protection arrangements were the most commonly cited explanations for the gap. In 2018, the median gender pay gap for full-time employees was 8.6 per cent nationally across all sectors, but in higher education it was 14.8 per cent, with 37 of the 120 universities reporting gaps in median pay of 20 per cent or more (Pells 2018). A sectoral analysis of academic gender pay in 2018 found that gender pay gaps by job level were zero with the exception of professorial level, where the gap was 6 per cent in favour of men. This finding was explained as a consequence of women comprising only 26 per cent of full professors, and by their more recent entry into this grade.

From 2010, there was a growing awareness among UK university administrators of gender pay gap performance. Sectoral joint employer-union working groups conducted research and disseminated the analysis throughout the university sector. The University and Colleges Union began an active campaign from 2015 onwards. Prior to compulsory reporting of the gender pay gap, a vigorous debate was already underway in higher education on the size of the gender pay gap and the reasons for it. Queen's University was not immune from this debate.

Queen's University academic salary scales

The UK higher education pay structure was reformed in the early 2000s into a single 51-point spine against which all academic and administrative roles are mapped. In August 2018, the scale ranged from £15,842 at one end to £61,618 at the top. In 2018, new university lecturers in their first academic post were typically appointed between point 35 (£38,460) and point 39 (£43,267) moving up the scale on an annual basis. The starting salary point is important as it determines future career earnings. There is some scope to advance more quickly at certain points in an academic career. For example, following a highly satisfactory completion of the probationary period, through accelerated promotion and on promotion to a higher grade. However, advances in these circumstances are modest, typically a one- or two-point progression. The UK framework was followed in QUB.

However, professorial salaries sit outside the 51-point pay spine in Queen's University, along with other institutions in the 24 research-intensive universities in the UK that comprise the Russell Group. Each university has its own professorial pay and progression arrangements determined according to free market criteria where supply and demand influence remuneration levels. A premium is accorded to skill scarcity and external achievement, for example Nobel prize-winning fellowship of bodies such as the British Academy and Royal Society.

Exceptional mechanisms also allow for pay advancement outside of the circumstances just described, though every university is different. Queen's University can apply the 'market supplement', normally used in cases of recruitment or retention, as an additional payment, decoupled from the salary scale and usually not reckonable for pension purposes. It is granted to new employees from higher-paying economies, such as Ireland, or for specialist and economically competitive skills that the university wishes to reward, for example from the technologies industry, medical services and the financial world. In theory, the negotiable market supplement tapers off over time as the individual advances up the salary scale to the point corresponding to the combined normal and supplementary salaries. The competitive nature of the market economy in UK universities means that issues of staff retention are often dealt with through such supplements, if progression to a higher grade is either not possible or an insufficient incentive.

In addition, line managers have the opportunity of putting forward the case of staff securing exceptional, externally recognised achievements for a supplementary pay award, which can be granted either as a one-off bonus or a one-point salary advance.

This route, the exceptional advancement scheme, is highly discretionary and relies on individual academics making their achievements known to their head of department or school over a sustained period of time. It also requires line managers to be willing to advance the case for financial advancement of individual staff members.

In 2016, professorial salaries were organised along four ranges in Queen's University, each with its own internal progression. New internally promoted professors entered Range 1 (3 progression points from £61,654). Professors recruited into the university would typically be appointed to Range 2 (6-point scale, from £69,729). Range 3 (5-point scale from £94,576), rewarded exceptional national or international achievement, such as Fellowship of the British Academy and recognised outstanding service to the university, for example as pro-vice-chancellor. Appointment at Range 4 (6-point scale from £109,483) recognises further exceptional and world-wide achievement but has rarely been used.

Progression in each of these ranges was determined through a triennial evaluation process. The outcome would not necessarily result in individuals advancing to the next point on the scale. In exceptional instances, a professor could obtain two increments, or move from the top of one range into the next. In addition, professorial salaries could also be enhanced through the informal mechanisms in place for other academic staff.

At the time of the Queen's University gender pay review (January 2017), women comprised 50 per cent of probationary lecturers (generally a three-year tenure track position), 47 per cent of lecturers and 35 per cent of senior lecturers or readers (Figure 7.2). Thus, there was a healthy pipeline in place for progression to professor. Over the course of the previous decade, women's share of professorial posts had increased from 14.5 per cent in 2006 to 22.5 per cent in 2017, reflecting the sectoral average at the time. However, that proportion had stagnated from 2011 when women comprised 22.2 per cent of the professorial body.

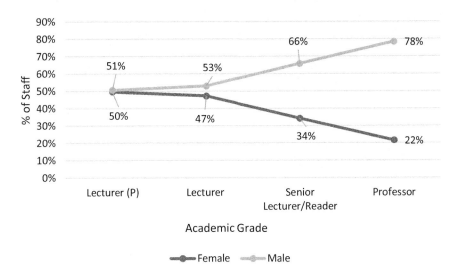

Figure 7.2 Gender representation in academic grades, QUB 2016

The 2014, Queen's University equal pay audit revealed an overall gender pay gap of 21.1 per cent in basic pay, and 22 per cent in total pay with total pay defined as basic pay plus payments (overtime, one-off discretionary awards and role-specific allowances, such as head of department/school) (Table 7.2). This was much higher than the mean gender pay gap across the sector of 14.1 per cent in 2014–2015 (New Joint Negotiating Committee for Higher Education Staff 2016).

Table 7.2 Percentage gender pay gap by employment category, QUB 2014

Employment Category	% Pay Gap – Basic Pay	% Pay Gap – Total Pay
Academic	13.7	14.1
Academic-related	5.1	5.4
Research	2.0	2.0
Technical	8.6	9.6
Clerical	−10.2	−9.4
Operational	16.0	25.4
Overall	**21.1**	**22.0**

Source: QUB 2017, Equal Pay Audit 2017

Gaps in total pay occurred in the university at spine points 2, 3 and 4 (professional support staff) where overtime and shift-working was a feature of employment, but there was no significant gender gap in basic pay. Similarly, there was no significant evidence of a gender pay gap among the academic grades on the 51-point pay spine. However, the gender pay gap at professor grade in Queen's was 11.4 per cent in both basic and total pay (Table 7.3).

Table 7.3 Percentage gender pay gap by academic grade, QUB 2014 and 2017

Grade	2014	2017	2014	2017
Lecturer	−0.01	1.2	−0.1	1.1
Senior Lecturer	−1.5	1.2	−1.4	1.1
Reader	2.4	2.9	2.7	2.9
Professor	11.4	10.6	11.4	10.6
Overall	**13.7**	**13.7**	**14.2**	**14.1**

Source: QUB 2017, Equal Pay Audit 2017

In line with UK national advice and guidance from the Equality Commission of Northern Ireland, overall pay gaps of more than 5 per cent are considered significant and are an indicator of the need for further investigation and interventions.

Queen's University data collection and analysis

Although the large gender pay gap had been known for some years, it was not until June 2016 that it became clear that it was an issue that would require a specific, focused and, as it turned out, seismic intervention by the university. On that date, the Times Higher Education Supplement reported that for full-time professors, Queen's had the largest gender pay gap in the UK, with female staff earning 14 per cent less than their male colleagues (Grove 2016). By 2016, Queen's had been involved with the UK Athena SWAN initiative, which aims to promote the careers of academic women, for over a decade. By 2016, the university had developed personnel systems to routinely report on gender-specific data relating to recruitment, appointment, progression, promotion and salary. These reports showed that, in promotion over the period 2010 to 2016 and in progression through the professorial ranges from 2009, the success rates for women had been more favourable than for men (Table 7.4). This outcome rested on the work of Queen's Gender Initiative in motivating women to apply for promotion through a unique mentoring programme and practical advice on preparing strong applications.

Table 7.4 Percentage success rates in promotions, QUB 2010–2015

Academic Year	Male	Female	Difference
2010–2011	50.0	53.8	+3.8
2011–2012	47.3	65.4	+18.1
2012–2013	37.0	53.3	+16.3
2013–2014	46.4	45.2	−1.2
2014–2015	32.7	36.0	+3.3
2015–2016	64.7	90.1	+25.4

Source: QUB Human Resources 2017 *Promotion success rates by gender* (unpublished)

Despite positive promotional outcomes and the 2015 professorial salary review, in which 70 per cent of female professors progressed compared to 54 per cent of males, the gender pay gap increased between 2015 and 2016. In December 2016, the Queen's vice-chancellor established a project group co-chaired by Professors Galligan and Millar to undertake a forensic analysis of the gender pay gap data and to make recommendations for its reduction to under 5 per cent by 2024. The group was asked to consider best practice in other UK universities, consult with the trade unions and professors, and to take legal advice in respect of the options proposed. At the time of this analysis (January 2017), the gap in basic pay had widened to 14.9 per cent.

The group's investigation identified multiple reasons for the pay gap and also ruled out some that might hold in other institutions. In particular, it found that:

1   although women were more successful in gaining promotions than men, a significantly smaller number of eligible female staff applied for promotion than eligible men;
2   although the number of female professors had increased from 22 to 47 between 2006 and 2016, the percentage of female professors remained at 22 per cent since 2011;

3   77 per cent of the female professors in 2016 had been promoted internally, compared to 64 per cent of men;
4   of the 115 professorial appointments over the decade, only 18 per cent had been women;
5   66 per cent of male appointments had occurred at salary point 3 in range 2 or higher, compared with 43 per cent of female appointments;
6   there was a much higher proportion of males (18%) in the two highest paid ranges than females (3%);
7   a significantly higher number and value of market supplements were paid to males, particularly in range 2; and
8   the Exceptional Advancement Scheme was dominated by male applicants (88%) and in positive outcomes (80%). No women were successful over six cycles of the scheme.

The group was also able to quantify the impact of these factors on the overall basic pay gap (14.86%) as well as on a 14 per cent pay gap found among range 2 professors. No gaps were evident in other ranges. Thus, the higher percentage of men at ranges 3 and 4 accounted for 7.5 per cent of the basic gap. In addition, market supplements, which were heavily skewed towards men, both in number and value, accounted for 1.9 per cent of the overall gap and 3.4 per cent of the range 2 gap.

The outcome of the analysis, and consultations with affected professors, unions and university decision-makers resulted in a 12-point plan agreed by the Queen's University Senate on 27 June 2017. The plan provided for a monitoring group headed by a pro-vice-chancellor and actions included reducing the pay bands in ranges 1 and 2; shortening the period of progress through range 1 from 9 to 4.5 years; a commitment to recruit professorial women and men to point 3 in range 2 as a minimum starting point; and a review of the application of the market supplement for new hires. In 2019, the effect of the plan had decreased the gender pay gap to 8.4 per cent.

Ireland context

The legal context for pay and equality issues in Ireland is provided in the Universities Act 1997 (Section 25.1) which confers universities with the authority to appoint such employees as it thinks appropriate, having regard to the efficient use of resources, its accountability requirements for expenditure of public monies and relevant policy relating to pay and conditions in the public sector. Section 25(4) of the Act stipulates that remuneration for university staff should be 'as may be approved from time to time by the Minister (for Education and Skills) with the consent of the Minister for Finance'. Hence, the government determines the pay structure and rates of pay in Irish universities, including Trinity College, Dublin.

The equality provisions in the 1997 Act are more general, with the only issue relating to staff being the more general references to promotion of equality of opportunity and the specific requirement for a university to have an equality policy (Section 36). More generally, the matter of equal pay is covered in national legislation by the Employment Equality Acts 1998–2015 which deal with equality in the workplace, including equal pay. The legislation confers the entitlement to equal pay for like work, prohibiting unequal treatment on nine specific grounds covered by the Act, including gender.

In relation to pay transparency, legislation on gender pay reporting (Gender Pay Gap Information Bill 2017) is progressing through the Houses of the Oireachtas (the Irish parliament) and is expected to be enacted in 2020. It is expected that the proposed legislation will require employers to disclose calculations on pay and benefit differences between men and women in their employment, along with the requirement to submit the details to a designated body and to publish the data on the university's own website. These planned provisions are similar to the UK requirements. The draft legislation indicates that reporting will initially apply to public and private sector employers with 250 or more employees, dropping within two years to include employers with 150 employees or more, and in the following year to those with 50 employees or more.

In contrast to the UK and Queen's University, the salary regime for academic staff in Trinity College is more structured and, arguably, less liable to variability in pay outcomes associated with more individualised pay structures. Although there was no legislation on wage transparency on the Irish statute books in 2017, there was some momentum in the higher education sector to examine gender inequalities in pay. This heightened awareness came from the engagement of Irish higher education sector with the issue of gender equality and the adoption of the Athena SWAN methodology and process. Trinity College, a leader in the application of Athena SWAN in Irish academia, voluntarily undertook a gender pay audit as part of the university's activities on gender equality. The analysis was undertaken by a group comprising: Director of Diversity and Inclusion, Tony McMahon, Professor Gail McElroy and Associate Professor Gaia Narciso.

Trinity College academic salary scales

In Trinity College, there are four distinct grades of academic staff, namely, assistant professor (equivalent to lecturer), associate professor (senior lecturer), professor in (associate professor) and professor of (chair/full professor). During the years of economic austerity since 2009, the entry academic grade scale (assistant professor) was reduced through the Financial Emergency Measures in the Public Interest (FEMPI) legislation. While some of the impact of these measures has subsequently been ameliorated, salaries at the time of the 2016 audit are shown in Table 7.5.

Progression through the relevant salary scale is incremental, with annual progression to the next scale point, subject to satisfactory performance. Progression across the salary scales can occur either through the academic promotion process, or through appointment to a higher scale following a competitive recruitment process.

Table 7.5 Salary scales, TCD 2016

Point	Assistant professor	Associate professor	Professor	Professor (chair)
1	€32,540	€69,349	€78,321	€106,516
2	€34,593	€73,272	€83,311	€112,445
3	€36,156	€77,124	€88,312	€118,403
4	€38,437	€80,916	€93,297	€124,361
5	€40,741	€84,717	€98,297	€130,320
6	€42,701	€88,512	€103,261	€136,276
7	€44,651	No further points	No further points	No further points
8	€46,615			
9	€48,632			
10	€50,708			
11	€52,738			
12	€54,852			
13	€56,901			
14	€68,063			
15	€70,251			
16	€72,439			
17	€76,948			

Source: Trinity College Dublin 2018, *Gender Pay Audit* (unpublished)

In addition to these standard processes for incremental progression, promotion and recruitment are similar to the situation in Queen's, there is an exceptional accelerated advancement scheme. Through this channel, staff may apply to the relevant academic promotions committee to progress along the scale by more than one increment in a given year. Likewise, there is a retention scheme where, in exceptional circumstances, the Provost may convene the relevant promotions committee to consider a candidate outside of the normal promotions round. Finally, the other exceptional academic pay measure in Irish universities is the departures framework which, subject to certain stringent conditions, permits the recruitment of exceptional academic staff on rates above the standard scales, for a limited term.

In Trinity College, as in other Irish universities, female representation decreases significantly at the higher academic grades. In 2016, 51 per cent of assistant professors, but only 22 per cent of chair professors in Trinity were women (Figure 7.3). This profile mirrors female representation in academic grades across all Irish universities, with 50 per cent of assistant professor equivalents and 19 per cent of chair professor equivalents.

Like Queen's University, female representation as chair professors while improving between 2012 and 2016 remains unsatisfactory (Figure 7.4) and is a major contributor to the gender pay gap.

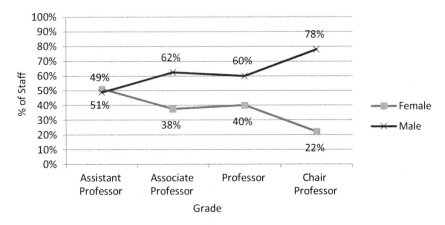

Figure 7.3 Gender representation in academic grades, TCD 2016

Source: Trinity College Dublin 2018, *Gender Pay Audit* (unpublished)

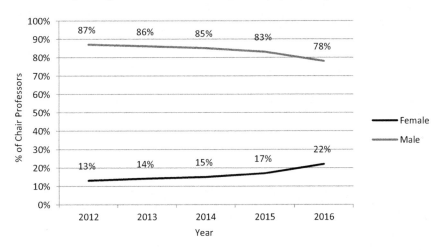

Figure 7.4 Gender representation in chair professors, TCD 2012–2016

Source: Trinity College Dublin 2018, *Gender Pay Audit* (unpublished)

Trinity College data collection and analysis

Trinity's gender pay audit involved a review of the remuneration of 3,465 staff who were in the employment of the University in 2016. The proportions of staff across grade categories were as set out in Table 7.6. The TCD gender pay audit, using annual earnings as the input data point, analysed all categories of employment in the University (academic, administrative, research and support staff). The analysis covered all staff, as well as full-time staff only, in order to standardise for part-time working and adjust the data for full-time equivalency. Finally, in order to investigate whether there was any gender pattern in pay progression for newly recruited staff, a cohort of newly recruited academic staff employed between 2004 and 2007 was identified and their pay progression up to 2016 was tracked.

Table 7.6 Staff representation by grade category, TCD 2016

Grade Category	% of overall staff population
Professional Services Staff	47
Academic Staff	26
Researcher Staff	23
Technical Staff	4

Source: Trinity College Dublin 2018, *Gender Pay Audit* (unpublished)

The overall gender pay gap across the university was estimated to be 9 per cent, based on total earnings in the period. In order to standardise for hours, when part-time employees were excluded from the calculations, the gender pay gap for full-time employees was estimated to be 3 per cent. Among academic staff specifically, median earnings were examined, since high-earning outliers can distort mean figures. Table 7.7 provides a breakdown of the median salaries for all academic staff in 2016, according to gender. As is clear from the table, the median is higher for male academics and this difference is statistically significant. In percentage terms, there is a 6 per cent pay gap between the median wages of men and women, with male academics earning more than female academics.

Table 7.7 Academic median salary for full-time and part-time staff, TCD 2016

		Female	Male	%Pay Gap
All Academic Staff	Median Annual earnings	€72,439	€76,948	5.9%
	Sample Size	409	509	
Full Time Academic Staff (only)	Median Annual earnings	€75,110	€76,948	2.4%
	Sample Size	296	417	

Source: Trinity College Dublin 2018, *Gender Pay Audit* (unpublished)

This is consistent with findings elsewhere and compares favourably with published data for comparable UK universities. Factoring in the nature of the contract (full time or part time) and adjusting for part-time work, by analysing only the earnings of full-time staff, the earnings gap is reduced, but nonetheless remains statistically significant.

In order to understand some of the determinants of the gender pay gap figures, a quartile analysis was undertaken for all staff. This analysis demonstrated a gender divergence at higher levels. More specifically, 'high earners' defined as any academic earning €90,000 or above, were examined. Among male academic staff, the proportion earning above €90,000 is close to 24 per cent, whereas the similar figure for female academic staff is just below 14 per cent. The figures in the €120,000–140,000 band reflect the gender profile of chair professors and this finding indicates that (lack of) progression of women to senior academic positions is a causal factor in the gender pay gap (Table 7.8).

Table 7.8 Academic staff quartile pay analysis, 2016

€000's	% of total female academics	% of total male academics
90–100	3.91	6.07
100–110	4.61	4.24
110–120	0.46	1.65
120–140	2.53	8.1
140–175	0.00	0.90
175+	2.30	2.92
Total	**13.81**	**23.88**

Source: Trinity College Dublin 2018, Gender Pay Audit (unpublished)

Finally, a timeline analysis was conducted to track the pay progression of a cohort of academic staff (those hired in the three years from 2004–2007) up to 2016. This analysis suggested that, while there did not appear to be a gender issue in starting pay, a gender gap emerged in the median wage after two to three years of service. This finding needs to be treated with caution since it may not be reliable due to the fact that the cohort size was relatively small.

Lessons and insights from the gender pay audits in QUB and TCD

Conducting a comprehensive and accurate gender pay audit is highly reliant on the quality of data available, and in this context both Queen's University and Trinity College encountered challenges which can be expected when this type of audit is being conducted for the first time. It should be noted that, in seeking payroll data for the purpose of gender analysis, these data have been gathered, processed and stored for a very different purpose than gender pay auditing. The core purpose of a payroll function is to pay employees accurately and on time, while the main reporting obligations tend to relate to internal financial governance and the requirements of external auditors. Hence, payroll processes (and human resource processes that feed into payroll), data sets and systems cannot be assumed to hold the type of data required for wage gap auditing. Conducting a gender pay audit could lead to adjustments to payroll information to provide a richer set of data for subsequent audits.

A second note of caution relates to interpretation of findings. The common standard measure of the gender pay gap, i.e. the difference in average hourly earnings between women and men, does not indicate or point to discrimination, or an absence of equal pay for equal value work. For example, if Queen's University had equal pay in all grades from lecturer to Range 4 professor, the average gender pay gap among the professoriate would still be over 7 per cent, due to the skewed nature of the male distribution compared to the female distribution. In this case, the gap cannot be interpreted as women being paid less than men. Rather it points to a systemic failure to get women into the more senior roles. A simplistic, and incorrect interpretation of data can result in a dialogue polarised around equal pay, in which fundamental issues, such as women advancing in leadership roles, women's under-representation in high-level high-paying jobs, the gendered nature of family care and the paucity of adequate childcare provision, are ignored.

The results of the gender pay gap audit in both universities provided greater insight into the sources, potential or real, contributing to pay inequality. The audit process contributed to learning in relation to the capacity of both universities to report and monitor gender pay differences. It also highlighted a range of issues and challenges for data collection and analysis for gender pay auditing. In both universities, it was not possible to determine hourly rates, and annual earnings were utilised to calculate gender pay differentials. For example, Trinity's overall gender pay gap, the adjusted gender pay gap figure of 3 per cent refers only to staff employed full-time at Trinity and is calculated on the difference in median annual salaries of all male and female full-time staff. While comparison of the average hourly rate is the universal standard methodology for calculation of the pay gap, it was not possible to utilise this methodology mainly because, as quasi autonomous and self-directed employees, weekly working hours are not defined for academic staff. Consequently, the removal of part-time staff from the Trinity sample, although necessitated by the nature of the available data, had the effect of reducing the overall sample size by about 20 per cent. This is far from ideal, especially since women are disproportionately more likely to work part-time (over 80 per cent of employees working part-time, across all grade categories, are women). For future audits, the aspiration would be to have pay data that is recorded to facilitate comparison with national and international pay gaps, but in the absence of contractual change in relation to working hours, this may need to be achieved through setting a normative working hours assumption.

Similar data challenges were present in Queen's University where efforts to identify the time taken, according to gender, to move from lecturer to professor were hampered by lack of clarity in the data. For example, it was often difficult to get an academic start date for staff who previously held a postdoctoral post at the university and start dates for academics who moved institutions to join Queen's. As a proxy, the date of the PhD was used to measure any inequality between males and females in the time taken to reach professorship. Also, while it was possible to obtain some tentative findings on the influence of maternity leave on progress, the sample size was much too small to draw definite conclusions. A gendered insight into pay progression is essential in order to achieve gender pay equality. Attempts to cross reference the indicative findings with other data points in relation to academic progression did not identify any systemic issue in relation to 'time to promotion' between male and female academic staff that would explain a gender pay divergence in early career. Other specific data challenges relate to the level of reporting available from the casual or hourly paid payroll and consistency in coding atypical posts.

Notwithstanding these challenges, the results of the gender pay gap audits in Trinity College and Queen's University have provided invaluable insights into the extent of any gender pay gaps among comparable categories of employees and an indication of the issues to monitor in terms of pay progression. Significantly, the data can also be used alongside other key human resource equality metrics, such as seniority profiles, recruitment trends and outcomes, as part of overall Gender Equality Plans.

Policy drivers impacting on gender pay from the experience of QUB and TCD

Both Trinity College and Queen's University have comprehensive equality and diversity policies which set out the institutional commitment to equality of opportunity and non-discrimination. These policies include specific human resource equality measures in relation to recruitment, advertising and selection, but do not specifically address equal pay. The respective salary structures and salary progression arrangements for academic staff in each institution are set out in detail earlier in this chapter. In addition, the following processes are also determinants of academic staff pay. Reviewing policy on these issues and monitoring the outcomes from process implementation of these policies will complement the existing data analysis. Typical processes that would be considered are:

- starting pay: the rate of pay for newly recruited or promoted staff;
- pay progression: employee pay progression can be through advancement along the incremental scale, or through promotion/appointment to a higher scale, as set out earlier. A key metric to consider is any gender differences in the time taken to progress through the grade structure;
- increments: generally paid annually subject to verification of satisfactory performance;
- accelerated advancement: certain grades within Trinity and all non-probationary staff in Queen's may apply to the relevant channels for their grade to advance along the scale by more than one increment in a given year;
- promotion: employees may seek promotion to a higher grade through the two universities' promotion procedures and the outcomes are generally reported to university governing bodies;
- time at grade: this can indicate a systemic bias operating in promotions and advancement practices;
- job requisitioning: decisions to create new posts, or to appoint staff replacements to existing roles are generally processed through a job requisitioning or posts approval process. In both universities, this is devolved to faculty and divisional level;

- provisions for specific retention or supplementation arrangements, in addition to standard promotion or pay progression schemes, present specific risks for gender equal pay decision-making and should be assessed as part of the gender pay audit process.

Conclusions

Comparing and contrasting the pay progression process

The gender pay gap cases of Trinity College Dublin and Queen's University Belfast illustrate two very different environments for tackling the issue. In the QUB case, market conditions mean that there can be a wide variation between universities on professorial pay. In Ireland, a more structured and centralised approach to pay determination is adopted allowing much less room for wage variance in the Irish higher education system. Despite operating in very different policy environments, the factors contributing to the gender pay gap in both institutions are broadly similar. One obvious shared characteristic is the lack of women at senior academic levels in both institutions, despite there being a relatively healthy pipeline for women's advancement. The question is, then, what is preventing women from making their way to the higher-paid echelons of a university career? Demonstrably, in both institutions, the valuing of the work of male academics over that of their female counterparts in promotions processes plays a part. Women's service in senior posts, when they finally make this grade, is likely to be shorter than that of their male colleagues. In tackling the gender pay gap, close attention needs to be paid to the gendered nature of the academic promotion and recruitment processes, particularly at full chair professorial level.

Both universities also demonstrate distortions in the exceptional pay reward mechanisms, though these are exhibited to a greater degree and scale in Queen's University. Success in an exceptional process, such as accelerated advancement and retention, relies on the subjective judgement of a small number of people, including an individual's line manager who is typically the head of department or school. These processes are not as widely promoted, or understood, as are public recruitment and standard academic promotion processes and, with the perceived lack of transparency, can create a risk of pay inequality.

The audit process

The need for, and quality of, the collaboration between data and process owners and Gender Equality Plan leaders is imperative. The source data to be analysed in a gender pay audit is unlikely to have been designed with gender disaggregated reporting in mind, so adapting processes and data to facilitate greater interrogation and monitoring over time will require collaboration towards a shared purpose.

A second key issue is in relation to how the available data are viewed. Disaggregation of data to the appropriate level, such as job categories and grades, and university, faculty and school-level analysis, is essential if one of the objectives of a gender pay audit is to use the findings as a basis for action. Using a number of different lenses, for example median figures and quartile analysis, to review the data and identification of trends, rather than one point in time analysis, is invaluable.

Finally, the audit process can be viewed as a lever for effective change and not just as a passive compliance or governance exercise. This chapter has highlighted the additional institutional insight that gender pay audits can provide over and above societal and legislative requirements. Analysis of the gender pay gap among comparable roles (in this case academic staff at various levels) using different lenses, provided more accurate insights into the nature of any gender pay gap and its causes, thus providing a basis for action to address it.

References

Department of Justice and Equality (2017) *National strategy for women and girls 2017–2020: Creating a better society for all*, Department of Justice and Equality, Dublin.

European Commission (2014) *Recommendation on strengthening the principle of equal pay between men and women through transparency*, 7 March 2014/124/EU. Available at: https://eur-lex.europa.eu/legal-content/EN/TXT/PDF/?uri=CELEX:32014H0124& from=EN

Government Equalities Office (2015) *Policy paper: Think, act, report*. Available at: www.gov.uk/government/publications/think-act-report/think-act-report

Government of Ireland (2016) *A programme for a partnership government 2016*. Available at: www.merrionstreet.ie/MerrionStreet/en/ImageLibrary/Programme_for_Partner ship_Government.pdf

Grove, J. (2016) University of Essex hikes salaries for female professors to eliminate gender pay gap, *Times Higher Education*, 2 June. Available at: www.timeshighereducation.com/ news/university-of-essex-hikes-salaries-for-female-professors-to-eliminate-pay-gap

HM Government (2010) *The equality strategy—building a fairer Britain*, Government Equalities Office, London. Available at: https://assets.publishing.service.gov.uk/govern ment/uploads/system/uploads/attachment_data/file/85299/equality-strategy.pdf

New Joint Negotiating Committee for Higher Education Staff (2016) *Higher education gender pay gap data*. Available at: https://uceastorage.blob.core.windows.net/ucea/ download.cfm/docid/new_jnches_-_higher_education_gender_pay_gap_data.pdf

Office for National Statistics (2019) *Gender pay gap*. Available at: www.ons.gov.uk/ employmentandlabourmarket/peopleinwork/earningsandworkinghours/bulletins/ genderpaygapintheuk/2019#the-gender-pay-gap (last accessed 14 January 2020)

Oireachtas (2017) *Irish human rights and equality commission (gender pay gap information) Bill*, 16 May. Available at: www.oireachtas.ie/en/bills/bill/2017/64/

Pells, R. (2018) Gender pay gap: How much less are women paid at your university? *Times Higher Education*, 6 April. Available at: www.timeshighereducation.com/news/ gender-pay-gap-how-much-less-are-women-paid-your-university

Queen's University Belfast (QUB) (2017) *Equal pay audit 2017*. Available at: www.qub. ac.uk/directorates/HumanResources/hr-filestore/Filetoupload,865185,en.pdf

Queen's University Belfast (QUB) Human Resources (2017) *Promotion success rates by gender 2010–2015* (unpublished).

Secretary of State for Education and Minister for Women and Equalities (2015) *Memorandum to the women and equalities select committee on the post-legislative assessment of the Equality Act 2010 (CM9101)*. Available at: https://assets.publishing.service.gov.uk/government/uploads/system/uploads/attachment_data/file/441838/Memo_to_Women_Equalities.pdf

Trinity College Dublin Human Resources (2016) *Academic pay scales 2016* (unpublished).

Trinity College Dublin Human Resources (2018) *Gender pay audit 2018* (unpublished).

UN Committee on the Elimination of Discrimination Against Women (CEDAW) (2017) *Concluding observations on the combined sixth and seventh periodic reports of Ireland*, 9 March, CEDAW/C/IRL/co/6-7. Available at: www.refworld.org/docid/596f48a94.html

Chapter 8

Men and masculinities in academia

Towards gender-sensitive perspectives, processes, policies and practices

Jeff Hearn

Introduction

Academia is a complex site involving many agents within multi-organisations in which the inter-organisational relations operate locally, nationally and transnationally. In seeking to understand the gender dimension of academia, it is necessary to understand gender power relations in societies and institutions. This in turn means developing an understanding of men and masculinities, as well as women and femininities. Thus, gender and gender relations are not synonyms for women; they not only concern women and girls but also men and boys, and further gender/sexual categories, notably LGBT*IQ+, including non-binary, agender and asexual people. This kind of relational gender power perspective applies in many arenas but takes particular forms in academia. Approaching gender dimensions in such ways is relevant to the conduct of academic institutions, organisations and management, research development and research processes and the specific doing of academic work.

Gender inequality in academia is often framed with a sole focus on women, either women's experiences or seeing women as the problem who need to be changed. The debate can also be framed in terms of complementary gender relations as problematic, hence change requiring gender mainstreaming, without any explicit commitment to feminist theory and practice. Less frequently, the focus can be shifted onto men as the problem and the need to change men within gender power relations. This chapter focuses on neither 'women as the problem' nor 'gender mainstreaming' as the solution. Rather it concentrates on gendering men, or 'the problem of men' in academia. In engaging with the problematic that men in academia are gendered too, discussion focuses on three key interconnected aspects: *perspectives* on studies of men and masculinities; *processes* in universities, higher education and science that can be analysed through a critical analysis of men and masculinities; and *policies and practices*: what is to be done individually, organisationally and nationally, in academia?

Changing perspectives on studying men and masculinities

Before proceeding to discuss some key features of recent studies on men and masculinities, three basic points should be noted. First, studies on men and masculinity are not new and have often studied men implicitly and/or without a clear critical stance; second, studying men and masculinity is, in itself, no guarantee of critical-ity; and third, the man or men question is well-documented in feminist and critical gender theory and practice.

The last 50 years have seen an expansion of critical research on men and mas-culinities, sometimes referred to as the sub-field of Critical Studies on Men and Masculinities (CSMM), as part of women's and gender studies (Hearn and How-son 2019). CSMM is a broad umbrella term for different kinds of studies of men and masculinities that are distinct from malestream studies (O'Brien 1981), which are opposed to non-gendered, non-feminist or anti-feminist scholarship. CSMM refers to critical, explicitly gendered studies of men and masculinities that engage with feminist critiques, but also some men's positive responses to feminism, and further critical perspectives such as poststructuralism, postcolonialism and drawing from gay, queer, trans, intersex and non-binary positions. Hence, studies within CSMM range across many perspectives, paradigms and disciplines, from masculine psychology to broad societal and collective analyses of men, includ-ing ethnographies of particular groups and activities of men and investigations of masculinities in specific discourses. Certain themes have been stressed, for example work and family, sometimes posed in contradiction with what are often assumed to be dominant definitions and priorities of men. Much research has been local, personal, bodily, immediate, interpersonal or ethnographic, on spe-cific groups of men and boys in different parts of the world. Increasingly, there is a further turn to the 'big picture' of globalisation (Connell 1993, 1998), world-centred approaches (Connell 2014), transnational patriarchies and transnational change (Hearn 2015). These diverse kinds of research studies are all relevant for the analysis and change of men and masculinities in academia.

More generally, the explicit 'naming men as men' (Hanmer 1990; Collinson and Hearn 1994) has been made, not to essentialise or reify men but to see men and masculinities as an object of critique and critical interrogation. The idea that the gender of men derives from a fixed, inner trait or core is antagonistic to CSMM. Accordingly, it is necessary to distinguish men as 'objects' of study, and men as 'subjects' or doers of studies. Importantly, the sub-field of CSMM is certainly not the preserve or property of men, as promoted in some ambiguous or anti-feminist versions of men's studies. Rather, CSMM comprise studies by all genders.

The broad critical approach to men and masculinities that has developed in CSMM can be characterised as: a critical explicit focus on men and masculinities, informed by feminist, gay, queer and other critical gender scholarship; understand-ing men and masculinities as gendered, socially constructed, not just 'naturally this way', variable and changing across, space, within societies and across the life course and biographies; emphasising men's differential relations to gendered power; spanning the material and the discursive in analysis; and taking account of the intersections of gender and other social divisions (Connell et al 2005).

Overall, CSMM encompass historical, cultural, relational, materialist, decon-structive, anti-essentialist studies on men and masculinities (Hearn and Pringle 2006). In debates in and around CSMM, the most cited approach is what can be called masculinities theory (Carrigan *et al* 1985; Connell 1995) in which various masculinities are framed in relation to the theorising of patriarchy and patriarchal relations. Within this approach, the concept of hegemonic masculinity has been central, while other concepts, such as complicit masculinity, are less well developed. Hegemonic masculinity has been defined as:

> the configuration of gender practice which embodies the currently accepted answer to the problem of legitimacy of patriarchy, which guarantees (or is taken to guarantee) the dominant position of men and the subordination of women.
>
> (Connell 1995, 77)

Key features of this approach centre on critiques of sex role theory together with an analysis of concepts of masculinities and power. The approach also emphasises men's unequal relations to men as well as men's relations to women and the implications of gay scholarship and sexual hierarchies more generally, distinguishing between hegemonic, complicit, subordinated and marginalised masculinities. This approach also calls for analysis of institutional and social, interpersonal and psychodynamic aspects of masculinities.

Masculinities theory has been extremely influential within CSMM and beyond, with applications and different interpretations of hegemonic masculinity in theoretical, empirical and policy studies (Connell and Messerschmidt 2005; Hearn *et al* 2012; Bridges and Pascoe 2014; Matthews 2016). There are also various critiques of masculinities theory and the concepts of masculinity and hegemonic masculinity, such as lack of clarity in what masculinity/ masculinities mean. Additionally, comparative, postcolonial, transnational, queer and other critical approaches complicate a unified theory of men and masculinities; and 'hegemonic masculinity' is often a heuristic device rather than a precise concept. Thus:

> the concept of hegemony has generally been employed in too restricted a way; the focus on masculinity is too narrow. Instead, it is time to go back from *masculinity* to *men*, to examine the hegemony of men and about men. The hegemony of men seeks to address the double complexity that men are both a *social category formed by the gender system* and *dominant collective and individual agents of social practices*.
>
> (Hearn 2004, 59, emphasis in original)

To summarise, CSMM involves, first, the critical gendering of men, the 'naming men as men' and, simultaneously, problematising and deconstructing masculinities and the social category of men.

Changing processes on men and masculinities in academia

Debates about gender in academia have typically focused on women and girls, as when discussing why more girls do not take up science, engineering and technology subjects. One might imagine that it is difficult to talk about academia without discussing the power, positions and constructions of men and masculinities, but that is not so. Instead, extensive scientific and popular debate on 'failing boys' in schools continues to be the focus. Men in academia remains unproblematised. Indeed, many debates and documents on gender equality in academia are strangely silent on questions of men, masculinities and male majorities, especially those that operate at senior and leadership levels. For example, there are many excellent studies and reports on gender and science (European Commission 2009; Caprile *et al* 2012), some funded by the European Commission. Yet few have much to say about men and masculinities and their part in maintaining inequalities within science and higher education systems. While many reports include a mass of highly relevant information, few if any demands are made on changing men, or masculinities. Consequently, men continue to be let off the hook. Men are typically an 'absent presence', even in critical studies of academia. Implicit references are often wrapped up in gender-neutral characterisations of institutions, as if there are 'non-gendered universities + women'. Without attending to such themes, how likely is it to lead to reduced gender inequalities in higher education? Naming men as men (Hanmer 1990; Collinson and Hearn 1994) and naming male privilege (Bulumulle 2015) is still an obvious, yet awkward and uncomfortable, task for many in academia.

Debates on gender equality in academia have focused on three main forms of gendered processes and politics:

• *gendered individuals*: Who does what? Who does academic work? Who are the leaders, inventors, followers, researchers, teachers, support workers? How are individual identities and careers gendered?;
• *gendered organising and organisations*: how academia is organised and managed within organisations and organisational cultures; and
• *gendered knowledge*: the relevance of gender for the construction of academic knowledge itself, in the research process and knowledge production.

Taking each of these processes in order: first, the gendering of men and masculinities in academia can be understood by way of the construction of individuals and their identities. Within academia there are many sites where different masculinities are reproduced: for administrators, academics, managers and students. In studying the conduct of jurisprudence in universities, for example, Collier (1998) catalogued different kinds of male academics and academic masculinities: the nutty professor; the administrator; the new entrepreneur; the sexual predator; the young man in a hurry; the infantilised intellectual; the empire builder; the aloof cynic; the gentleman intellectual; the academic couple; even the profeminist (Collier 2002). Arguably, the new entrepreneur and the young man in a hurry have become more prominent in the neoliberal university, where age and status are no longer so strictly self-reinforcing. To this list, one might note further academic masculinities in all subject areas such as: the misogynist, the stealer of ideas; the unsuccessful academic; the non-researching research manager; the gatekeeper; and the equality supporter, whether active, passive or simply hypocritical.

The focus on the individual is not only a matter of male academic identity, it also concerns individual careers and evaluations. For example, there is now significant evidence from Swedish surveys of the relative advantages that accrue to male doctoral students compared to their female counterparts. This is in a range of areas: health, stress, parenthood, discrimination, sexual harassment, integration in the academic environment, doctoral work and career coaching. The overall results indicate a more positive, supportive doctoral educational environment for men than women (HSV 2003, 2008; UKÄ 2016; Hearn and Husu 2019). Individual academic evaluation may be gender-biased in various ways, for example, with scoring of men higher than women in assessing CVs and differential letters of recommendation (Madera *et al* 2009). A more complex process is raised by a study of 168 life scientists in ecology and evolutionary biology, showing clear differences in publication rates between men and women in early careers, with consequences for subsequent citation (see Chapters 1 and 2). The use of the apparently neutral h-index as a measure of research performance (the number of published papers, h, by a given scientist that have received 'h' or more citations) favours men. The h-index is highly correlated with the quantity of research output. Women assessed thus are likely to suffer in comparison with men (Symonds *et al* 2006). Men still tend to publish more papers than women, even after accounting for mitigating factors (Ding *et al* 2006). These processes interconnect with organisational contexts.

Second, gendering men and masculinities in academia is important in terms of how academic institutions and workplaces operate. Historically, academic organisations have been characterised by the relative age, class and ethnic homogeneity and homosociality of certain men. Homosociality encapsulates men's greater valuation of men, and preference for men and men's company (Lipman-Blumen 1976), the transfers of power and information, emotional charge, and emulation and imitation between men; and the dispensability of individual men. It is a useful concept to consider the ways of organising of men in academic management. Similarly, the notion of 'cultural cloning' (Essed and Goldberg 2002) has been applied more intersectionally to analyse working in and between academic institutions. The historical legacy and current reality of men-men relations, men's networks and male bonding are obvious in most academic institutions. The legacy of homogeneity and homosociality of certain men has only been displaced partially in relatively recent times. Even with moves to more technocratic forms of management (Hearn 2001), academia remains predominantly a site of men's power, privilege and mutual support (Bulumulle 2015).

Contemporary academia continues much of this legacy, but with some further features. For a start, academia is characterised by strong age, ethnic and gender-differentiation, both vertically and horizontally. In many cases, there are relatively fixed layers of older professorial and senior staff, predominantly men, together with shifting, temporary and often more diverse populations of women and men members among students and less well-established staff. Furthermore, some academic institutions and social sites, such as some university departments and conferences, involve both formality and informality, that also bring social and interpersonal ambiguities. In some extreme instances this provides room for men's harassment and misuse of power towards typically younger students and researchers. These, in turn, may mean the presence of hierarchical, age, gender, social, sexual and intense emotional dynamics. In sum, academia houses both strong pressures and opportunities to conform and, at least in some academic traditions, occasions for subversion of that conformity.

A key aspect of the gendered operations of academia is how men act as managers, gatekeepers and leaders more generally. Considered in a broad international perspective, there are very large national and societal variations in the extent to which men dominate professoriates, headships of departments, rectorates and decision-making bodies responsible for awarding research funding (European Commission 2019). In some EU countries, for example Belgium, Croatia, Cyprus, Czech Republic, Estonia and Greece, such key positions are still overwhelmingly 'men's business' (European Commission 2019) (see Chapter 1).

Gendered processes in research and funding are not just about individual careers. They are more embedded organisational processes. These include, not only the relative rate of research funding success of women and men applicants, but also relative gender rates of application (affected by position, status and organisational support and facilitation), relative rates and patterns of publication, citation and funds awarded, according to gender. Some studies of funding processes, for example, Wennerås and Wold's (1997) study showed how men were favoured in the allocation of state funding of medical research in Sweden. However, a similar UK study by the Wellcome Trust (Wellcome Trust 1997), while not finding gender bias, noted women's lower rate of application for research funding. Such studies have been influential in questioning and sometimes reforming assessment and selection procedures. A meta-analysis of 21 studies found evidence of robust gender differences in grant award procedures:

> Even though the estimates of the gender effect vary substantially from study to study, the model estimation shows that all in all, among grant applicants men have statistically significant greater odds of receiving grants than women by about 7 per cent.
>
> (Bornmann et al 2007, 2)

In many countries, basic information is still lacking on the gendering of these processes and the part that different men play as gatekeepers in research funding decisions (European Commission 2009).

Men's managerial power and influence, along with managerial masculinities in academia, encompass the impact of men's actions on appointments, promotions, distribution of academic resources and priorities. Two particular issues of interest are: the transition from being primarily a senior researcher to an academic manager; and the question of which particular women, with which particular gender positioning, are supported and sponsored by men in academic management. Masculine or masculinist cultures may also be reproduced at the level of departmental or research teams, in terms of local work cultures: as 'family' (for example, patriarchal, paternalist) or 'gang' (for example, sporty, nerd), which may undervalue or exclude women's contribution and leadership.

Third, the gendering of men and masculinities extends to knowledge production, research content, theory development, concepts, research directions and priorities. The institutional structures and contexts of academia have always had differential impacts on men's and women's opportunities to engage in academic activities (Bowling and Martin 1985; Schiebinger 1987). The relevance of explicitly gendered thinking on men and masculinities is relatively well-researched and recognised in relation to technology (Cockburn 1985; Willinsky 2000; Lohan and Faulkner 2004) and, to some extent, in relation to medicine (Rosenfeld and Faircloth 2006). For example, cardiovascular disease has often been presented as a male disease but is in fact a major disease of women; osteoporosis is sometimes seen as a female disease but is a major disease of later male life. Until the late 1990s, women were routinely excluded from scientific studies since it was assumed that the results would apply equally to males and females. This assumption was shown in many instances to be wrong (Greenspan *et al* 2007).

Moreover, each facet and stage of the research process and knowledge production, in terms of both substantive academic and theoretical practices, is susceptible to gendered structuring, positionings and interactions of men and masculinities. Shifting this process means paying greater attention to the gendered aspects of research content and sex/gender analysis in scientific knowledge production; and challenging assumptions of gender neutrality within supposedly 'objective' mainstream scientific excellence. It also calls for the further development of critical studies on men and masculinities themselves (see Chapter 14).

Changing policies and practices on men and masculinities in academia

Naming men as men in academia is both a matter of analysis and of policy and practice. So, what is to be done by and with men? How can men contribute to gender equality and how are men affected by gender (in)equality in academia? Men are not a homogenous group and the long-used binary assumptions no longer prevail.

Individual and interpersonal change

One arena for action is to focus on changing individuals and interpersonal relations. Men in academia are probably not so very different to other men. Some may be a little more intellectual, work-oriented, more defended, more defensive and they may be able to engage in complex forms of resistance. Men's practices can be seen as paralleling closely how men may respond to gender equality more generally on a spectrum from outright rejection and hostility to welcoming;

anti-feminist, unhelpful to facilitative, profeminist (Messner 1997; Egeberg *et al* 2009). Men move along such dimensions in gendered practices according to political and organisational pressures and conditions. Men, as a social group, are relatively privileged but some men seek to act against gender inequality, supporting women and appointing feminists. Unreconstructed men persist, as when, for example, supposedly 'critical' male academics say proudly they know nothing about gender.

There are many ways in which men can avoid being concerned with or resist gender issues and gender equality. Typical expressions used to avoid and resist 'naming men as men' in academia include:

'We are all just individuals'
'We are all just human beings, we are all equal'
'Men and women are no different, so . . .'
'Men and women are very different, so . . .'
'I am first and foremost a manager, professor, administrator . . .'
'I just try and be fair, and judge people on their merits'
'Here it is just a question of competence'
'Here we are just one big happy family . . .'
'Class, race, religion, sexuality etc. are more important'
'I am gay, so this is not key for me'
'I am a father, I take care of my children, do my bit at home'
'I don't have time for feminism or gender equality, they're old fashioned'
'I don't know anything about gender . . .'

There are men in academia who may be familiar with and even embrace feminism and gender equality but cannot be relied upon to act against men's interests or to demonstrate solidarity with women. Men acting against gender inequality are less usual: appointing feminist women, supporting women, critically examining men in their own scholarly work. They have a key role to play in breaking silence, in being persistent.

Common pitfalls in mixed-gender groups in academia, as elsewhere, are many and varied. They include 'hogging the show' and being the continual problem-solver; focusing only on task and content, to the exclusion of giving support and acknowledging one's own and others' feelings; negativity and falling back on formal power positions; listening only to other men; intransigence and dogmatism; condescension and paternalism; using sexuality to manipulate women; and seeking attention and support from women while running the show; storing key information for their own use; and speaking on behalf of others (Moyer and Tuttle 1983). These have a good deal in common with the five 'master suppression techniques' described by Ås (1978) namely: making invisible, using ridicule, withholding information, double binding, and heaping blame and putting to shame—later supplemented by objectifying, and using force and the threat of force. Against such actions, Moyer and Tuttle (1983) were early advocates of responsible actions for men to oppose 'mansplaining'. Recommended actions include: limiting talking time to a fair share; not interrupting; being a good listener; not speaking on every subject; not putting others down; and intervening to interrupt others' oppressive behaviour. Such actions can all contribute to nurturing more democratic group and organisational processes.

Organisational change

At the organisational level, systemic and structural change is still needed. According to the ETAN report (European Commission 2000), the principles of gender mainstreaming in scientific institutions are: building equality into the culture and organisations, treating employees as whole persons, respect and human dignity (anti-discrimination), participation and consultation, and visioning. The main tools recommended for realising these goals include: gender equality indicators, gender proofing and gender impact assessment, ownership of gender equality within all organisational levels, gender monitoring for employers, enacting EU member-state laws on gender balance in decision-making and access to public records, removing the laws impeding women's scientific careers, providing awareness-raising and training.

Structural gender change in universities also requires changing men and masculinities. Local and national targets for maximum numbers of men in academic management, evaluation committees and similar bodies need to be set. If there are more women in academic management and gatekeeping, there will be less men there. Such changes might increase the likelihood of more research funding flowing to women and into fields where women are under-represented with less to men and for fields where men are over-represented. Changing men in academia, academic leadership and academic evaluation means ensuring that men have academic and professional knowledge and training on gender and power issues and do not reproduce sexism and gender domination in their own actions and behaviour. It also means changing dominant models of masculinity in academia, for example, by way of gender equality training and similar interventions to address questions of male identity and men's prejudices, behaviours and gender awareness. It also calls for an awareness of how academic organisations can reproduce dominant male values, and ways of promoting positive change. These interventions would likely have further impacts on men's own research and teaching.

Many further organisational policies and actions follow from naming and deconstructing men, such as reviewing a culture of long hours' work and normalising caring masculinities at home and work (Scambor et al 2013 and Chapter 5). Instituting policy and practice on issues of sexuality, gender identity, harassment, bullying and violence; and attending to men's intersectional relations, for example in relation to age, class, mental health and sexuality are equally important (Hearn and Collinson 2009). Importantly, resource allocation policy can be linked to gender equality, for example, shifting budgets in inverse proportion to the ratio of men to women. In summary, it is necessary to investigate how men can assist in *not* blocking, *not* resisting, gender equality policies, to ask men where they stand and to change men!

National and transnational change

Finally, there is the question of national and transnational contexts. Personal experience attests that the situation on men, masculinities and gender equality can appear to be different in different countries, with distinct national policy frameworks. Academia is increasingly sustained by transnational reserve armies of postdoctoral academic labourers pursuing gendered and generational precarious, mobile 'early' careers through short-term research projects and part-time teaching, sometimes over an extended period and multiple sites or continents (Hearn and Husu 2019; Murgia and Poggio 2019 and Chapter 2). In this academic world, control may easily shift from direct patriarchal management in universities towards greater self-monitoring by more docile or supposedly 'autonomous' academics, existing within transnational academic patriarchies.

Furthermore, academia is increasingly subject to internationalisation, transnational trends and influences. These include moves to neoliberal management, work intensity, monitoring and surveillance, with less unit resources and more standardised measures. Academic institutions are positioning themselves in terms of competitive status through league tables and the prioritising of publications (Chapter 14). There is also the domination of north/west/anglo 'knowledge' and an obsession with 'excellence' in research. In the contemporary academic world, the individual academic institution is not necessarily the primary or most important unit. It exists within tighter inter-organisational relations between universities, through networks, partnerships and associations. Scientific knowledge production and global academic value chains are developed through a mix of scientific hubs and dispersed transnational networks. All these developments are to be understood more fully by highlighting critical analysis and practice in relation to men and masculinities. Men and masculinities now operate within the complex relations between transnational neoliberal academic patriarchies, neoliberal (supposedly 'autonomous') universities and constructions of neoliberal, individual and individualist 'autonomous' masculinities (Hearn 2017). These conditions demand new, creative responses for changing men nationally and transnationally. The problem of men in academia is national and transnational, not just a matter of individual male academics or individual male-dominated universities and academic institutions.

Conclusion

This chapter shifts the debates on gender-sensitive academia to encompass critical approaches to men and masculinities. This means addressing critical research studies and theoretical developments, both general and more focused on academia, along with changes in policy development and everyday practice. The interventions outlined here are on and around men and masculinities at many levels. They collectively assist movements towards more gender-sensitive academic institutions. By shifting the perspective from a sole focus on women as the 'problem' to be reformed, or versions of gender-neutral, gender mainstreaming and structural change where men and masculinities are distinctly and strangely absent, knowledge production itself is likely to become less patriarchal, less sexist, less ungendered and ultimately more scientific.

References

Ås, B. (1978) Hersketeknikker, *Kjerringråd*, 3, 17–21.

Bornmann, L., Mutz, R. and Daniel, H. (2007) Gender differences in grant peer review: A meta-analysis. *Journal of Informetrics*, 1 (3), 226–238.

Bowling, J. and Martin, B. (1985) Science: A masculine disorder? *Science and Public Policy*, 12 (6), 308–316.

Bridges, T. and Pascoe, C. (2014) Hybrid masculinities: New directions in the sociology of men and masculinities, *Sociology Compass*, 8 (3), 246–258.

Bulumulle, K. (2015) *Interrogating what is male privilege in the academy*, Doctoral dissertation, University of Adelaide, Adelaide.

Caprile, M., Addis, E., Castaño, C., Klinge, I., Larios, M., Meulders, D., Müller, J., O'Dorchai, S., Palasik, M., Plasman, R., Roivas, S., Sagebiel, F., Schiebinger., L., Vallès, N. and Vázquez-Cupeiro, S. (eds) (2012) *Meta-analysis of gender and science research: Synthesis report*, European Commission, Brussels.

Carrigan, T., Connell, R. and Lee, J. (1985) Towards a new sociology of masculinity, *Theory and Society*, 14 (5), 551–604.

Cockburn, C. (1985) *Machinery of dominance: Women, men, and technical know-how*, Pluto, London.

Collier, R. (1998) 'Nutty professors', 'men in suits' and 'new entrepreneurs': Corporeality, subjectivity and change in the law school and legal practice, *Social & Legal Studies*, 7 (1), 27–53.

Collier, R. (2002) The changing university and the (legal) academic career—rethinking the 'private life' of the law school, *Legal Studies*, 22 (1), 1–32.

Collinson, D. and Hearn, J. (1994) Naming men as men: Implications for work, organizations and management, *Gender, Work and Organization*, 1 (1), 2–22.

Connell, R. (1993) The big picture: Masculinities in recent world history, *Theory and Society*, 22 (5), 597–623.

Connell, R. (1995) *Masculinities*, Polity, Cambridge.

Connell, R. (1998) Masculinities and globalization, *Men and Masculinities*, 1 (1), 3–23.

Connell, R. (2014) Margin becoming centre: For a world-centred rethinking of masculinities, *NORMA: The International Journal for Masculinity Studies*, 9 (4), 217–231.

Connell, R., Hearn, J. and Kimmel, M. (2005) Introduction, in M. Kimmel, J. Hearn and R. Connell (eds), *Handbook of studies on men and masculinities*, Sage, Thousand Oaks, CA, 1–12.

Connell, R. and Messerschmidt, J. (2005) Hegemonic masculinity: Rethinking the concept, *Gender & Society*, 19 (6), 829–859.

Ding, W., Murray, F. and Stuart, T. (2006) Gender differences in patenting in the academic life sciences, *Science*, 313 (5787), 665–667.

Egeberg Holmgren, L. and Hearn, J. (2009) Framing 'men in feminism': Theoretical locations, local contexts and practical passings in men's gender-conscious positionings on gender equality and feminism, *Journal of Gender Studies*, 18 (4), 403–418.

Essed, P. and Goldberg, T. (2002) Cloning cultures: The social injustices of sameness, *Ethnic and Racial Studies*, 25 (6), 1066–1082.

European Commission (2000) *Science policies in the European Union: Promoting excellence through mainstreaming gender equality: A report from the ETAN network on women and science*, European Commission, Luxembourg.

European Commission (2009) *The gender challenge in research funding: Assessing the European national scenes*, European Commission, Luxembourg.

European Commission (2019) *SHE figures 2018*, European Commission, Brussels.

Greenspan, J., Craft, R., LeResche, L., Arendt-Nielsen, L., Berkley, K., Fillingim, R., Gold, M., Holdcroft, A., Lautenbacher, S., Mayer, E., Mogil, J., Murphy, A. and Traub, R. (2007) Studying sex and gender differences in pain and analgesia: A consensus report, *Pain*, 132, S26–S45.

Hanmer, J. (1990) Men, power and the exploitation of women, in J. Hearn and D. Morgan (eds), *Men, masculinities and social theory*, Unwin Hyman/Routledge, London, 21–42.

Hearn, J. (2001) Academia, management and men: Making the connections, exploring the implications, in A. Brooks and A. Mackinnon (eds), *Gender and the restructured university*, Open University Press, Buckingham, 68–89.

Hearn, J. (2004) From hegemonic masculinity to the hegemony of men, *Feminist Theory*, 5 (1), 49–72.

Hearn, J. (2015) *Men of the world: Genders, globalizations, transnational times*, Sage, London.

Hearn, J. (2017) Neoliberal universities, patriarchies, masculinities, and myself: Transnational personal reflections on and from the global North, *Gender, rovné přiležitotosti, výzkum [Gender and Research]*, 18 (1), 16–41. Available at: www.genderonline.cz/uploads/9ca00c579277882deab7f476e0833abafb2a3248_gender-01-2017-stat-1-hearn.pdf

Hearn, J. and Collinson, D. (2009) Men, diversity at work, and diversity management, in M. Özbilgin (ed), *Equality, diversity and inclusion at work: A research companion*, Edward Elgar, Cheltenham, 383–398.

Hearn, J. and Howson, R. (2019) The institutionalization of (critical) studies on men and masculinities: geopolitical perspectives, in L. Gottzén, U. Mellström and T. Shefer (eds), *The Routledge international handbook of masculinity studies*, Routledge, London, 19–30.

Hearn, J. and Husu, L. (2019) Age-gender relations in the academic profession: Putting the challenges of entry and early career into context, in T. Adams and M. Choroszewicz (eds), *Gender, age and inequality in the professions*, Routledge, London, 193–212.

Hearn, J., Nordberg, M., Andersson, K., Balkmar, D., Gottzén, L., Klinth, R., Pringle, K. and Sandberg, L. (2012) Hegemonic masculinity and beyond: 40 years of research in Sweden, *Men and Masculinities*, 15 (1), 31–55.

Hearn, J. and Pringle, K. (2006) *European perspectives on men and masculinities: National and transnational approaches*, Palgrave Macmillan, Houndmills.

HSV [Högskoleverket] (2003) *Doktorandspegeln 2003*, HSV Rapport, 28 R, Stockholm.

HSV [Högskoleverket] (2008) *Doktorandspegeln 2008*, HSV Rapport, 23 R, Stockholm.

Lipman-Blumen, J. (1976) Toward a homosocial theory of sex roles: An explanation of the sex segregation of social institutions, in M. Blaxall and B. Reagan (eds), *Women and the workplace*, University of Chicago Press, Chicago, 15–31.

Lohan, M. and Faulkner, W. (eds) (2004) Men and masculinities, *Special Issue on Masculinities and Technologies*, 6 (4).

Madera, J., Hebl, M. and Martin, R. (2009) Gender and letters of recommendation for academia: Agentic and communal differences, *Journal of Applied Psychology*, 94 (6), 1591–1599.

Matthews, C. (2016) Exploring the pastiche hegemony of men, *Palgrave Communications*, 2, article 16022.

Messner, M. (1997) *Politics of masculinities*, Sage, Thousand Oaks, CA.

Moyer, B. and Tuttle, A. (1983) Overcoming masculine oppression in mixed groups, in *Off their backs . . . and on our own two feet*, New Society Publishers, Philadelphia, 24–29.

Murgia, A. and Poggio, B. (eds) (2019) *Gender and precarious research careers: A comparative analysis*, Routledge, London.

O'Brien, M. (1981) *The politics of reproduction*, Routledge & Kegan Paul, London.

Rosenfeld, D. and Faircloth, C. (eds) (2006) *Medicalized masculinities*, Temple University Press, Philadelphia.

Scambor, E., Wojnicka, K. and Bergmann, N. (eds) (2013) *Study on the role of men in gender equality*, European Commission, Brussels.

Schiebinger, L. (1987) The history and philosophy of women in science: A review essay, *Signs*, 12 (2), 305–332.

Symonds, M., Gemmell, N., Braisher, T., Gorringe, K. and Elgar, M. (2006) Gender differences in publication output: Towards and unbiased metric of research performance, *PLoS One*, 1 (1), e127.

UKÄ [University Chancellor's Office] (2016) *Doktorandspegeln 2016. En enkät om studenternas studiesituation*, UKÄ Rapport 18, Stockholm.

Wellcome Trust (1997) *PRISM women and peer-review: An audit of the Wellcome Trust's decision-making process*, Wellcome Trust, London.

Wennerås, C. and Wold, A. (1997) Nepotism and sexism in peer-review, *Nature*, 387, 22 May, 341–343.

Willinsky, J. (2000) Tempering the masculinities of technology, in N. Lesko (ed), *Masculinities at school*, Sage, Thousand Oaks, CA, 253–282.

Chapter 9

Unconscious bias in academia

A threat to meritocracy and what to do about it

Jadranka Gvozdanović and Jemimah Bailey

Introduction

The belief that academia is a meritocracy (Scully 1997) has been a long-standing tenet of university life, drawing on ideals that position academic institutions as gender-neutral organisations, where academic advancement is the result of a combination of hard work, talent and merit (Nielsen 2016). Meritocracy means that within academia all individuals should experience the same opportunities for advancement, irrespective of gender:

> Advocates of meritocracy stress that in true meritocratic systems everyone has an equal chance to advance and obtain rewards based on their individual merits and efforts, regardless of their gender, race, class, or other non-merit factors.
>
> (Castilla and Benard 2010, 543)

Recent literature confirms that gender continues to have an impact on advancement and opportunity in academic institutions, particularly when it comes to recruitment and promotion pathways (Chapters 3 and 4). The complexities of these procedures, practices and decision-making processes have been explored by a growing body of researchers (Van den Brink and Benschop 2012) illustrating the gendered practices in recruitment and selection procedures. The study by O'Connor and O'Hagan demonstrates a broad lack of awareness of the gendered nature of the subjective constructions of excellence (2015). As outlined by Foley and Williamson, an increasingly common explanation for the perpetuation of such gendered inequalities is that 'women face routine discrimination arising from unconscious (or implicit) bias, defined as attitudes or stereotypes that affect perceptions and decisions in a non-conscious manner' (Foley and Williamson 2018, 35).

In an early age educational environment that simplifies the world's complexities by attaching to them a reductionist number of classifying labels, these labels become internalised as stereotypes, leading to selective perceptions that accord with internalised concepts. Children recognise stereotypes by the age of six and behave in accordance with them by the age of nine (Rippon 2019). These stereotypes are culturally entrenched and reinforced in sociocultural settings. The connections made in the brain by such formative experiences can be overcome, but changing conditioned behaviour is a painstaking and slow process. This holds for individuals and for social structures, which in turn relate to prevailing power relations. Academia hinges on power structures legitimised by achievement and merit. Assessing achievement is the key issue to guarantee progress and access to resources, raising the question of whether this is conducted in a fully meritocratic way.

Since Berger and Luckmann's (1966) research, data in psychology, cognitive neuroscience and social science have shown that concepts about social groups are constructed (Schiebinger 2014) and that the human brain is plastic and permeable (Rippon 2019). Yet internalised concepts are extremely difficult to mitigate and statistics show that progress is extremely slow in spite of several decades of accumulated knowledge about skewed perception and judgement of women and minorities. Valian's (1998) work provided telling evidence on how social stereotypes influence individual behaviour. Twenty years after Valian's study, these inequalities are still in place (see Chapter 1), representing a major loss of talent. As argued elsewhere in this book, gender equality is an essential component of a fair and democratic society and, just as importantly, gender equality also enhances the relevance and validity of research and education so that both can better respond to global challenges and meet the diverse needs of society.

This chapter investigates the key areas in which meritocracy happens to be circumvented and provides examples of best practice which have been introduced in academic institutions to mitigate and eliminate bias. Its primary focus is on gender bias, since women are as well-educated and as gifted as men, yet they experience many more obstacles in their careers than their male peers. It is also important to acknowledge that other forms of unconscious bias connected with, for example, race, class and sexuality also intersect with gender. The chapter starts by examining the definition, causes and impact of unconscious bias in general, then moves on to detail the problem of unconscious bias in academia and to explore some of the strategies adopted to tackle it.

Awareness of unconscious bias and its impact

What is unconscious bias?

Unconscious bias is also referred to as implicit bias and occurs:

> when we make judgements or decisions on the basis of our prior experience, or own deep-seated thought patterns, assumptions or interpretations, and we are not aware we are doing it.
>
> (Royal Society 2015, 2)

This type of bias can contribute to various forms of inequality and, in the case of gender inequality, it can result in the needs and viewpoints of different genders being absent, overlooked or dismissed. When it comes to research, there is a danger that unconscious bias can lead to gender-blind or gender-biased research. In relation to recruitment and assessment of individuals (see Chapter 3), it can hamper objective and fair judgement, thereby undermining claims of meritocracy.

Why does unconscious bias exist?

Broadly speaking, individuals respond on the basis of internalised schemas used to make the task of processing information efficient and manageable. However, these useful cognitive 'shortcuts' can also mislead since they reinforce information that confirms expectations. Recipients pay less attention to contradicting information, thereby introducing or reinforcing bias. Bias is at play in multiple everyday situations and there are many areas that are influenced by bias, among them ethnic and regional identity, race, age, class, sexuality, faith beliefs, body ability and gender, in all of which intersectionality effects may also prevail (Gvozdanović and Maes 2018). Part of the explanation for this process is the way in which the human brain operates at both conscious and unconscious levels, captured by Kahneman's 'dual processing model'. Kahneman (2011) explains that the brain is constantly taking in a massive volume of information and, when only a tiny portion of this information can be processed consciously, the vast majority of it is processed subconsciously. The subconscious mind seeks to simplify and to make assumptions and is not adequately skilled at the type of rational or analytical thinking required for making good decisions, since it jumps to conclusions and is influenced by irrational and biased assumptions.

What are the roots of unconscious bias?

Unconscious or implicit bias is developed and maintained from experience, culture and processing of information from sources of external communication such as the media. Hence, through observed patterns of behaviour for example, certain occupations are associated with a particular gender, which subsequently becomes hard-wired into the unconscious brain. The risk is that these observed patterns frequently lead to assumptions that only certain groups of people have the innate qualities that make them suitable for certain roles such as nurse, judge, housekeeper, astronaut or professor. The unconscious brain:

> begins to expect [these patterns] with the result that other patterns or combinations start to feel less "normal" and more challenging to process. If left unchecked this can lead us into (at best) lazy stereotypes and, at worst, prejudicial or stereotypical behaviours.
>
> (Royal Society 2015, 2)

The media can also reinforce and sometimes challenge unconscious bias, for example by reinforcing gender stereotypes in advertisements or current affairs coverage of events and issues. Another important element is the influence of families and close circles of friends who make up an individual's 'in-group', those who identify with one another based on factors such as gender, ethnicity, geography and other demographics, leading them to judge those outside the 'in-group' more harshly. Consequently, it is important to become aware of when the unconscious mind might be influencing behaviour and decisions.

How does unconscious bias affect behaviour?

There are particular circumstances when individuals are more likely to be influenced by unconscious bias, such as when cognitively overloaded, physiologically under-resourced, emotionally charged, dealing with complexity or contradictory information and when under time pressures. All these circumstances can increase the chance of acting on the short-cuts in judgement created by the unconscious mind. Behaviour can be influenced at the interpersonal level (for example, warmth or lack of warmth towards and from colleagues); in recruitment and work allocation; listening; providing feedback or performance evaluations; informal networking, coaching and giving or receiving advice. Academic processes are not free of unconscious bias where important career-impacting decisions are made, for example in academic recruitment, retention and advancement, as well as in the allocation of research funding (Chapters 3 and 4).

Unconscious bias in academia

In a recent investigation initiated by CNRS, French and Canadian cognitive psychologists investigated 40 selection processes in different scientific disciplines over two years and found that committee members who associate 'science' and 'male' in association tests had a positive bias towards male candidates applying for scientific directorships (grade A professorships) (Régner et al 2019). These results are in line with previous research that established an inverse relationship between the percentage of women in science and stereotypical association of science with men (Miller et al 2015). The League of European Research Universities published a paper outlining the evidence for how implicit (or unconscious) gender bias creates a 'significant impediment to women's advancement in an academic career' (Gvozdanović and Maes 2018, 3). Many of the factors identified in the LERU report are also explored elsewhere in this book (see discussion of SHE figures 2018 in Chapter 1). Some key findings highlighted by Gvozdanović and Maes (2018) are detailed later in the chapter.

Findings on bias in recruitment and career advancement processes

Recruitment and selection

Standards of meritocracy can be circumnavigated in a number of ways. For example, despite the official adoption of rules of transparency in academic organisations, internal policies and processes allow pre-selection of candidates, even when posts are openly advertised (Nielsen 2016; Van den Brink 2010; Husu 2000). Research into professorial appointments shows that the commonly used mechanisms in recruitment and appointment are often disadvantageous for the appointment and careers of academic women (Van den Brink 2011; Van den Brink and Benschop 2011). 'Those mechanisms include academic networks that are predominantly male and the way in which scientific excellence is defined' (Gvozdanović and Maes 2018, 11). Not only are female candidates expected to perform better in order to be judged the same (Heilman and Haynes 2008; Kaatz *et al* 2014) but expectations and requirements of international mobility and employment at overseas institutions place an additional strain on women during a life phase when they could typically be making decisions about or having children.

Some national research authorities have adopted regulations to discount for career breaks, which more often, though not exclusively, affect female researchers:

> The UK research evaluation system Research Excellence Framework (REF), through which research funds are distributed to universities, explicitly allows for discounts in the number of publications relative to the time available, to cover circumstances such as career breaks and parental leave. Similar rules are applied in Germany.
>
> (Gvozdanović and Maes 2018, 13)

Both publication output (Maliniak *et al* 2013; West *et al* 2013) and teaching evaluations (McNeill *et al* 2014) have been shown to be rated in a gender biased way, which disadvantages female candidates. Alongside this, recommendation letters for female candidates have been shown to contain more negative language, unexplained statements and faint praise (Trix and Psenka 2003; Madera *et al* 2009). The Massachusetts Institute of Technology Report found that 'the proportion [of a letter] devoted to intellectual brilliance compared to temperament is much less for women than for men' (2011, 14).

Research evaluation

Gvozdanović and Maes (2018) indicate that female researchers secure less funding than their male counterparts, particularly when it comes to starting grants, which is likely to have a detrimental impact on early stage careers. A study by Lee and Ellemers (2015) of research applications in the Netherlands found clear evidence of bias in evaluation and success rates (by 4 per cent favouring male applicants) along with the use of biased language in instructions and evaluation sheets. Male applicants scored significantly higher on 'quality of researcher' evaluations. This gave them better success rates, though they did not score any higher than women on the 'quality of proposal' evaluations.

Working conditions

Working conditions can be shaped and reshaped by academic institutions and it is here that leadership (see Chapter 11) holds some responsibility. Evidence points to female scholars being continually disadvantaged through holding precarious contracts (Chapter 2) and by the gender pay gap (Chapter 7). This contrasts with evidence that male and female researchers do equally well under comparable circumstances and when given equivalent resources (Faniko *et al* 2016). Why do universities not treat male and female researchers as fully equal? Causes for unequal treatment include differences in the type of institution, teaching load (typically higher for women scholars), funding and unequal amounts of research assistance (Ceci and Williams 2011). All these factors have an impact on research productivity and affect women's career prospects (Chapter 4), sometimes influencing them to leave the academic world altogether, often at a significant point in their career.

Precarious contracts

Precarious working contracts include contracts of under 12 months, student contracts and hourly paid teaching or research contracts for non-students. These are a major source of uncertainty for early stage researchers and academics. Across the EU, 8.1 per cent of female, compared with 5.2 per cent of male, researchers are reported as in precarious contract positions (European Commission 2019). The impact of such arrangements is explored in detail by Murgia and Poggio, who note that 'women more often occupy precarious positions, either working part-time or working in conditions that lack stability or opportunities for career advancement' (2018, 3). Precarious contracts are endorsed by senior academics, leaving early stage scholars vulnerable to exploitation, particularly when those scholars are at a life stage when decisions about having children are also being made (see Chapter 5). Becoming a parent is usually accompanied by a career break, and this affects women more often than men, particularly in the absence of supporting measures to help the returning new parent resume their research. Disadvantageous working circumstances also inhibit publication productivity, which is in turn linked to less high-profile citations (Van den Besselaar and Sandström 2017). Lower productivity leads to less research funding and lowers the chances for accessing a leading role in academia. This vicious circle is a major effect of precarious positions, more often associated with women than men.

Addressing unconscious bias in universities

Gvozdanović and Maes (2018) identify three key functions and factors crucial to mitigating the effect of bias: leadership, vision and strategy; structural measures; and effective implementation.

Leadership, vision and strategy

First, Gvozdanović and Maes (2018) identify the crucial role that leadership plays within academic institutions in tackling the effects of unconscious bias:

> Leaders are better placed than anyone else to explain why change is necessary . . . and [to] provide incentives for supporting change while upholding and safe-guarding academic excellence.
>
> (Gvozdanović and Maes 2018, 15)

The authors note that leadership is founded on taking responsibility at a local institutional level, arguing that 'knowledge about implicit bias and how to mitigate or prevent it should be an integral part of leadership training' (Gvozdanović and Maes 2018, 16). LERU universities express this commitment by appointing an equality representative to governing bodies, adopting Gender Equality Plans as part of their university strategies and by introducing bias training and bias observers. For example, the University of Zurich offers a module on gender, diversity and bias awareness in its leadership development programme, which is open to all university staff who have a leadership role. The University of Amsterdam offers leadership workshops and implicit bias workshops. Targeted online training for awareness-raising and action against bias in selection processes, complementing its diversity strategy, is provided by the University of Heidelberg. Action taken by the University of Freiburg to demonstrate the engagement of institutional leadership included: the signing of the German Diversity Charter in 2010 to emphasise its commitment to equality and diversity; the installation of a vice-rectorate for research integrity, gender and diversity in 2014; and regular equality, diversity and inclusion training (Buitendijk *et al* 2019). At the University of Edinburgh, the endorsement of implicit bias awareness and training by the principal (equivalent of university rector) demonstrated senior-level commitment to tackling the issue and led to senior staff taking part in face-to-face training sessions, alongside the development of an online training programme for other staff in the university. It was evaluated by an external assessor and the impact of the training was shown to have led to improvements in unconscious bias knowledge, pro-equality efficacy and a decrease in family versus career stereotyping for women (Gvozdanović and Maes 2018).

Structural measures

Second, alongside the importance of leadership is the value placed on monitoring change, or lack of it, at an institutional level, reviewing the status of the policies and procedures and putting in place the supports and training programmes to tackle inequalities on a systemic basis:

> At structural level, the university requires mentoring programmes and training courses of different kinds. Training courses for leadership and committee members should demonstrate how intended and unintended inclusions and

exclusions follow from established practices. . . . Awareness about potential bias is the crucial first step towards reducing bias in individuals and organisations. . . . Awareness raising can act as a catalyst to change.

(Gvozdanović and Maes 2018, 16–17)

As an example of this type of action, the University of Oxford implemented unconscious bias training with the senior management team, which led to a complete overhaul of recruitment procedures for statutory professorships. At Trinity College, Dublin a specific structural measure to address unconscious bias in the recruitment process was introduced with the assignment of unconscious bias observers to selection committees for senior appointments. Observers monitor biased behaviours and recommend actions to address them, thereby improving the fairness of the recruitment system. Such adverse behaviours include devoting more time to some applicants than others; asking different questions of different candidates at interview; making assumptions about candidates based on stereotypes and discussing candidates informally. Observers are also part of academic shortlisting and interview panels in the Department of Chemistry at the University of York while 'gender vanguards' are used in a similar way at KU Leuven (Gvozdanović and Maes 2018). The University of Heidelberg also has unconscious bias observers on selection committees and their judgement is part of the decision-making process in professorial appointments. Targets for improvement of equality structures are formulated as part of the university strategy and faculties formulate specific targets to be reached within three or six-year periods. Yearly progress reports are discussed in the university senate. The University of Freiburg has integrated its diversity strategy into the university's strategic development planning. This means that with each five-year planning cycle the progress of equality initiatives is monitored and assessed. At KU Leuven, annual monitoring evaluates the 'inflow and through-flow of staff and students with diversity characteristics' (Buitendijk *et al* 2019, 52).

Effective implementation

Third, Gvozdanović and Maes (2018, 18) explore the measures needed for effective implementation which require transparency, accountability and monitoring: 'Monitoring needs to accompany and steer any processes . . . implies regular analysis of gender disaggregated data'. The authors highlight the importance of creating an environment which encourages individuals to make themselves accountable for the outcomes and create the conditions for decision-makers to act in line with the goal of mitigating unconscious bias. Partners in the EU-Horizon 2020 Systemic Action for Gender Equality (SAGE) project (2019) also integrated the key functions and factors, identified by the LERU paper, into their Gender Equality Plans (GEPs). The European Commission defines a Gender Equality Plan as:

a set of actions which start by conducting audits of procedures and practices to identify gender bias; move on to identifying and implementing strategies to address bias; and also set targets and monitor progress via specific indicators.

(EIGE 2016, 1)

The SAGE project recognised that substantial structural change in higher education institutions is needed for gender equality to be realised and it provided an effective example of using a cascade approach to raising awareness of unconscious bias and securing top-level support for change. The SAGE institutional GEPs were developed and implemented as part of this process of structural change.

Gender Equality Plans help with the structural transformation of an academic institution. This requires that the plans be embedded into an institution's structures, systems and cultures; followed up with the monitoring of activities, including resistance, and making ongoing adjustments as necessary. This process recognises that change is never completed, but part of an ongoing cycle (Chapter 10). One part of the SAGE GEPS was the roll-out of unconscious bias training within partner institutions. This was on the basis that unconscious bias and gender awareness sessions should be scheduled for all levels, ideally starting at senior management level and cascading to lower levels. Top down attendance sends a signal to other levels to ensure buy-in and demonstrates commitment to the institutional GEP.

All the SAGE institutions ran unconscious bias training workshops, targeting different groups within the organisations. Some found that gathering the qualitative data on the existing gender culture through focus groups also served as a method for raising awareness of gender equality issues more generally and overcame some ideological issues. Alongside the bias awareness training, institutions ran seminars presenting gender disaggregated data and demonstrating the impact of inequality. SAGE partners produced documents and tools to support the implementation of their GEPs. For example, the SAGE team at Science Po Bordeaux designed a guide on unconscious bias for those involved in selection and recruitment committees. Other institutions organised sessions on career progression for female academics, gender in the curriculum and gender in research. The SAGE (2019) project also produced an online course on *Creating a gender-sensitive institution*, which includes a session on unconscious bias awareness with further examination of the processes involved in mitigating the impact of unconscious bias: www.tcd.ie/tcgel/internationalprojects/SAGE/creating_a_gender_sensitive_ institution/index.php

The impact of unconscious bias awareness training

There are a number of approaches for tackling bias at individual level, including unconscious bias awareness training and 'perspective taking' which involves getting participants to reflect empathically on the experiences of those facing prejudice or disadvantage. Devine *et al* (2017) implemented a 'habit-breaking' gender bias intervention at the University of Wisconsin which led to the proportion of women hired by departments increasing by 18 per cent. Alongside information on how unconscious bias functions, participants discussed specific case studies and learned five evidence-based strategies that have been shown to counteract unconscious bias. These five strategies were first implemented by Devine *et al* (2012) in an intervention aimed at reducing racial bias. They include:

- stereotype replacement, whereby participants recognise stereotypical responses within themselves and wider society, label these and replace with non-stereotypical responses;
- counter-stereotypic imaging, which involves imagining counter-stereotypic 'others' (for example a female firefighter) to provide positive exemplars;
- individuating, which relies on obtaining specific information about individuals, to encourage evaluation of them based on personal, rather than group, attributes;
- perspective-taking, by speaking in the first person as if they were a member of a disadvantaged group, to mitigate automatic assumptions about that group; and
- increasing opportunities for contact, a strategy to increase exposure to 'out-group' members.

This approach supports the observation by Atewolugun *et al* (2018) on the effectiveness of interactive training sessions. According to their review, there is a mixed picture when it comes to the effectiveness of unconscious bias training. It is effective for awareness-raising of bias but the evidence for its ability to change behaviour is limited. The authors recommend the adoption of bias reduction strategies using: counter-stereotypic examples to challenge unconscious stereotype endorsement; bias mitigation strategies such as structured interviews to reduce the impact of bias to empower recipients to change their behaviour. Crucially they argue for unconscious bias training being used as part of a wider programme:

> For organisational level change to happen, organisational structures, policies and procedures must be targeted directly, perhaps overhauled . . . [training] should be treated as just one part of a comprehensive strategy for achieving organisation-wide change.
>
> (Atewolugun *et al* 2018, 9)

Repelaer van Driel (2015) carried out an experiment using a mock hiring methodology, asking participants to evaluate real assistant professor applications, imagining that they were an university employer. Participants were randomly assigned to one of four groups where, prior to applicant evaluation: they read information on the under-representation of women in academia (the impact of unconscious bias via statistics); information on unconscious gender bias (theory of unconscious bias); both of these; or no information (control). Their findings suggest that educating participants about unconscious bias theory is more effective for reducing gender bias in hiring than using statistics to illustrate the impact of unconscious bias. A meta-analysis of diversity training carried out by Bezrukova *et al* (2016) revealed that:

> the positive effects of diversity training were greater when training was complemented by other diversity initiatives, targeted to both awareness and skills development, and conducted over a significant period of time.
>
> (2016, 3)

The report from the Chartered Institute of Personnel and Development concurs with this perspective, noting that while:

> training is often well received by participants and can have short-term results, it doesn't usually show a sustained impact on behaviour and emotional prejudice, and alone is not sufficient to create a diverse and inclusive organization.
>
> (2019, 25)

The EU FP7 INstitutional Transformation for Effecting Gender Equality in Research (INTEGER) Project (2011–2015) sought to address gender imbalances in STEM, at both institutional level and faculty, school and department levels through the implementation of Gender Action Plans. Three institutions were involved, including Trinity College Dublin (TCD), The National Centre for Scientific Research (CNRS) in France and Šiauliai University in Lithuania. As part of the INTEGER project, TCD carried out an intervention to address unconscious bias at all levels of the university, from the highest-level senior management team, to heads of school and academic staff, in a six-step process:

1 secure top-level buy-in from the highest-level decision-makers (university provost or rector);
2 engage decision-makers: unconscious bias briefing by external gender equality champion to influence and persuade key decisions makers (senior management team/college officers);
3 train the trainers to build capacity to ensure a broader reach and further sustainability via a three-day training programme by an external consultant;
4 disseminate the evidence through events to present the current research literature on unconscious bias and stimulate discussion;
5 cascade the message through unconscious bias briefings provided for senior promotions team, junior and senior promotions committees, recruitment panels, principal investigators and anyone who manages or recruits staff;
6 institutionalise the process and build unconscious bias sessions into recruitment and promotion decision-making.

Among the tools emanating from the INTEGER project was a case study video on how to go about raising awareness of and addressing unconscious bias. This is available at: www.integer-tools-for-action.eu/en/resource/case-studies

Conclusion

Insofar as unconscious bias plays a role in assessment procedures, for example in recruitment, promotion or funding decisions, it presents a challenge to prevailing meritocratic principles in academia. Meritocracy implies that access to power and resources is granted to those who deserve it. Academics get tenure, secure scarce research funding and publish in prestigious journals through rigorous competition which should naturally drive excellence to the top. The reality is that recognition of excellence on the basis of pure merit does not always work well in practice and can leave talent unrecognised because of the barriers to recognition created by systemic bias (Chapter 3) and other factors. This causes a tremendous loss of potential in academia and in the wider society.

Inequalities resulting from unconscious bias are an institutional problem that require monitoring and structural change to tackle them. Once the problematic areas have been identified, measures with a specific timeframe and allocated accountability can be undertaken in parallel with awareness-raising training for leadership at various levels and staff, especially in recruitment and promotion committees. Early career researchers, often employed on precarious contracts, present a particular challenge to gender equality in academia. Transparency is key to institutional governance, as is monitoring and training in connection with GEPs. Leadership and leaders' vision for gender equality are critical in understanding and challenging unconscious bias by providing the driving force for the required changes.

Isolated initiatives are unlikely to have a sustainable impact on tackling gender inequality and unconscious bias. Collecting data and monitoring change, or the lack of it, is a crucial tool in creating transparency, identifying problem areas and tracking the effectiveness of measures to tackle unconscious bias. There is evidence that unconscious bias can be reduced:

> when a sophisticated, habit-breaking design that is long-term and includes awareness-raising and bias mitigation strategies is used . . . [these] should be treated as one step towards achieving organisational change, through awareness raising, unconscious bias change and motivation to act.
>
> (Atewolugun *et al* 2018, 38–42)

It is vital that unconscious bias is tackled not just at an individual level but also systemically at an institutional level, where policies and practices can be introduced to mitigate unconscious bias.

> 'Only with targeted counterbalancing activities can university populations truly represent the societies they serve so that talent is not wasted'
>
> (Buitendijk *et al* 2019, 11)

References

Atewolugun, D., Cornish, T. and Tresh, F. (2018) *Unconscious bias training: an assessment of the evidence for effectiveness*, Research Report 113, Equality and Human Rights Commission, London.

Berger, P. and Luckmann, T. (1966) *The social construction of reality: A treatise in the sociology of knowledge*, Doubleday, Garden City, NY.

Bezrukova, K., Spell, C., Perry, J. and Jehn, K. (2016) A meta-analytical integration of over 40 years of research on diversity training evaluation, *Psychological Bulletin*, 142 (11), 1227–1274.

Buitendijk, S., Curry, S. and Maes, K. (2019) *Equality, diversity and inclusion at universities: The power of a systemic approach*, LERU Position Paper, League of European Research Universities (LERU), Leuven.

Castilla, E. and Benard, S. (2010) The paradox of meritocracy in organizations, *Administrative Science Quarterly*, 44 (4), 543–576.

Ceci, S. and Williams, W. (2011) Understanding current causes of women's underrepresentation in science, *Proceedings of the National Academy of Sciences*, 108 (8), 3157–3162.

Chartered Institute of Personnel and Development (2019) *Diversity management that works: An evidence-based view*, CIPD, London.

Devine, P., Forscher, P., Austin, A. and Cox, W. (2012) Long-term reduction in implicit race bias: A prejudice habit-breaking intervention, *Journal of Experimental Social Psychology*, 48 (6), 1267–1278.

Devine P., Forscher, P., Cox, W., Kaatz, A., Sheridan, J. and Carnes, M. (2017) A gender bias habit-breaking intervention led to increased hiring of female faculty in STEMM departments, *Journal of Experimental Social Psychology*, 73, 211–215.

EIGE (2016) Roadmap to gender equality plans in research and higher education institutions, EIGE, Vilnius. Available at: https://eige.europa.eu/sites/default/files/gear_roadmap_01_shortguide.pdf

European Commission (2019) *SHE figures 2018*, Directorate-General for Research and Innovation, Luxembourg.

Faniko, K., Ellemers, N. and Derks, B. (2016) Queen bees and alpha males: Are successful women more competitive than successful men? *European Journal of Social Psychology*, 46, 903–913.

Foley, M. and Williamson, S. (2018) Managerial perspectives on implicit bias, affirmative action and merit, *Public Administration Review*, 79 (1), 35–45.

Gvozdanović, J. and Maes, K. (2018) *Implicit bias in academia: A threat to meritocracy and to women's careers—and what to do about it*, League of European Research Universities (LERU), Leuven.

Heilman, M. and Haynes, M. (2008) Subjectivity in the appraisal process: A facilitator of gender bias in work settings, in E. Borgida and S. Fiske (eds), *Beyond common sense: Psychological science in the court-room*, Blackwell Publishing, Oxford, 127–155.

Husu, L. (2000) Gender discrimination in the promised land of gender equality, *Higher Education in Europe*, 25, 221–228.

Kaatz, A., Guerrez, B. and Carnes, M. (2014) Threats to objectivity in peer review: The case of gender, *Trends in Pharmacological Sciences*, 35 (8), 371–373.

Kahneman, D. (2011) *Thinking, fast and slow*, Penguin, Allen Lane, London.

Lee, van der R. and Ellemers, N. (2015) Gender contributes to personal research success in the Netherlands, *Proceedings of the National Academy of Sciences*, 112 (40), 12349–12353.

Madera, J., Hebl, M. and Marn, R. (2009) Gender and letters of recommendation for academia: Agents and communal differences, *Journal of Applied Psychology*, 94 (6), 1591–1599.

Maliniak, D., Powers, R. and Walter, B. (2013) The gender citation gap in international relations, *International Organisation*, 67 (4), 889–922.

Massachusetts Institute of Technology (2011) *A report on the status of women faculty in the schools of science and engineering at MIT*, MIT Press, Cambridge, MA.

McNeill, L., Driscoll, A. and Hunt, A. (2014) What's in a name: Exposing gender bias in students' ratings of teaching, *Innovative Higher Education*, 40 (4), 291–303.

Miller, D., Eagly, A. and Linn, M. (2015) Women's representation in science predicts national gender-science stereotypes: Evidence from 66 nations, *Journal of Educational Psychology*, 107 (3), 631–644.

Murgia, A. and Poggio, B. (2018) *Gender and precarious research careers: A comparative analysis*, Routledge, London.

Nielsen, M. (2016) Limits to meritocracy? Gender in academic recruitment and promotion policies, *Science and Public Policies*, 43 (3), 386–399.

O'Connor, P. and O'Hagan, C. (2015) Excellence in university academic staff evaluation: A problematic reality? *Studies in Higher Education*, 41 (11), 1943–1957.

Régner, I., Thinus-Blanc, C., Netter, A., Schmader, T. and Huguet, P. (2019) Committees with implicit biases promote fewer women when they do not believe gender bias exists, *Nature Human Behaviour*, 26 August, 525–537, doi: 10.1038/s41562-019-0686-3

Repelaer van Driel, R. (2015) *Women in science: The effect of training on gender bias reduction in academia*, unpublished Masters Thesis, Faculty of Social and Behavioral Sciences, Leiden University.

Rippon, G. (2019) *Gender and our brains: How new neuroscience explodes the myths of the male and female minds*, Pantheon. Available at: www.youtube.com/watch?v=uqR4 cw9Amlg

Royal Society (2015) *Unconscious bias briefing (Prof Uta Frith)*. Available at: https://royalsociety.org/~/media/policy/Publications/2015/unconscious-bias-briefing-2015.pdf

SAGE (2019) *Systemic action for gender equality*, Horizon 2020 SWaFS Project. Available at: www.tcd.ie/tcgel/international-projects/sage.php

Schiebinger, L. (2014) *Women and gender in science and technology*, Routledge, London.

Scully, M. (1997) Meritocracy, in R. Freeman and P. Werhan (eds), *Blackwell encyclopedic dictionary of business ethics*, Wiley-Blackwell, Oxford, 413–414.

Trix, F. and Psenka, C. (2003) Exploring the color of glass: Letters of recommendation for female and male medical faculty, *Discourse & Society*, 14 (2), 191–220.

Valian, V. (1998) *Why so slow? The advancement of women*, MIT Press, Cambridge, MA.

Van den Besselaar, P. and Sandström, U. (2017) Vicious circles of gender bias, lower positions, and lower performance: Gender differences in scholarly productivity and impact, *PLoS One*, 12 (8), 1–16.

Van den Brink, M. (2010) *Behind the scenes of science: Gender practices in the recruitment and selection of professors in the Netherlands*, Amsterdam University Press, Amsterdam.

Van den Brink, M. (2011) Scouting for talent: Appointment practices of women professors in academic medicine, *Social Science & Medicine*, 72 (12), 2033–2040.

Van den Brink, M. and Benschop, Y. (2011) Gender practices in the construction of academic excellence: Sheep with five legs, *Organization*, 19 (4), 507–524.

Van den Brink, M. and Benschop, Y. (2012) Slaying the seven-headed dragon: The quest for gender change in academia, *Gender, Work and Organization*, 19, 71–92.

West, J., Jacquet, J., King, M., Correll, S. and Bergstrom, C. (2013) The role of gender in scholarly authorship, *PLoS One*, 8 (7), 1–6.

Chapter 10

Change management to initiate and accelerate gender equality

Jemimah Bailey and Eileen Drew

Introduction

One of the central purposes of the Horizon 2020 Systemic Action for Gender Equality (SAGE) project was the implementation of Gender Equality Plans (GEPs). This was in recognition that substantial structural change in academia is needed before gender equality can be achieved. GEPs were developed and implemented as part of this process of structural change in each SAGE implementing institution namely: Instituto Universitário De Lisboa (ISCTE-IUL), Portugal; International University of Sarajevo (IUS), Bosnia and Herzegovina; Kadir Has University, Istanbul (KHAS), Turkey; Sciences Po Bordeaux (SciPo), France; Università degli Studi di Brescia (UNIBS), Italy, under the guidance of the SAGE Coordinating partner Trinity College, Dublin (TCD). In order to facilitate the adoption and integration of the GEPs, a *SAGE Model for Institutional Change* was designed. This model was informed by the work of organisational change experts such as Kotter (2012) and Kanter (1977, 1989) and the experiences, learning and outputs of the FP7 2011–2015 INstitutional Transformation for Effecting Gender Equality in Research (INTEGER) project.

This chapter starts by presenting some of the key themes found in change management literature, particularly those pertaining to gender equality in universities. It then presents the *SAGE Model for Institutional Change* detailing the nine key components to support the management of change in the creation of a gender-sensitive institution. The chapter draws upon SAGE project evaluation reports and an online focus group conducted with SAGE project partners to collect their descriptions of, and reflections on, the change process in promoting gender equality in their institutions.

Change management and gender equality

The achievement of gender equality can be regarded as both a challenge and a mechanism for change in research-performing organisations, implying systemic, integrated, long-term approaches rather than piecemeal short-term measures. There is a growing body of research that outlines the specific challenges, particularly in a European context, driven by the European Union's commitment to gender mainstreaming, adopted in the 1990s as the principal strategy for increasing gender equality:

> Gender mainstreaming is a structural transformation strategy that aims to transform organisational processes and practices by eliminating gender biases from existing routines.
>
> (Benschop and Verloo 2011, 283)

Danowitz presents some of the key organisational issues that need attention if gender equality is to be achieved in academia, pointing out that 'changing universities to achieve gender equality ultimately means changing organisational structures and cultures and, at times, the larger policy spheres in which they function' (2008, 96). She argues that there are five key factors that must be tackled in the advancement of equality, to ensure that gender equality measures are part of deep cultural change within universities:

* gender equality measures must be grounded in the university's basic values and strategic action plan;
* various constituencies within the university must buy in or accept the proposed gender equality measures;
* gender equality initiatives must be tailored to the particular needs of the university and must be adapted to its mission and culture;
* gender equality initiatives must be linked to major programmes and endeavours;
* a gender equality monitoring system with accountability must be put in place to assess short-range and long-range outcomes (Danowitz 2008, 97).

Established literature on institutional and organisational change within the academia has generally focused on the challenges of adapting to an increasingly globalised and neoliberal world and meeting the demands of expanded access to third-level education. As O'Connor *et al* note: 'neoliberalism values competition, metrics and financial profit, over collective interests, cooperation and community' (2019, 723). One aspect of neoliberalism which has had particular impact in the higher education sector is managerialism, resulting in the adoption of managerial practices drawn from the corporate world. The entrepreneurial university (Clark 1998, 2004) and Sporn's model of university adaptation (1999) elaborate on how higher education institutions change their structures in response to environmental forces. Sporn's review of the current environment for higher education notes that universities:

> are still in the process of finding the right balance between demand and response. This is further triggered by stark societal developments like digitalisation, immigration and integration and inequality.
>
> (Sporn 2019, 52)

She suggests that for successful organisational transformation, it is necessary for higher education institutions to use the theories and approaches (including strategic planning, leadership, vision and mission, accountability and impact) offered by organisational studies to steer change efficiently and effectively.

This chapter draws upon organisational change management literature to explain the components deemed relevant to promoting gender equality, demanding new policies, behaviours and actions to meet the many challenges that resist such change in the university sector. Kanter (1989) saw the combination of five major building blocks (Figure 10.1) present in organisational changes, to increase the capacity to meet new challenges. These are described in some detail later in the chapter, with examples of contemporary relevance in academia.

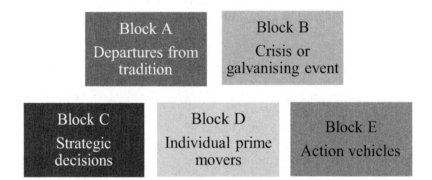

Figure 10.1 Building blocks for change
Source: Moss Kanter (1983)

Block A: Departures from tradition

These can be orchestrated by innovators, or just happen to the organisation in a passive way. Such departures can provide the university with an incentive to solve new problems or replace existing methods with more productive ones. For these departures to arise, the institution should be loosely enough controlled to promote innovative interventions, in this case a Gender Equality Plan (GEP). However, in themselves, even successful departures (including GEPs) do not produce major change in the absence of other building blocks.

Block B: Crisis or galvanising event

This refers to external forces such as interventions from higher education funders, or political changes such as Brexit and internal forces provoked by national or sectoral policy changes, or the attitudes of employees. These can be used deliberately to create a change climate. For example, large-scale Japanese organisations have been known to identify, or even create, crises in order to galvanise marketing strategies.

Block C: Strategic decisions

Strong leaders of change are needed to articulate direction by creating a vision, allowing themselves and others to see more clearly the steps to take, building on present capacities and strengths to get there. This can often involve a series of smaller decisions. The process is assisted by more integrative systems, innovations, communication channels and team mechanisms to keep gender equality ideas circulating. These forms of coalitions and cooperative traditions make it easier to get moving. Strategic decisions supporting gender equality help to set in motion the next two major blocks in effecting change.

Block D: Individual 'prime movers'

No strategy, no matter how brilliant or responsive, can succeed without someone giving it a push—hence the role of change agents who remain committed to the vision, keeping up the momentum and pushing beyond the actions of the innovating team. Prime movers, or champions, raise the new concept or practice on every possible occasion, in every speech, at every meeting, contributing to a shared vision of gender equality. The message is clear and unequivocal, indicating firm commitment. Where change emanates from outside, for example, via the EU or government regulation, it must be internalised in a way that demonstrates how the necessary change will meet organisational needs, for example with targeted Gender Equality Plans, now required in all Irish higher education institutions (HEA 2016). This requirement provides a signal about the direction of change and the need to adapt the organisation's culture in response to the national funding body (Chapter 12).

Block E: Action vehicles

These are the mechanisms that allow the new action possibilities to be articulated as actual policies and procedures, structures such as teams, communication channels, appraisal measures, work recognition or rewards that should be incorporated into a Gender Equality Plan. Collectively, these building blocks pave the way for significant institutional change which is further examined in terms of Kotter's eight-step change model (2012), which provides a useful source of change management theory and practice. Kotter's model was used to drive structural change for gender equality during the FP7 INTEGER project (2011–2015) and led to the development of the approach adopted by the SAGE project. Kotter's influence on the INTEGER (2015) project is outlined here (Figure 10.2).

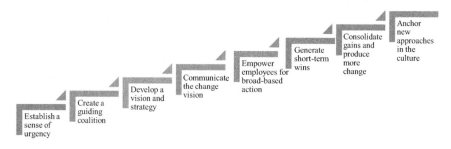

Figure 10.2 Eight-step change model
Source: Kotter 2012

Step 1: Establish a sense of urgency to spark the initial motivation. Like Kanter (1983), Kotter (2012) recommended identifying potential threats or opportunities, developing future scenarios, generating discussions and providing people with convincing reasons for supporting change, aligned with support from external stakeholders. He stressed that this requires high-level buy-in along with time and energy.

Step 2: Create a guiding coalition through strong leadership and visible support from key people (stakeholders and leaders) in the organisation's hierarchy, bringing them together as a change coalition, working as a team to build urgency and momentum for change, appealing for their emotional commitment.

Step 3: Develop a vision and strategy that people can understand and remember through determining the values that are central to change and providing a short summary of what the vision should be.

Step 4: Communicate the change vision by sending a powerful and frequent message to all involved, addressing people's concerns and anxieties openly and honestly, applying the vision to all operations and leading by example.

Step 5: Empower employees for broad-based action by identifying any processes or structures that are barriers to change, thereby assisting them towards executing the vision to move change forward. This can be achieved through new appointments, examining the structures, job descriptions and performance and compensation systems, recognising and rewarding people engaged in change, identifying resistors, helping them and generally removing barriers, human or otherwise.

Step 6: Generate short-term wins early in the change process to help convince critics and negative thinkers, via smaller, inexpensive and achievable targets, having reviewed the pros and cons of each change initiative. Kotter also advocated rewarding the people who help in achieving these targets.

Step 7: Consolidate gains and produce more change by looking for more things to improve, based upon previous successes, analysing every win by asking what went right and what needs improvement? Setting goals to continue building momentum, adopting a continuous improvement philosophy (*kaizen*) and keeping ideas fresh by bringing in new change agents and leaders to form a coalition.

Step 8: Anchor new approaches in the culture to ensure that they are part of the core of the organisation, hence the values behind the vision show in day-to-day work through continuous improvement in every aspect of the organisation. For Kotter (2012), leaders, new and existing staff, have to continually support the change by talking about progress and success stories, incorporating change ideals in hiring and training new staff and acknowledging key members' contributions.

INTEGER and change management theory

During the FP7 INTEGER (2015) project, institutional partners in Ireland, France and Lithuania used their project resources to create a sense of urgency and to reinforce the high-level policy shift that each institution had to activate, drawing upon key actors, as change agents, in their individual implementing institutions: Trinity College, Dublin (TCD) Ireland; the Mission des Femmes in (CNRS), France and the Siaulai University, Lithuania. A key lesson learned from INTEGER was that senior management need to be committed to the changes and to demonstrate this visibly. The underlying vision in each INTEGER institution was enshrined in the acronym INstituting Transformation for Effecting Gender Equality in Research and the design of a specific INTEGER logo that reflected and disseminated this. Alongside the use of the acronym and logo and in order to make the necessary gender equality actions more accessible and comprehensible Trinity College, Dublin (TCD) designed the visual metaphor of the INTEGER wheel, as the roadmap action plan framework to be followed. The INTEGER wheel was then adapted for use in the other INTEGER partner institutions. (It was further adapted and refined in 2015 for use as the SAGE wheel.)

INTEGER introduced important and timely communications in the form of: cascading, networking, conferences, exchanges of experience, site visits, presentations of survey findings and recommendations for action and, most importantly, adoption of the INTEGER project's objectives by the university's governing bodies. The TCD project partners produced a video *Driving Excellence through Gender Equality* featuring the provost and vice provost pledging their support for gender equality and diversity in the university. This served a number of functions in addition to communicating change, it represented a short-term win and demonstrated the buy-in of senior management. To further anchor and reinforce the university's strategic commitment to gender equality, TCD ensured that the Athena SWAN initiative was incorporated into the university's strategic plan 2014–19. Further information on Athena SWAN is provided in Chapter 12.

Initially, change within TCD was driven by internal forces underpinned by WiSER's mantra of: *recruiting, retaining and progressing women students and staff in STEM.* To change attitudes and behaviours that impede progress towards gender equality, namely perceptual, emotional, cultural and cognitive blocks, external expert speakers were invited to lead unconscious bias awareness sessions in all three INTEGER institutions. TCD adopted a cascade process, working from the top down with key segments of the university, including the promotion committees. The INTEGER experiences and outputs were harnessed and built upon still further to inform the next phase of transformation and testing of the SAGE (Systemic Action for Gender Equality) model of actions in GEPs.

The SAGE model for institutional change

The *SAGE model for institutional change* (Figure 10.3) built upon the theories of change management experts such as Kanter (1989) and Kotter (2012) along with the experiences of the 2011–2015 INTEGER project, to identify the key components for effective management of change towards gender equality in academia.

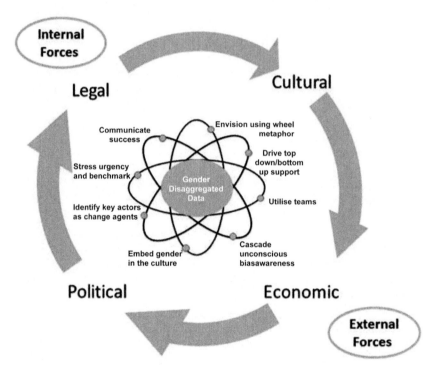

Figure 10.3 SAGE model for institutional change

Gender disaggregated data

The requirement to monitor gender equality using detailed and accurate data, disaggregated by gender, is at the core of the change management process (Danowitz 2008). Robust data collection provides both the evidence that gender inequalities exist; how pronounced they are; the benchmarking required to measure progress; and to provide comparisons with other institutions. This transparent data collection allows institutions to assess 'whether time and resources are being expended effectively or just wasted' (Kang and Kaplan 2019, 583).

During the INTEGER project, data were deemed essential to defining the problem and identifying opportunities. Each INTEGER institution embarked upon a thorough data collection exercise, through focus groups and surveys, and a review of policies, procedures and practices to identify barriers to gender equality and draw up the actions necessary to address these. Given that the experience garnered during the INTEGER project illustrated how data are essential to outlining the problem and detecting areas for action relating to gender, the collection, analysis and presentation of gender-disaggregated data were placed at the core of the *SAGE wheel* and the *SAGE model for institutional change*. Data collection underpins all the actions that form the Gender Equality Plan (GEP) for the unit (centre, department, school, faculty) and institution.

Each SAGE institution embarked on a thorough data collection exercise through focus groups and surveys and conducted a review of policies, procedures and practices, in order to identify barriers to gender equality and to draw up the actions necessary to address these. This involved collecting gender-based:

- quantitative data on student numbers at all levels; staff numbers of all grades and categories; a gender profile of decision-makers; committee representation; take-up of leave arrangements;
- qualitative data on attitudes, experiences of promotion processes, career aspirations, work-based culture.

Quantitative data help to address the 'what?' question while only qualitative data can address the 'why?' and 'how?' questions, critical to addressing gender inequalities. Hence the most relevant, targeted actions need to be based on a combination of the two types of data. What follows are the responses collected in a SAGE project focus group with partners, conducted via skype. These responses have been anonymised to protect identity and confidentiality. The SAGE partners described this process as a vital starting point:

> *'You can see where the institution is and where it wants to go—that's a huge thing'.*
> *'Collecting gender-disaggregated data, very basic but very important'.*

The practicalities of collecting gender disaggregated data relied on a range of departments, including human resources, student offices and research and evaluation officers. Some of the SAGE partners experienced problems in collecting this gender-disaggregated data. Despite declared support from senior management, some staff were reluctant to allocate the time and resources necessary for this task.

Part of the gender disaggregated data collection involved conducting a survey on the gender culture of the institution. In some cases, this data collection tool proved difficult to administer. For example, if an institution was small, the issue of the anonymity of responses arose:

> *'There was a problem related to anonymity, due to the small number of staff'.*

Collecting data also allows for benchmarking to compare trends and patterns, policies and processes with other similar organisations. This helps identify existing inequalities and future changes which can then be monitored. Different institutions face different priorities and challenges which is the reason that Gender Equality Plans need to be appropriate and realistic for the specific environment of the individual institution. This reinforces Danowitz's view that 'gender equality initiatives must be tailored to the particular needs of the university and must be adapted to its mission and culture' (2008, 97).

Stress urgency and benchmark

Moss Kanter's concept of 'departures from tradition' and Kotter's emphasis on establishing a sense of urgency can be seen as the initial driving forces for change. Sporn (1999) reiterates this by highlighting how universities adapt their structures in response to environmental forces. 'A key element . . . was the notion of crisis or opportunity that created the impetus for change to both the institutional and societal environment' (Sporn 2019, 38). Danowitz (2008) emphasised that gender equality measures must also be linked to major programmes such as the Athena SWAN awards in the UK and Ireland. SAGE partners reported that involvement in the project itself also provided momentum for action:

> 'The project gave us a more orderly framework for things that were already going on at the university. The external context is very 'anti gender' in [country], but internally we had already been doing some things'.

Identify key actors as change agents

Kanter (1989) stressed that change agents need to be the right people, in the right place at the right time, to support innovation, encourage building of coalitions and teams to design and implement visions. In doing so, they must influence and persuade those who will be instrumental in bringing about change. The INTEGER experience illustrated that key actors as change agents in the partner institutions played a major role in driving the project forward. Similarly, SAGE partners found that there were key individuals who helped to drive the change forward:

> 'Once you convince the rector your life gets a lot easier. The head of human resources was also a key person for us'.

Drive top-down and bottom-up support

Kotter refers to the 'guiding coalition' as vital for success, crucial in seeking buy-in and commitment from senior managers (presidents, deans and so on) to embark upon, or endorse, the necessary actions. Equally, it is essential to activate grass-roots support from those who may serve on teams and/or become change agents. As O'Connor's account of change within higher education institutions recognises that:

> those in senior positions were much more open to arguments concerning the development of the university, whereas those below this level were much more driven by personal agendas.
>
> (2019, 836)

Recognising that top-strategic-level buy-in was critical to ensuring changes at all levels, each INTEGER institution invited their president, director, rector or provost to attend and present at INTEGER 'Exchange of experience' project meetings to which distinguished guest speakers from the US and EU were invited to present the case for institutional transformation for gender equality and embedding gender into the university's culture.

The support of senior management, particularly from the director or rector, was crucial to SAGE implementation in all institutions, in addition to human resources staff, given their involvement in the critical areas of recruitment, career development and staff training. The SAGE partners generally found that if the senior management supported the gender equality initiatives this provided essential momentum:

> *'When we wanted to get something done or we had resistance (which we did) we would communicate that to the director and things would get sorted out'.*
> *'The changes came from a top down direction. We tried to disseminate from some high authority places. . . . It is too hard to change from the ground up, as that would mean changing the mind of a lot of people. So we went for the short cut through using the high-up positions, to communicate and then instruct'.*

This suggests that, at least initially, top-down support serves as a more effective driver than bottom-up support towards gender equality implementation.

Utilise teams

Setting up a Gender Equality Plan implementation team is important to achieve: a shared ownership of the vision; broader engagement; and diverse perspectives (gender, age, discipline, seniority, academic, professional and so on). Team members need to be invited to join on the basis of sharing the team's workload towards achieving actions and the organisational gender equality vision. Teams act as the structural drivers of the institutional change process in academia, with members appointed to implement the GEPs and monitor gender equality. Team members have to act as advocates for gender equality initiatives; work to overcome resistance encountered; and pave the way for lasting transformation.

All INTEGER partners formed teams to effect changes, though membership changed, as members exited and were replaced by new entrants. Team membership required a commitment to the process in their role as prime movers. One of the 'lessons learned' from INTEGER was that implementation teams should include mixed genders, junior and senior staff, academic and non-academic staff (management, administrative and technical):

> *'The secret is to involve many people so that they are aware what is the purpose* [of the plan] *and who the coordinator talks to for this or that'.*

The value of creating a diverse GEP implementation team was reinforced by the SAGE experiences, where this approach had not been taken. One partner explained how, although they attempted to work as a team, the small size of the institution made it challenging:

> *'We found it easier to go individually from one person to another to get the cooperation we needed'.*

The same team member reflected that with hindsight, they would have tried a different approach, to find more people to help with the project. Another team member from a different institution also agreed with this:

> *'We didn't form an institutional-wide team . . .* [with hindsight] *I would create a team all over the university, take more of a ground-up approach'.*

Cascade unconscious bias awareness

Rolling out a programme of unconscious bias awareness training to staff connects with Kotter's emphasis on communicating the change vision and the justification for positive interventions to address bias. Providing training in unconscious bias awareness and its impact is an important first step in communicating the relevance of gender inequality in higher education institutions. It is also important that it is part of a much broader commitment:

> to create systems and environments in which bias and stereotyping are either less likely to become initiated, or are prevented from resulting in discrimination even when they are active.
>
> (Kang and Kaplan 2019, 580)

Experience from the INTEGER project demonstrated that unconscious bias and gender awareness sessions need to be scheduled for all levels, ideally starting at the top (senior management) and cascading to lower levels. Top-down attendance is symbolic and sends a signal to other levels to ensure attendance. As Kang and Kaplan point out:

> if everyone else in an organisation appears to value diversity, we are more likely to act like we value diversity ourselves . . . the most important source of such normative change is that of a group's leaders.
>
> (2019, 582)

To change attitudes and behaviours that impede progress towards gender equality, namely, perceptual, emotional, cultural and cognitive blocks, external experts and speakers were invited to lead unconscious bias awareness sessions in all three INTEGER institutions. TCD adopted a cascade process, working from the top-down with key segments of the university including the promotions committee.

All SAGE institutions ran unconscious bias training workshops targeted at different groups within their organisations. Some found that gathering the qualitative data on the existing gender culture through focus groups also served a method for raising awareness of gender equality issues more generally and contributed to overcoming some ideological issues:

> *'The common prejudice or stereotype is that gender is related to women only, so it's not men's problem'.*

Alongside the unconscious bias awareness training, institutions also ran seminars presenting the gender disaggregated data and explaining the impact of inequality. These training events also seemed to be a site where resistance or scepticism about the change process and its value to the institution were revealed:

> *'We had to use the literature that proves that gender equality gets the whole institution to a higher and more efficient level'.*

The experiences of the INTEGER project also provided information on resistance to change, with the lesson learned that some resistance is inevitable. Emphasising the evidence base for good practice, and the benefits to the broad institutional community, helps to maximise support. As is clear from the experiences of the SAGE partner institutions, any efforts to generate significant change are likely to be met with resistance from some quarters and resistance is an inevitable part of the change process. Strategies for managing resistance to change have been dealt with at length in the FESTA project, which produced the *Handbook on Resistance to Gender Equality in Academia* (2016).

Envision using SAGE wheel metaphor

For Kotter (2012, 71), 'Vision refers to a picture of the future with some implicit or explicit commentary on why people should strive to create that future'. Hence, developing a clear vision and the strategies to achieve that vision play a crucial role in the change process. As previously noted, the underlying vision in each INTEGER institution was enshrined in the acronym/logo and through the use of the INTEGER Wheel, which acted as a roadmap for the GEP.

In the case of the SAGE project, the SAGE wheel model for Gender Equality Plans was used to illustrate the range of actions that can be employed to drive gender equality in higher education institutions. Integrative actions to implement change, utilising training and communication are required for people to learn how to use or incorporate the new actions. Kanter recommended devices such as cascading, networks, conferencing, road shows and informal visits to relay information from the converted to prospective and necessary participants. These mechanisms create momentum and critical mass in convincing people to adopt new practices leading to appropriate and timely gender actions.

SAGE partners reported finding the SAGE wheel a useful tool in identifying potential actions for the development of each individual institution's GEP:

> 'The SAGE model [was] extremely useful as a guideline'.

Despite having the resource of the SAGE model to draw on, some of the SAGE partners reported finding it hard to communicate the purpose of the project to the wider institutional audience.

Embed gender in the culture

Kotter (2012) advocated anchoring new approaches in the culture and consolidating gains to produce more change, by hiring or promoting people who can implement the change and reinvigorating the process with new projects. For Kang and Kaplan (2019, 581), 'Gender inclusive workplace cultures are those that create a positive social climate for people of all gender identities'. The institutional culture needs to be, or become, in tune with the vision of gender equality, otherwise nothing will change. Hence the need to make gender more visible, including LGBTQ+ issues, through diverse speakers/films/events, drawing attention to gender-related issues, such as harassment. Measures to address language, for example in recruitment adverts and promotion calls, need to be gender sensitised. This is a critical stage for building awareness of an inclusive culture that values diversity. In 2019, the Trinity Centre for Gender Equality and Leadership adopted the slogan: 'gender matters-whatever your gender' as part of its contribution to the TCD equality trail. The language and message should, wherever possible, be included in all the institution's plans, reviews and mission statements.

In TCD, it became clear that in order to anchor and institutionalise the gains from INTEGER, and build upon them, required an external stimulus. This was provided by the establishment of an Athena SWAN national committee which led, in turn, to the extension of the Athena SWAN awards to all Irish universities and institutes for higher education. SAGE institutions also produced documents and tools to support the implementation of their GEPs. For example, a guide for those involved in recruitment, and a manual of good practice was produced. Other focus group members referred to career progression, gender in the curriculum and gender in research.

> 'We have a lot of students who have babies, so we refurbished a room for them to use for baby changing; it is highly utilised'.

Communicate success

Kotter (2012) advocates generating short-term wins and anchoring new approaches in the culture by highlighting the connections between new behaviours and organisational success. The communication of 'small wins' (Correll 2017, 744) is an important part of the incremental route to gender equality since this 'approach can produce important changes in the short run, such as reducing the biases women experience during workplace evaluations, and this change can inspire larger change' (Correll 2017, 745).

INTEGER introduced an important and timely action vehicle to communicate successes through: cascading, networking, conferences and exchanges of experience, site visits, presentations of survey findings/recommendations for action and, most importantly, their adoption by governing bodies (council and board). It also sponsored a media training event run in 2014 to assist INTEGER partners in communicating their message. A similar event was run for SAGE partners in 2018. This enabled SAGE partner institutions to communicate the successful implementation of their GEPs though their institutional social media accounts, communication events, as well as networking with colleagues both internally and externally:

> '*Once we started, the institution realised it could be useful*'.

Evidence emerged of a growing awareness of the SAGE project through, in a number of cases, SAGE teams being proactively approached, internally and externally, for their inputs. The crucial role that communication plays in facilitating a wider support for gender equality measures goes in tandem with the need for SAGE team members to convince colleagues that, not only would improvements in gender equality benefit the institution, but that gender equality was not a threat to academic merit:

> '*A lot of them saw the gender equality agenda as taking something out of a merit-based university. They were very cautious and some expressed a fear of a merit-based system being attacked from the gender equality side. We needed to make an efficient way to explain how the two can co-exist . . . merit and gender equality are not* [mutually] *exclusive*'.

Accepting that generating significant change is likely to be met with opposition from some quarters is important in overcoming that resistance. Creating and learning new systems, processes and structures takes time, as people build up their competence through integrating knowledge and applying it to their actions. As Hultman concludes:

> overcoming resistance is essentially a process of impacting people's facts, beliefs, feelings, values, and behaviour. Some methods for dealing with facts

and beliefs are to verify facts, clarify beliefs, challenge unviable beliefs, and suggest more viable beliefs.

(2003, 12)

In the context of the SAGE project, team members worked hard to challenge the belief that gender inequality undermines meritocracy.

Conclusion

This chapter has outlined the role played by change management theories and the lessons learned from previous gender equality initiatives in developing the *SAGE model for institutional change.* Alongside this, the chapter has presented the reflections of the SAGE team members on putting the model into practice, as they worked towards implementing institutional GEPs. The SAGE process is perceived as a starting point for gender equality by the SAGE team members, who are realistic about how much change can be achieved during a three-year project, particularly when academic careers in some countries can take many years to develop:

> *'We have only two female professors and a low representation of women. You're not going to solve that in three years'.*
> *'A three-year project is too short a time to implement such change. The time for career change is very long, so it's hard to see change in three years. Not just for accepting the idea that gender is something we should invest in, but career change is very lengthy process'.*

However, the value of the SAGE model is best summed up by the team member who said:

> *'The SAGE model gave us directions where to start – collecting data – and four areas of action. You need someone to guide you . . . it provides a structure, but you need guidance too'.*

References

Benschop, Y. and Verloo, M. (2011) Gender, change, organizational change and gender equality strategies, in E. Jeanes, D. Knights and P. Martin (eds), *Handbook of gender, work and organization,* John Wiley & Sons, Chichester.

Clark, B. (1998) *Creating entrepreneurial universities: Organizational pathways of transformation.* Issues in higher education. Elsevier Science, New York.

Clark, B. (2004) *Sustaining change in universities: Continuities in case studies and concepts,* McGraw-Hill Education, London.

Correll, S. (2017) Reducing gender biases in modern workplaces: A small wins approach to organisational change, *Gender and Society,* 31 (6), 725–750, doi:10.1177/08912432 17738518

Danowitz, M. (2008) Gender equality as organizational change: Frames, challenges, and strategies in the EU and US, in S. Grenz, B. Kortendiek, M. Kriszio and A. Löther (eds), *Gender equality programmes in higher education: International perspectives*, VS Verlag, Wiesbaden, 87–100.

FESTA (2016) *Handbook on resistance to gender equality in academia*, Female Empowerment in Science and Technology Academia: FESTA. Available at: www.festa-europa.eu/public/handbook-resistance-gender-equality-academia

HEA (2016) *HEA national review of gender equality in Irish higher education institutions*, Higher Education Authority, Dublin.

Hultman, K. (2003) Managing resistance to change, *Encyclopedia of Information Systems*, 3, 693–705.

INTEGER (2015) *Institutional transformation for effecting gender equality in research*. Available at: www.integer-tools-for-action.eu/en/resource/lessons-learned

Kang, S. and Kaplan, S. (2019) Working towards gender diversity and inclusion in medicine: Myths and solutions, *Lancet*, 393, 579–586, doi.org/10.1016/S0140-6736(18)33138-6

Kanter, R. M. (1977) *Men and women of the corporation*, Basic Books, New York.

Kanter, R. M. (1989) *The change masters corporate: Entrepreneurs at work*, Allen and Unwin, London.

Kotter, J. (2012) *Leading change*, Harvard Business Review Press, Cambridge, MA.

O'Connor, P. (2019) An autoethnographic account of a pragmatic inclusionary strategy and tactics as a form of feminist activism, *Equality, Diversity and Inclusion: An International Journal*, 38 (8), 825–840, doi.org/10.1108/EDI-12-2018-0227

O'Connor, P., Martin, P., Carvalho, T., O'Hagan, C., Veronesi, L., Mich, O., Saglamer, G., Tan, M. and Caglayan, H. (2019) Leadership practices by senior position holders in higher educational research institutes: Stealth power in action, *Leadership*, 15 (6), 722–743, doi.org/10.1177/1742715019853200

Sporn, B. (1999) *Adaptive university structures: An analysis of adaptation to socioeconomic environments of US and European universities*, Higher education policy series No. 54, Taylor and Francis, Philadelphia.

Sporn, B. (2019) Adaptive university structures—from theory to practice and back, in P. Teixeira, A. Veiga, M. Machado, P. da Rosa and A. Magalhães (eds), *Under pressure: Higher education institutions coping with multiple challenges*, Koninklijke Brill NV, Leiden.

Chapter 11

Understanding leadership in higher education as a tool for change in relation to gender

Andrew Power

Traditional leadership theories

A substantial volume of work has been written on the subject of leadership and many theories developed to explain it. Bennis and Nanus (1985) suggest that leadership is the most studied yet least understood topic of any in the social sciences. Many theories have been put forward including: 'great man' theory; trait and behaviourist theories; situational leadership; and contingency, transactional and transformational leadership theories. Feminist theories of leadership have brought much-needed and timely perspectives to the field (Rosener 1990; Klenke 1996; Loden 1985). In considering the emergence of female leaders, much is made of the benefits of diversity when constructing boards or leadership teams. Ironically, this view of leadership is strangely reminiscent of the discredited 'great man' theory of leadership. This theory held that the ability to be a great leader was something a person was born with rather than a set of skills that could be learned. The examples were frequently military leaders and thus built on the narrative of heroic leaders. An echo of this approach today can be seen in the way sporting heroes and their achievements are frequently discussed. This has sometimes led to a similarly reductive view of the different traits that women leaders may possess.

Two themes emerge with the first being a diminishing belief that leaders are born rather than made. Over time, it gradually became accepted that leadership skills could be studied, learned, or improved. The second development is the acceptance that leaders are not hermetically sealed or self-contained. Their leadership skills depend on outside forces such as the environment, the context or their relationship with their followers. Leadership is understood as a process of acknowledging, understanding and shaping these external factors.

An acknowledgement that leadership skills could be learned has led to a large and profitable training industry for managers, targeted mainly at the private sector. This was capitalised on in higher education through the creation and provision of Master's in Business Administration (MBA) (2018) programmes, the most frequently conferred master's degree in the United States (Byrne 2014). An even larger private leadership industry has emerged, for example *The Leaders Institute* or *Dale Carnegie* (www.leadersinstitute.com or www.ireland.dalecarnegie.com).

The private sector led the way and dominated research and the development of leadership theory. Much of it has been popularised in management books or delivered in a practitioner-friendly form via company training sessions. Despite the fact that higher education has been providing leadership training to the business community there has been less impetus towards developing leadership development programmes within universities themselves. In more recent years, organisations such as AdvanceHE (www.lfhe.ac.uk/) in the UK have begun to address this with a number of specific programmes. Formed from the merger of related organisations in 2018, including the Leadership Foundation, one of the programmes which continues to be run in Higher Education Institutions, in the UK and Ireland, is the Aurora Leadership programme. The Aurora programme supports women and their institutions through a series of leadership workshops, mentoring and motivating interventions from senior female role models. In addition to the formal aspect of the programme the development of a network of early career women in higher education is a key benefit to participants.

The second theme of the research, that leaders must take greater control of their environment, is also easier for the leader in the private sector to conceptualise. For all the uncertainty of the market, a leader in the private sector has a clearer set of objectives and a smaller number of variables than a public sector leader or administrator. It is also likely that a private sector leader will have more control over the management of resources and more motivational levers at their disposal than in the public sector. In higher education, measures of success or failure are more complex and longer term. In addition, the connection between the funding of a department or the promotion of an individual academic are not tied in the same direct way to outputs. Simply setting targets, such as one that the gender or ethnic composition of the senior academic leadership reflects the student population or indeed the broader academia, is a positive but insufficient step. Targets have the advantage of being easier to introduce and they tend to meet less resistance from the dominant group who see them as less threatening. Targets are less threatening because they are difficult to enforce and slow to achieve change. More positive actions, such quotas, meet much more resistance as they are seen to undermine the dominant group. They are, however, a way to effect change more quickly.

A target-led approach can mean that the time taken to effect change can be longer and that changes are limited to organic or incremental change. Building leadership capacity, and more specifically increasing the number of senior female leaders within higher education, has been slow when left to the more passive approach of targets and aspirations. More positive approaches to achieving change are required and some are explored later. One approach to recruitment which has gained traction in the corporate technology sector and was imported from professional sports is the Rooney Rule (Fox 2015). Dan Rooney, former US ambassador to Ireland, 2009 to 2013, sought to address the fact that the majority of players in the US National Football League (NFL) were African American but almost none were head coaches. Rooney mandated that a minority candidate must be shortlisted for all interviews. In 2014 Microsoft and other IT companies have adopted the rule in relation to gender for appointments to their boards (Branson 2018). Approaches in Irish higher education have included requiring interview panels to be gender balanced and gender blind screening of CVs is becoming more common. Nevertheless, there is a need to develop the necessary knowledge and experience in institutions for making significant change.

O'Connor (2019) has questioned the gender competence of senior leaders in Irish HE and suggested that the lack of experience or knowledge amongst the predominately male leadership is one cause of this inertia. O'Connor draws attention to the recommendation of the Irish Higher Education Authority that in the appointment of all line mangers 'a requirement of appointment will be demonstrable experience of leadership in advancing gender equality' (HEA 2016, 47). The limited instances of positive action, whilst attracting some resistance and occasional controversy may be quicker to yield results and may seed change in the system. An example of this, in the Irish context, is the Senior Academic Leadership Initiative (SALI) (https://hea.ie/funding-calls/senior-academic-leadership-initiative/) (see Chapter 12). This competitive process funded by the Irish Higher Education Authority provided for up to 45 (20 appointments in 2020) new and additional senior academic leadership posts to be awarded over three years from 2020 to accelerate gender balance at senior levels.

The public sector and focus on implementation

If leadership theories have been a preoccupation of researchers in the private sector then implementation theories hold a corresponding place in the public sector. Implementation refers to what happens between the establishment of a government intention and its consequent impact (O'Toole 1997). The public sector focus notes that policies announced at the top of the hierarchy have failed to be consistently implemented by those who are designated to deliver them.

In his review of the implementation literature, Matland (1995, 146) argued that it lacks a theoretical structure and despite a very large number of case studies, most writers fall into the 'top-down', or 'bottom-up', view of implementation. The top-down theorists, such as Pressman and Wildavsky (1984), were clear that policy sets the goals and implementation is about how those goals are satisfactorily and accurately executed. This resonates with ideas of a hierarchical leadership system with a 'great man' setting the rules. Bottom-up theorists such as Lipsky (1980) and his concept of a 'street-level bureaucrat' echo the transformative model of leadership where the followers, or subordinates, play a more important role in the process. The impact of external factors on the success or otherwise of administrative implementation were considered by Mazmanian and Sabatier (1983). They addressed factors such as public support, socio-economic conditions, support from sovereigns and the attitudes of constituency groups, analogous to the thinking demonstrated in situational or contingency leadership theories. However, the premise that if the system is designed correctly then the desired results will follow rarely refer to leadership as a significant factor in successful implementation.

Their only reference to leadership is when they discuss the importance of the commitment of those engaged in implementation, whilst acknowledging that 'leadership skill remains a rather elusive concept' (Mazmanian and Sabatier 1983, 35).

The top-down hierarchical approach has shifted to a more inclusive, change-driven, transformational approach. This change in implementation theory increasingly sees the street-level bureaucrat, citizen and service user as an important part of the implementation process. This has relevance for alternatives to male leadership in universities, particularly when considering the question of whether women manage differently to men. The top-down approach emphasised a formal, structural way to lead where the power relationship was vertical and directional, which in turn played to the traditional hierarchical approach associated with male leadership. The shift to bottom-up leadership opened up the possibility of a more collaborative or participatory style of leadership, often linked to, or expected of, female leaders. A discussion of the emergence of alternative styles of leadership pioneered by female leaders is detailed by Drew (2008).

Leadership in the public sector

The task of leadership has become more complex in an organisational climate of shared power and openness. Public sector leaders face additional difficulties, relating to contextual complexity (Brunner 1997), first identified and described in relation to the difference in role between the leader of paid employees and those in a voluntary organisation:

> issues on contextual complexity apply to mission, organisational and environmental culture, structure, types of problems, types of opportunities, levels of discretion and a host of other critically important areas.
>
> (Van Wart 2003, 215)

Within the public sector, goals may be more complex, less measurable, or more susceptible to change. For example, the clarity of a private sector goal such as profit maximisation is likely to be absent and replaced by a more nebulous goal such as improved university ranking or more integrated research innovation. This contextual difference has contributed to the lack of crossover of some leadership theories, from the private to the public sector. Some believe that leadership does not, and should not, exist in the public sector, arising from the notion that administrative leadership in the public sector is driven entirely by political forces and bureaucracy (Van Wart 2003). Hence, leadership is the sole preserve of the political leadership and the role of public servants, at all levels, is to implement the will of government. In a review of leaders in the British public sector (Blackler 2006) chief executives in the NHS saw themselves as little more than conduits for central government policies and targets, rather than as reformers.

This is also evident in the Irish higher education sector, through initiatives to address change: linking research funding to gender balance; requiring senior appointees to have experience in advancing gender equality; the Senior Academic Leadership Initiative (SALI); and the requirement for HEIs to obtain Athena SWAN certification. All of these were driven by the Higher Education Authority (HEA), the Department of Education and Skills or by the Minister for Higher Education. None were led by the academic institutions who continue to see their role as implementors rather than leaders.

Irish academia is in a time of change, with debates about the funding mechanism for higher education, the changing role of providers, the merging of some institutions and the general shifting landscape of provision with gender equality sought in leadership roles. There is opportunity in times of flux to make radical change but the signals are mixed. On the one hand initiatives on research funding, as developed by Doona in Chapter 12, is positive, as is the SALI initiative. On the other hand, recent opportunities to appoint the first woman to the position of president of an Irish University or Technological University has not materialised. The growing awareness of gender imbalance as an issue and the adoption of the Athena SWAN Charter is to be welcomed, but until institutions move from data collection and monitoring to the more direct approach of promoting more women as leaders, progress will remain incremental.

Van Wart (2003, 221) offers a range of definitions of leadership specific to the public sector, ranging from bureaucratic 'the process of providing the results required by authorized processes in an efficient, effective, and legal manner'; motivational 'developing and supporting followers'; political 'aligning the organization with its environment', public service 'dedicated to the common good'; or a combination of all of these. This language is different from the language of private sector leadership theory. There is no discussion of the transactional nature of the relationship between leader and follower nor is there a sense of the transformational nature of the leader as an agent for change. This is important since the gendered nature of leadership is often characterised by a distinction between male (transactional, direct, task orientated) and female (transformational, participative, people orientated) (Rosener 1990).

Leadership throughout the public sector has focused less on change and more on doing the same tasks more efficiently, effectively or accountably. In Ireland, for example, the effectiveness of the public sector is regularly reported on by the comptroller and auditor general, whose annual reports provide an insight into the efficiencies of the organs of the state. Callahan (2007) expressed concern that the accountability burden is undermining performance since more time is now spent on the administrative burden of documenting rather than on improving performance. Horan (2007) commented that over-reporting is an increasing feature and obligation of senior managers in the public sector. In the specific case of higher education this approach has found expression in the importation from the broader public sector of much of the ideas of New Public Management (Tolofari 2005; Broucker and De Wit 2015). In addition to increasing metrics for expected activities such as research and publications the language of: performance; service delivery; management by objectives; and management by incentive, are now part of the landscape of performance metrics and agreements between academic institutions and the state.

While recognising some of the advantages which result from New Public Management, two problems arise from this transformation in thinking. First, changes which saw recipients of public services as consumers rather than citizens resulted in some inappropriate behaviours as systems designed for profit maximisation were applied to situations requiring service optimisation. In the case of higher education it is problematic to think of students as customers and yet issues such as recruitment, retention, progression and, of course, student fees, feed into this thinking. Second, while some management theories and techniques were imported from business schools and the private sector, theories of leadership which were advancing in the private sector were largely ignored by the public sector. An obvious example is the impracticality of applying a sales culture of targets, bonuses and so on, when higher education does not see itself in the business of sales. Another change is the growing recognition of the diversity of the customer base. Businesses may have slowly begun to see that if their leadership team better reflected the diversity of their customers, they might gain a better insight into how best to meet their needs. This could be seen as 'good for business'. In academia, the same link between leadership insight to the growing diversity of the student population has not been recognised nor has it been applied to systematic considerations of gender.

The current emphasis on control and measurement runs contrary to the idea of leadership, which is about movement and change. Despite the contextual differences in the public sector, effective leadership is essential. Mobilising public organisations to accomplish their mandated purpose is constrained by ministerial ability to provide leadership for multiple agencies and functions for which they are responsible. Government may provide the public servant or agency with vague or conflicting goals and, inevitably, with insufficient resources. Leadership is also important to prevent capture by external interest groups of the public agenda for their own purpose. Finally, leadership in the public sector is important because the citizens whose will is served by the public servant may not have the knowledge or information to achieve the solution to their issue (Behn 1998a, 1998b).

Women and leadership

Despite the many advances in leadership theory there is still a strongly held idea of 'heroic individualistic' leadership. This means that successful female leaders may be compared unfavourably with their male counterparts or, as 'unicorns', rare, unusual and exceptional individuals. Lack of female leaders in the workplace has less to do with the nature or ability of women and everything to do with the gendered nature of the workplace. Women face a range of gendered assumptions and stereotypes about their fitness for leadership, which are then translated into discriminatory norms and organisational practices in areas such as recruitment and promotion (Marshall 1984). Examples of the consequences of these gendered assumptions are noted in Chapters 3, 4 and 7, which refer to gendered recruitment, career progression and the gender pay gap respectively.

There is a lack of female leadership at the highest levels of academia world-wide (Morley 2013). In the EU, only 15 per cent of rectors or vice-chancellors are women (European University Association 2016). Manfredi (2017) argues that universities need to tackle the invisible barriers which prevent women from pro-gressing into senior roles, namely: the gendered construction of leadership and the impact of unconscious bias (see Chapter 9) which results in women being con-stantly judged less favourably than men; and the cumulative disadvantage they face throughout their careers.

The gender construction of leadership refers back to the traditional understand-ing of leadership. A more evolved understanding of leadership styles appropriate to the business or academic environment brings with it a demand for more diverse skills. Drew (2008) discusses how feminine leadership brings an added dimension rather than being a replacement of a more traditional approach. The adoption of more open, collaborative styles of leadership, with greater emphasis on consensus and equality, not only give opportunities to women leaders to exercise their skills but also allow male leaders to learn from and develop their own style of leader-ship. Examples of female leaders who have achieved positions of leadership in universities are rare, but it is possible to detect a distinctive voice. Professor Rich-ardson, the first female vice-chancellor of the University of Oxford called for the education of future leaders who can 'think critically' and 'act ethically' in order to better deal with issues like financial crises. She also acknowledged the impor-tance of diversity in universities stating, 'in an increasingly complex world, the best may not be those who look and sound like ourselves' (BBC News 2016). The first female president of Harvard challenged those women who achieve success in leadership positions to maintain this distinctive voice: 'sustain our commitment to fairness and justice for women here and around the world' (Faust 2014).

Difficulty in achieving leadership responsibilities in universities is often com-pounded by a gendered division of labour in academia, with women more likely to have greater teaching, administrative and pastoral responsibilities. These tend to be less valued than research (Manfredi 2017). This topic is also the subject of Chapter 4 (Kinahan *et al*). Positive action is one way in which change can be accelerated. In Ireland, state funding of academia is now linked to the proportion of women at full professorial level and the setting of a gender target of 40 per cent by 2024 (HEA 2016). Instigating gender change in an organisation has often been portrayed as the responsibility of the aspiring female leader, thus absolv-ing the organisation of some of the responsibility. Branson (2018) is critical of the long list of books authored by successful female leaders offering self-help, since they fail to address organisational change, for example Sandberg (2013). Burkinshaw and White (2017) argue that while interventions aimed at helping women break through the glass ceiling are common, the gendered power relations in universities have not changed. Their study indicated that while older, and more senior, female leaders had learnt to fit in and accommodate the prevailing culture, younger women in the leadership pipeline questioned if the price of accommodating the organisational culture to progress their careers was worthwhile.

Manfredi (2017) recognised that a one-off focus on positive action may not be enough to tackle structural and systemic gender issues across institutions. Developing a framework could enable institutions to learn from the application of positive action, to reflect on their practices and on how merit is constructed and assessed. This involves setting aspirational targets to increase gender diversity in senior roles across an institution as well as adopting positive action in recruitment and promotion. It also calls for the recognition of issues such as unconscious bias (Chapter 9) or organisational blind spots. This virtuous circle leads back to the setting of new targets to close the gender gap in leadership roles.

Women's leadership often involves working within, around and underneath institutional, cultural and societal contexts. Blackmore and Sachs (2007) discuss how this leadership style, born of a hostile environment, may well involve a process of both performing and reforming, of simultaneously working within existing institutional arrangements and structures, while also arguing for new ways of organising and modelling new forms of leading. Their view of leadership is more about articulating and sharing ideas and understanding when to take action. They suggest an almost subversive approach to working outside, against and within the system. In addition to mentoring and communication they emphasise the importance of six elements identified by Day (2004) for successful leadership: achievement, care, collaboration, commitment, trust and inclusivity. Many of these elements should form part of a positive mentoring process. Mentoring, and the more active approach of sponsorship, could be part of the informal, individual driven, and the formal, organisational driven, approaches to building leadership capacity. Mentoring schemes driven by a university, such as in the Aurora Women's Leadership programme, provide a network of mentors and mentees. Female leaders demonstrate a sensitivity to the context of interpersonal relations, habits and customs that determine the meanings and associated expectations of formal rules. Blackmore and Sachs (2007) note that this social capital often came from outside rather than within their organisations (unions, social movements, professional organisations, community networks).

Leaders and followers

Leadership, strategy and change are different ways of looking at the same phenomenon. To lead is to move or change and strategy involves planning for such change. Leadership can reside in the follower and not just in the leader. In this way, leadership can be seen as a series of leadership acts rather than as a distinct role. Looking at leadership as a process between a series of actors in which all participants play a vital role, where leadership skills are nurtured and developed, has a resonance in the public sector environment, since teams are less likely to change quickly and developing teams is more productive than seeking to replace members. Problems are often long-term and systemic rather than resolvable by short-term actions. In academia, teams of colleagues, based either on departmental and faculty structures, or on research interests, are likely to be stable over a number of years. This environment would benefit most from a style of shared leadership where relationships develop over time. O'Connor *et al* (2019) explored the specific power relationships in research environments in which power is often covertly exercised by those with control over strategic direction and resources and what they describe as 'stealth power' is frequently male dominated. This is clearly unproductive and undermining of trust. Seeing leadership in higher education as a long-term relationship between individuals who bring their diverse skills and knowledge to a problem requires more conscious effort than a top-down direction but is considerably more productive.

Kramer (1995) argues that leadership is a form of relationship not dependent on the specific traits of an individual, building on the ideas of the transactional model of leadership. There is a relationship or transaction between follower and leader which is dynamic and changeable. Transformational leadership is based on the idea that the essential function of leadership is to produce adaptive or useful change (Kotter 1990; Van Wart 2003) and the leadership style adapts to the needs of the task or situation. The fusion of transactional and transformational leadership has emerged from studies which build a unified theory of leadership containing both relationship-building and change management elements of leadership. For example, Hooper and Potter (1997) talk about 'transcendent leaders' who can engage emotionally with their followers and transcend change.

This concept can be traced back to Parker Follett (1868–1933) who looked at lateral relationships across organisations and envisaged what would now be recognised as matrix-style organisations. This move away from a traditional hierarchical organisation focused on the informal relations within an organisation and a more dynamic set of power relations (Graham 1995). Parker Follett developed the concept of 'power with' rather than 'power over' and coined the phrase 'win-win approach'. This approach to problem solving or conflict resolution within an organisation embraced a range of views and can be seen as a precursor to understanding that diversity provides a mechanism for a broader understanding of issues. Discussing Parker Follett's work, Rusch (1991) attributed concepts such as transformational leadership, the interrelationship of leadership and followership, and the power of collective goals of leaders and followers to her lectures of 1927. This work expanded on the concept of hierarchical organisations and opened the possibility of more collaborative matrix style organisations, where the collaborative, networking and participative skills which Rosener (1990) associated with female leaders, were more valued. In higher education there are examples of this where staff may have a direct departmental or faculty manager but need to build similar productive relationships with the chairs of committees or research groups.

Seeing leadership as a relationship necessitates considering the role of the follower, involving a two-way process requiring effort, energy and a belief in common purpose, by both parties:

Corporations and government agencies everywhere have executives who imagine that their place on the organization chart has given them a body of followers, and of course it has not. They have been given subordinates. Whether the subordinates become followers depends on whether the executives act like leaders.

(Gardner 1990, 3)

Followers are as intrinsic a part of the leadership process as leaders, where the role of leader might move between individuals. Rost (1991) argued that a new view of followers is necessary, in which a follower has an active role and must make a choice to perform that role. It is also possible that followers can be transformed into leaders and leaders into followers. This rotation of leadership, or the building of leadership skills within all members of the team, is well suited to an academic environment where organisational change is often slow and opportunities for formal progression limited. The opportunity to build up the skills of leadership in a matrix environment rather than imposing a constant hierarchy, provides the opportunity to maximise the skills of all.

Distributed leadership (Gronn 2002) offers some guidance, relying as it does on 'concertive action' where people pool ideas and expertise, so producing services and leadership energy that is greater than the sum of their individual capacities. Distributed leadership can take the form of spontaneous collaboration on tasks. Leadership is evident in the interaction and relationships in which people with different skills, expertise and from different organisational levels coalesce to pool expertise and agree conduct for the duration of the task. It also exists in shared roles which emerge between two or more people, involving close joint working 'within an implicit framework of understanding' and emergent 'intuitive understandings'. Finally, it can exist in the institutionalisation of structures, working together for example via committees. The advantages of distributed leadership amount to 'an overall widening of the net of intelligence and organisational resourcefulness' (Gronn 2002, 37). The concepts of shared and distributed leadership are also discussed by Brookes (2007). In addition to empowering the traditional 'follower' this concept requires a considerable change to the traditional 'leader' who may see the process as undermining or threatening. However, for those open to seeing the first role of leadership as being to create new leaders, the opportunities for men and women to learn and grow in their leadership skills provides a pool of potential leaders for the organisation as a whole.

Peck and P. 6 state that 'the governance and management of many public services have been increasingly subject to tight surveillance, detailed central rule-making about how decisions should be made in an attempt to eliminate uncertainty' (2006, 21). They argue that this is misguided and that implementation in the public service is a creative process of change and adaptation. The aversion to risk in the public sector may have its roots in a conservatism or caution in dealing with public funds, where there is little or no perceived reward for instigating innovative change. The changeable nature of public policy, resulting from regular changes in government, may also play a part, or that the problems facing the public service are seen as just too complex (Van Bueren *et al* 2003). Dunoon (2002) suggests that management is about ensuring stability and continuity and that leadership is concerned with change and transformation. The emphasis on management rather than leadership in the public sector may derive from the fact that a management approach can produce tangible, measurable results. Leadership involves more risk and less certain outcomes. Academia has been willing to take on the many initiatives which have been initiated centrally or politically. It is now time for universities and institutes to demonstrate their ability to move beyond the implementation of reports and to do what centres of learning do best, innovate, change and grow. Academic institutions value their independence and autonomy; with that comes the responsibility to show their capacity for leadership. Comparing the approach to leadership in the public sector against the approach of the private sector, the issue comes down to adaptability, responsiveness and risk. Changes in thinking about leadership in the public sector have been slow whereas the private sector continues to be more agile in its ability to respond to changing circumstances. Some of the limitations to adaptability and responsiveness in the public sector are structural, such as contracts of employment, while others are as a result of the nature of the services supplied. It can be argued that some aspects of the public service merit risk aversion but in the case of higher education change and innovation is clearly needed.

Conclusion

The study of leadership in the public sector and higher education has been limited in the past, relative to the private sector. This may have been due in part to the different nature of the environment, less appetite for risk and a relative lack of autonomy. This is changing and one of the motivations is the recognition that the gender imbalance in senior positions in higher education is neither acceptable nor sustainable. This chapter suggests that the slow pace of change achieved by past attempts at developmental initiatives and goal setting should be augmented by a more positive approach to change. A greater appetite for risk and reward, more common in the private sector, could challenge the *status quo* and achieve real change. Building leadership capacity and skills throughout the academic staff, linking resources to a gender balanced leadership teams, seeding leadership posts in areas of specific gender imbalance, are all positive moves to achieve a community of academic leaders more reflective of the student population they seek to inspire.

References

BBC News (2016) *New Oxford vice-chancellor urges 'open-minded' students.* Available at: www.bbc.com/news/uk-england-oxfordshire-35290156

Behn, R. (1998a) The new public management paradigm and the search for democratic accountability, *International Public Management Journal*, 1 (2), 131–164.

Behn, R. (1998b) What right do public managers have to lead? *Public Administration Review*, 58 (3), 209–224.

Bennis, W. and Nanus, B. (1985) *Leaders: The strategies for taking charge*, Harper & Row, New York.

Blackler, F. (2006) Chief executives and the modernisation of the English national health service, *Leadership*, 2 (1), 5–30.

Blackmore, J. and Sachs, J. (2007) *Performing and reforming leaders: Gender, educational restructuring, and organizational change*, State University of New York (SUNY) Press, Albany.

Branson, D. (2018) *The future of tech is female: How to achieve gender diversity*, New York University Press, New York.

Brookes, S. (2007) Are public leaders up to standard? *CSL Leadership Review*, 1 (4), 211–224, Centre for Studies in Leadership, University of Guelph, ON.

Broucker, B. and De Wit, K. (2015) New public management in higher education, in J. Huisman, H. de Boer, D. Dill and M. Souto-Otero (eds), *The Palgrave international handbook of higher education policy and governance*, Palgrave Macmillan, London.

Brunner, R. (1997) Teaching the policy sciences: Reflections on a graduate seminar, *Policy Sciences*, 39 (2), 217–231.

Burkinshaw, P. and White, K. (2017) Fixing the women or fixing universities: Women in HE leadership, *Administrative Science*, 7 (30), 1–14.

Byrne, J. (2014) Why the MBA is now the most popular masters, *Poets and Quants*, 26 May. Available at: http://poetsandquants.com/2014/05/26/why-the-mba-is-now-the-most-popular-masters/

Callahan, K. (2007) *Elements of effective governance: Measurement, accountability and participation*, CRC Press, Boca Raton.

Day, C. (2004) The passion of successful leadership, *School Leadership and Management*, 24 (4), 425–438.

Drew, E. (2008) Leadership for business excellence: The gender perspective, in K. Foley and P. Hermel (eds), *The theories and practices of organization excellence: New perspectives*, SAI Global, Sydney, 269–293.

Dunoon, D. (2002) Rethinking leadership for the public sector, *Australian Journal of Public Administration*, 61 (3), 3–18.

European University Association (2016) *More women become university leaders—equality still far away*. Available at: https://eua.eu/news/41:more-women-become-university-leaders-equality-still-far-away.html

Faust, D. G. (2014) *History of presidency: 'It can be otherwise'*, Harvard University Press. Available at: www.harvard.edu/president/speech/2014/it-can-be-otherwise

Fox, A. (2015) How the Rooney rule succeeds and where it falls short, *ESPN Magazine*. Available at: https://abc7ny.com/sports/how-the-rooney-rule-succeeds-and-where-it-falls-short/730588/

Gardner, J. (1990) *On leadership*, The Free Press, New York.

Graham, P. (1995) *Mary Parker Follett—prophet of management: A celebration of writings from the 1920s*, Harvard Business School Press, Boston, MA.

Gronn, P. (2002) Distributed leadership, in K. Leithwood, P. Hallinger, K. Seashore Louis, G. Furman Brown, P. Gronn, W. Mulford and K. Riley (eds), *Second international handbook of educational leadership and administration*, Kluwer, Dordrecht.

HEA (2016) *National review of gender inequality in Irish higher education institutions*, Higher Education Authority, Dublin.

Hooper, A. and Potter, J. (1997) *The business of leadership*, Ashgate, Aldershot.

Horan, A. (2007) Governance and performance: Some dilemmas, *Administration*, 55 (1), 195–224.

Klenke, K. (1996) *Women in leadership: A contextual perspective*, Springer, New York.

Kotter, J. (1990) *A force for change: How leadership differs from management*, Free Press, New York.

Kramer, R. (1995) Carl Rogers meets Otto Rank: The discovery of relationship, in T. Pauchant (ed), *In search of meaning: Managing for the health of our organizations, our communities, and the natural world*, Jossey-Bass, San Francisco, 197–223.

Lipsky, M. (1980) *Street-level bureaucracy: Dilemmas of the individual in public services*, Russell Sage Foundation, New York.

Loden, M. (1985) *Feminine leadership or how to succeed in business without being one of the boys*, Time Books, New York.

Manfredi, S. (2017) Increasing gender diversity in senior roles in HE: Who is afraid of positive action?, *Administrative Sciences*, 7 (2), 1–14.

Marshall, J. (1984) *Women managers: Travellers in a male world*, Wiley, Chichester.

Masters Programs Guide (2018) Available at: www.mastersprogramsguide.com/rankings/popular-masters-degrees/

Matland, R. (1995) Synthesizing the implementation literature: The ambiguity-conflict model of policy implementation, *Journal of Public Administration Research & Theory*, 5 (2), 145–175.

Mazmanian, D. and Sabatier, P. (1983) *Implementation and public policy*, University Press of America, Lanham, MD.

Morley, L. (2013) *Women and higher education leadership: Absences and aspirations*, Leadership Foundation for Higher Education, London.

O'Connor, P. (2019) Creating gendered change in Irish higher education: Is managerial leadership up to the task? *Irish Educational Studies*, doi:10.1080/03323315.2019.1697951

O'Connor, P., Martin, P., Carvalho, T., O'Hagan, C., Veronesi, L., Mich, O., Saglamer, G., Tan, M. and Caglayan, H. (2019) Leadership practices by senior position holders in higher educational research institutes: Stealth power in action, *Leadership*, 15 (6), 722–743, doi.org/10.1177/1742715019853200

O'Toole, L. (1997) Implementing public innovations in network settings, *Administration & Society*, 29 (2), 145–174.

Peck, E. and P. 6 (2006) *Beyond delivery: Policy implementation as sense-making and settlement*, Palgrave Macmillan, Basingstoke.

Pressman, J. and Wildavsky, A. (1984) *Implementation*, University of California Press, Berkeley.

Rosener, J. (1990) Ways women lead, *Harvard Business Review*, 68, November–December, 119–125.

Rost, J. (1991) *Leadership for the twenty-first century*, Praeger, Westport.

Rusch, E. (1991) *The social construction of leadership: From theory to praxis*, paper presented at the Annual conference on research on women and education, 7–10 November, San Jose.

Sandberg, S. (2013) *Lean in: Women, work and the will to lead*, Knopf, New York.

Tolofari, S. (2005) New public management and education, policy futures, *Education*, 3 (1), 75–89.

Van Bueren, E., Klijn, E. and Koppenjan, J. (2003) Dealing with wicked problems in networks: Analyzing an environmental debate from a network perspective, *Journal of Public Administration Research and Theory*, 13 (2), 193–212.

Van Wart, M. (2003) Public-sector leadership theory: An assessment, *Public Administration Review*, 63 (2), 214–228.

Chapter 12

Addressing gender inequality in academia

The role of Irish funding agencies

Annie Doona

Introduction

The story of Irish higher education could be summarised as 500 years of male dominated mono-cultural stasis followed by 100 years of near glacial progress, following the admission of the first female students to Trinity College Dublin and University College Dublin in the early 1900s. A number of areas of inequality still exist, including the under-representation of women in senior academic posts. The landscape of higher education in Ireland, as elsewhere, is complex and multi-dimensional. Its many players include academic presidents, funders, regulatory bodies, policymakers and politicians, private equity, influential individuals and of course students, as individuals, teams and as represented by student unions. This chapter examines the role of funding agencies for Irish higher education institutions in a changing landscape and how they will implement their stated policies. Do they see themselves as advocates and agents of change or as observers in which their role is to monitor and report? If the former, then what actions can they take, what levers do they control and are they willing to use their influence and resources, including the threat of withholding funding, to challenge preconceptions of how things should be done? Irish HEA statistics show that, despite the fact that women held 52 per cent of all lecturing posts, they occupied only 18 per cent of professorial posts in Ireland in 2013, rising to only 26 per cent in 2018. Ireland has yet to appoint a female university president and only three of the 11 Institutes of Technology (IoTs) are currently led by women. Pay grades also reflect the promotions imbalance, with women accounting for just 31 per cent of those paid over €106,000 in universities and only 21 per cent of those in IoTs in 2018 (HEA 2019a).

The Irish *National Strategy for Higher Education to 2030* contains no reference to gender equality, though it does reference access to learning for under-represented groups and disadvantaged groups, stating that: 'Higher education institutions will recruit, develop and retain high-quality staff, fully accountable for their performance to a strong and dynamic leadership' (DoES 2011, 27). Absent from the document is any reference to the under-representation of women in senior posts in higher education. Over the last five years, however, there have been major changes in Ireland within higher education in the promotion of gender equality. This is evident at sectoral, national and institutional policy levels. A number of developments have altered the national discourse. The first involved legal cases taken by a number of individual women academics in pursuit of promotional opportunities (Irish Human Rights and Equality Commission Report 2014). The second was the national adoption by the HEA, in 2015, of the Athena SWAN programme of awards to progress gender equality and as a means of stimulating change. Additionally, in 2013 the Irish Research Council (IRC), the main funding body for cross-disciplinary research, published its *Gender Strategy and Action Plan 2013–2020*. It focused on the streamlining and development of strategies to tackle gender imbalances across its programmes.

During this period a number of higher education institutions began to publish strategic plans that referenced gender, or published specific gender strategies (IADT 2019; TCD 2014; UCC 2017). The HEA Review of 2016 reinforced the political motivation to effect real change leading to a *Gender Action Plan for Higher Education* (HEA 2016). The establishment of a Government Equality Taskforce built upon the work of this review (HEA 2018). Among its recommendations for action was the announcement of a Senior Academic Leadership Initiative (SALI) to fund 45 women-only senior posts in higher education institutions. This initiative was introduced in response to statistics demonstrating that if the current pace of change in promoting women into senior posts continued, the imbalance would persist for another two to three decades. The initiative was also part of a commitment from the female Minister of State for Higher Education to tackle gender inequality in higher education institutions. The granting of the first 20 posts, 15 to universities, two for technological universities and three to institutes of technology, were announced in January 2020, following a competitive application process and assessment of the applications by an international panel of experts in the field of gender equality in higher education. The SALI initiative bolsters the stated aim of the government to have 40 per cent of chair professors posts held by women by 2024 (HEA 2019b).

The SALI initiative was not universally welcomed. Whilst some leaders and lecturing staff in higher education, both male and female, regarded it as a necessary step to tackle gender imbalances, others viewed it as tokenism and feared that it would not address the fundamental issues of culture, attitudes and equality. Some also expressed a concern that the women appointed to these posts would be ghettoised, regarded as second-class professors appointed on the basis of gender rather than academic merit. In 2019, the HEA set up a Centre of Excellence in Gender Equality to monitor its own progress around gender equality and progress in the sector. Its stated objective is: 'to ensure sustainable acceleration towards gender equality through centralised support for HEIs and dissemination of good practice' (HEA 2019c). The Centre is currently responsible for the SALI initiative, in place since the research for this chapter took place.

The key developments outlined previously refer directly or indirectly to the role of funding as a way of progressing gender equality. The actions were specifically targeted at women, ranging from actively encouraging them to apply for funding or posts, women-only programmes, and progress towards gender equality in the allocation of state funding for higher education institutions and research.

The gender equality policy context

The adoption of the Athena SWAN Charter in 2015 marked a turning point in the formalisation of progress towards addressing gender imbalance. Institutions that sign up to the Athena Swan Charter are required to carry out a self-assessment, analysing gender imbalances across a range of areas. These include an examination of gender-related policies, such as availability and take-up of flexible working arrangements, recruitment and promotion procedures and outcomes and staffing levels according to gender. This is accompanied by a Gender Action Plan, addressing any areas of concern arising from the self-assessment. The institution applies for an award based on its self-assessment and the robustness of its Gender Action Plan. It is also a requirement for institutions to hold an Athena SWAN award before individual departments or schools can apply for their awards. The HEA requires that all Irish HEIs must achieve an institutional Athena SWAN Bronze award to be eligible for funding by the end of 2020, with a requirement to have attained a Silver Award within seven years (HEA 2016, 291). Furthermore, progress around gender equality is required as a pre-requisite for research funding:

> Within three years, research funding, as part of the Strategic Dialogue process, Higher Education Institutions will be at risk of funding being withheld if they are not addressing gender inequality sufficiently.
>
> (HEA 2016, 91)

As a result of this report, a Gender Equality Taskforce was set up in 2017. It published a three-year action plan to identify good practice and highlight, as well as address, areas that needed improvement. The *Gender Action Plan 2018–2020* states that: 'All HEIs shall submit their institutional gender action plan to the HEA and provide annual progress updates' (HEA 2018, 21). This led to a strategic dialogue whereby Irish HEIs must set and review targets annually with the HEA articulated via a Compact, a set of agreed targets and performance indicators, which include monitoring of the Gender Action Plan through a system of follow-up evaluation and performance monitoring, linked to funding. With funding linked to institutional performance, it could be withheld if institutions fail to meet the agreed KPIs and targets as set out in their Compact (HEA 2018).

The research

The research for this chapter was carried out between May 2018 and January 2020, gathering the views of leaders of the key funding bodies on the relationship between gender and funding. It was important to ascertain whether a threat to withhold funding for non-compliance could be a feasible and useful tool to promote gender equality. First, a desk-based review of the key policy documents was used to analyse specific commitments to the withholding of funding as a mechanism for influencing change towards achieving gender equality. Published frameworks provide the written declaration to use funding as a way of furthering gender equality. Second, a key question was how willing were funding bodies to implement the policy to affect meaningful change? To address this question, face-to-face semi-structured interviews were carried out with four leaders of funding bodies: the Department of Education and Skills (DoES); Irish Research Council (IRC); Higher Education Authority (HEA); and Health Research Board (HRB).

Policy documents: a context for change?

Overall, the political framework since 2015 has recognised the importance of funding as an incentive to address gender imbalances in higher education. One important dimension to affecting change is how the leaders of Irish HEI funding agencies see their role in implementing policies, and how effective they believe funding incentives to be. Key stakeholders were identified in four of the main funding bodies—the Department of Education and Skills, the Higher Education Authority, the Irish Research Council and the Health Research Board. At the time of the research interviews, all heads of these institutions were male. Before presenting the research and its findings, a short description of each of these five agencies is provided.

Department of Education and Skills

The Department of Education and Skills (DoES) is responsible for education and training. It produces an annual *Action Plan for Education*. The DoES (2019) plan includes reference, amongst its strategic priorities, to the need to address the gender-staffing imbalance in higher education. The DoES has a number of sections with specific responsibilities, including higher education. A Minister of State for Higher Education was appointed to lead a number of initiatives to address gender imbalance, including the SALI initiative.

Higher Education Authority

The Higher Education Authority (HEA) is the state body that leads on the strategic development of the Irish higher education and research system, with the objective of creating a coherent system of diverse institutions with distinct missions, responsive to the social, cultural and economic development of Ireland and its people, supporting the achievement of national objectives. The HEA has played a major role in commissioning and publishing strategic reports and policies on gender inequality. In 2019, it set up the Centre for Excellence in Gender Equality. The HEA is the statutory agency responsible for the allocation of exchequer funding to the universities, Institutes of Technology (IoTs) and other higher education institutions. The priorities of the HEA's *Strategic Plan 2018–2022* include the implementation of the recommendations of the *Report of the Expert Group*, the *HEA National Review of Gender Equality in Irish Higher Education Institutions* and the *Gender Equality Taskforce*.

Science Foundation Ireland

Science Foundation Ireland (SFI) funds research in the areas of science, technology, engineering and mathematics. SFI seeks to remove and mitigate any existing or perceived factors that may limit the participation of women in research Sciences, Technology, Engineering and Mathematics (STEM) careers and to redress gender imbalances amongst SFI award holders, of whom 26 per cent were female (SFI 2018). One of SFI's key performance indicators (KPI) targets is to increase the proportion of female research award holders to 30 per cent by 2020. This aim would facilitate the retention of excellent female researchers within academia, thereby increasing excellence in research and impact by continuing to fund meritorious researchers regardless of gender, through widening the pool of potential applicants.

The Health Research Board

The Health Research Board (HRB) is a state agency that funds and supports research and provides evidence to prevent illness, improve health and transform patient care. It published a *HRB Policy on Gender in Research Funding* (2019), outlining its intention to support both women and men to realise their full potential in order to ensure equality of opportunity and to maximise the quantity and the quality of research. The policy states that the HRB will work to achieve a greater gender balance throughout its research funding programmes and practices by: promoting gender equality within its own administration of research funding; and within the research teams that it funds; fostering the integration of sex and/ or gender into research and innovation content; and assuming a greater national responsibility for promoting gender equality in health research.

Irish Research Council

The Irish Research Council (IRC) is the body in Ireland that funds research across a range of disciplines. The IRC actively promotes gender equality in research funding and has set up a scheme to promote gender equality in research. It has published its own *Gender Strategy 2013–2020* and is committed to reviewing and monitoring gender in research, including the numbers of women researchers and the amounts of funding they receive (IRC 2013).

These five funding bodies comprise the institutional framework for policymaking in relation to gender equality in higher education in Ireland. As such, they have considerable opportunity to shape future action and innovation in this area, making the interviews with four of their leaders particularly timely.

The interviews

The interviews were based around the following questions:

- How do funders see their role?
- Is the threat of withdrawal of funding a good incentive in achieving gender equality?
- Is the overall approach characterised as carrot, stick or both?
- What levers do funders have to make change happen?
- What happens if gender targets are not met?
- What are the likely challenges and resistances to implementing the funding approach?

All interviews were carried out face-to-face and were recorded and transcribed. The responses are outlined in the following sections.

How funders see their role

Interviewees were asked how they perceived their role in relation to funding and gender. All stated that they had a leadership and strategic role and outlined the importance of buying into and owning the problem and the solutions relating to gender. As one said:

> 'I think it's important to be seen as taking ownership of the issue but the question I would ask is the sector taking ownership, does the sector accept that it is a really significant issue [gender equality] that needs to be addressed, or is it a question of what is being done to them, being imposed?'

Another recognised that their organisation 'needed to take a leadership role in this'. The issue of leaders taking control themselves was a recurring theme:

> 'A key role for my organisation is an oversight role, an enabling role, but not doing the 'in the trenches' stuff that you are doing in the institutions'.

One leader pointed out that his organisation did not have a specific brief around funding individual institutions, stating that their focus was on the overall extent of sex and gender research content in applications for funding. He did state, however, that he was very conscious of his role as an influencer of gender equality.

All interviewees believed their role to be developers of policy and to ensure that initiatives were in place as part of their policy in relation to gender. All believed that they had a role in influencing the culture and that changing the organisational culture lay at the heart of ongoing strategic and structural transformation.

One leader said he recognised that these cultural differences might be granular, down to departmental level, as well as at institutional level:

> *'I think there are issues like different cultures within disciplines and depart-ments in institutions where women have been in a minority. There are certain practices that have become part of the culture and disadvantaged women such as meetings in the evenings or early morning'.*

One participant believed that changing the culture might take a long time, saying that:

> *'A lot of the structures, but above all the culture that is in place, is the product of a long time and is not going to be undone with a five year plan'.*

Another also highlighted the role of culture:

> *'We need to ask the question about the culture of higher education and whether male dominated roles are perpetrating what you hope are legacy bad prac-tices, concerned that the culture of higher education isn't what it should be on account of male dominated practice and a nationwide lack of gender balance'.*

The belief that changing culture and attitudes lies at the heart of ongoing strategic and structural transformation was evident in all responses. All four interviewees spoke about their role as influencers, but expressed a view that until institutional leaders identified and rewarded good practice, no real change would be effective. All interviewees reiterated that their organisations had a monitoring and review responsibility to ensure that the recommendations and required actions, identified in key policy documents, were implemented.

A carrot or stick approach?

Leaders of the HEA and the DoES acknowledged that ultimately they had the power to impose funding sanctions for the higher education institutions that do not make progress in gender equality. These two interviewees, who identified their potential to utilise the withholding of funding as a sanction, were asked what specific incentives (carrots) or sanctions (sticks) they had at their disposal. The DoES and HEA identified specific monetary sanctions and the imposition of additional formal monitoring for those HEIs deemed not to be performing well. They also referred to progress on Gender Action Plans by HEIs.

All the interviewees were supportive of the Athena SWAN accreditation requirement and the withholding of funding, with one saying that:

> *'Ultimately it is about outcomes but if you want to play evaluation in a sys-tem you have to be able to tell that system that this is how the outcome will*

be judged. That is why we ended up having an evaluation mechanism like Athena SWAN'.

Another pointed out:

'In terms of realism, it's hard to see how gender could be addressed in the timeframes set but if no timeframes are set no progress will be made so Athena Swan accreditation is an important first step'.

All of the interviewees believed that there is also a need for positive measures, funding rewards as well as imposing sanctions. One stated that if the whole of academia had to be *'dragged kicking and screaming'* to realise gender objectives, on account of the risk that they might lose funding, then real change and commitment might be limited. He did accept, however, that there had to be consequences for those not making progress and that one clear sanction was monetary loss. He went on to say that he recognised that this approach came with challenges. When pressed on whether the approach of the four institutions was mainly carrot or stick, all interviewees identified the need for a mixture of both approaches. The overall response was that they preferred the carrot approach alongside institutional ownership of the gender equality issue at a local level. However, they all stated that they would use the stick approach as necessary.

What funding levers are available?

Interviewees were asked about their ability to use the stick as a lever, in terms of whether it was feasible and possible to withhold funding. One pointed out that one way this could happen was through use of Compact, where targets and actions are reviewed annually by the HEA and an international panel. At this point funding could be withheld from HEIs. Another referenced performance review, pointing out that:

'Performance dialogue is important, in that there can be a number of priorities including gender in these discussions. The role of the Department [DoES] is in saying we want that issue to be front and centre and there to be real reasons for people who clearly are not compliant or who do not understand the need for change'.

He also pointed out that there had to be real consequences for inaction, given the government's stated commitment to gender equality. All interviewees approved the approach advocated by the Report of the Gender Task Force Expert Group (HEA 2018) relating to the withholding of funding. An example given was institutions not achieving Athena SWAN accreditation within the required time. One interviewee stated:

'The funding leverage is very powerful and can help to progress things that might not happen so quickly otherwise'.

Interviewees were also asked if they supported positive action initiatives, specifically funding incentives or reward for good progress. One leader pointed out that his organisation already had a number of positive actions as part of its gender strategy and action plan. These included campaigns to highlight the achievements of women researchers, gender-blind research assessments and a requirement for research proposal assessment panels to be comprised of at least 40 per cent women. Career breaks, due to looking after children and other family members were included when assessing an applicant's record of accomplishment. Another interviewee believed that:

> 'Lobbying for any uplift in research funding has to be cross departmental and cross agency so that the Irish Research Council can expand their programmes as well as Science Foundation Ireland and the Health Research Board'.

They all supported the use of funding as an incentive and stated that many of their organisational processes already implemented this. Most were committed to consistently reviewing their funding practices to ensure fairness and equity. Statistics on the awarding of funding, by gender, are also gathered and reviewed in all organisations. One interviewee stated his support for a positive funding approach, positing the idea of:

> 'rewarding or incentivising those institutions that have shown that they can embrace this agenda, that they are changed and forging ahead'.

Another participant pointed out that, at the time of the interview, the Gender Task Force was looking at rewarding those bodies that had made good progress. He supported this and believed it would be helpful if there were some measures to reward good performance, alongside the sanctions.

Interviewees were asked about quotas and sanctions for not meeting targets, for example, the withholding of funding if an institution did not reach 50:50 senior academic posts within an agreed timeframe. The Report of the Gender Task Force Expert Group (HEA 2016) had referenced quotas for academic promotions, based on a flexible cascade model where the proportion of women and men to be promoted or recruited is based on the proportion of each gender at the grade immediately below. The HEA refers to: 'A minimum of 40 per cent women and 40 per cent men to be full professors at the appropriate pay scales' to be achieved by the end of 2024. One leader pointed out that his organisation had set targets for female membership of assessment panels and individual scholarships for researchers, but it had not used quotas in the awarding of funding. He did state that he wanted:

> 'very much to try and work with the stakeholders such as the HEA, to ensure that the IRC makes a positive contribution to the landscape in this area'.

Another interviewee was interested in the complexities of the system and whether the introduction of quotas would be effective. He pointed out that there had been considerable discussion in the Gender Task Force Expert Group's work on that issue (HEA 2018). In particular, using a cascade model of appointing women to senior posts where they became available, would still take two decades for gender equality to be reached. He did point out that there were actions that were not quotas that could be considered:

> 'There have been examples in other EU foundations, other states, where they have pushed the envelope on the civil service into level roles, for example if two candidates are equivalent, preference can be given to the female candidate under gender equality objectives'.

This begs the question as to why this would not be feasible in Irish academic institutions. Quotas did not appear to be something that any of the four institutional leaders were keen to introduce. Instead, rewards for good practice, which are only minimally in place at present, via funding from the HEA, could be developed. The current performance review system does allow for the withholding of funding but the new system was only partly in place in 2019. None of the interviewees reported any withholding of funding to institutions, to date.

All interviewees restated that without the situation where gender balance was supported, encouraged and led from the top, real change could not happen. They favoured buy-in and a cultural shift as the real and sustainable agent of change. They all had concerns about the length of time it would take to effect change. All four interviewees expressed the view that a robust system of sanctions and rewards, based on real evidence, was needed alongside every opportunity and support being given to individual institutions to change.

Challenges and resistance

Interviewees were asked to outline any challenges that they might face in implementing national policy towards gender equality. More specifically, they were asked to identify structural challenges to implementing change, particularly around contractual issues preventing institutions from meeting their targets. For example, in seeking to increase female representation in senior posts, or institutions not being able to implement the flexible cascade model, would funding be withheld?

All interviewees confirmed that some current practices might be difficult to change quickly, but all felt that this was an area that could be achieved in partnership with the key stakeholders. They were also concerned that external factors, such as changes in political leadership or personnel in key roles, could pose challenges and might lead to slippage on the gender issue. All pointed out that progress made has been under the strong leadership of the current female Minister of State for Higher Education. As one interviewee stated:

> 'It could slip back, the main progress that has been made to now has been at the level of attention it gets'.

He pointed out that unless gender actions are enshrined in policy and monitored then the focus on gender may change in the future saying: *'The challenge is to keep it there as a high priority'*.

All leaders noted that the major issues were inaction, apathy and even hostility from some institutions and their leaders. One said:

> *'I heard one president saying* [that] *many institutions had to be dragged kicking and screaming into this'*.

Getting institutional leaders firmly 'on board' with the equality agenda was defined by one interviewee as producing an action plan and taking real actions and ownership of the issue to initiate change. So the overall message here is that before cultural and attitudinal change happens, behavioural change, led by public body initiatives, must pave the way.

Academia in Ireland has faced a number of funding challenges over the last 20 years. Interviewees were asked if they had any other comments to make on funding and gender equality. One interviewee summed up the main challenge:

> *'It is well recognised that we are right down the league tables in terms of funding of higher education and my question is – what is the impact of that on gender equality?'*

Conclusions

The current policy frameworks for using funding as a sanction-led initiative in the battle for gender equality have been in place since Athena Swan was instigated in 2015. Subsequent reports and policy documents have outlined the expectation placed on higher education to improve its performance in relation to gender equality, particularly in women's representation in research and senior academic posts. Annual performance reviews are, in theory, linked to funding. Mechanisms exist for the withholding of funding where satisfactory progress against targets has not been met. Some positive action initiatives, including SALI, have been introduced in the last year, recognising that without these innovations, gender parity in senior posts will take decades to achieve.

Leaders of the four funding organisations all had a well-founded awareness of, and individual commitment to, gender equality. Their stated preference was for the changing of cultures, the winning of hearts and minds rather than the threat of withholding funding and telling institutions what they must do. Although the use of quotas was not the preferred option, all leaders favoured positive action initiatives, or had already introduced them. The approach in general was that good leadership and commitment from the funding bodies they represented had to be matched by strong leadership in the institutions themselves. All interviewees believe that there is an opportunity to utilise funding as both a sanction and a reward, although no evidence was presented of this happening to date. All recognised that failure to do so would mean another two decades of no real progress and continued dependence on the goodwill and commitment of individual leaders. In 2020, when the first round of HEA performance reviews will take place in Ireland, assessment of progress by individual HEIs, with their Gender Action Plans and progress towards the achievement of Athena SWAN, will be part of the assessment criteria. Using funding as both a sanction and a reward, with support from the CEOs of the State funding bodies, will be critical to this process.

References

DoES (2011) *National strategy for higher education to 2030*, Report of the Strategy Group, Department of Education and Skills, Government Publications Office, Dublin.

DoES (2019) *Empowering through learning: Action plan for education 2019*, Department of Education and Skills, Dublin.

HEA Expert Group (2016) *HEA national review of gender equality in Irish higher education institutions*, Higher Education Authority, Dublin.

HEA Expert Group (2018) *Gender action plan 2018–2020: Accelerating gender equality in Irish higher education institutions*, Higher Education Authority, Dublin.

HEA Expert Group (2019a) *Higher education institutional staff profiles by gender 2019*, Higher Education Authority, Dublin. Available at: https://hea.ie/assets/uploads/2019/07/Higher-Education-Institutional-Staff-Profiles-by-Gender-2019.pdf

HEA Expert Group (2019b) *Senior academic leadership Initiative (SALI) Call for applications—2019 Promoting gender balance at senior academic levels in the higher education sector*. Available at: https://hea.ie/assets/uploads/2019/06/FINAL-Call-document-2019-06-21.pdf

HEA Expert Group (2019c) *Centre of excellence for gender equality*, HEA, Dublin. Available at: https://hea.ie/policy/gender/gender-equality-centre-for-excellence/

HRB (2019) *HRB policy on gender in research funding*, Health Research Board, Dublin. Available at: www.hrb.ie/funding/funding-schemes/before-you-apply/all-grant-policies/hrb-policy-on-gender-in-research-funding/

IADT (2019) *Strategic plan 2019–2023*. Available at: www.iadt.ie/content/files/IADT_Strategic_Plan_WEB_AW.pdf

Irish Research Council (2013) *Gender strategy and action plan 2013–20*, Irish Research Council, Dublin. Available at: http://research.ie/resources/publications/gender-strategy-and-action-plan-2013-2020/

Irish Human Rights and Equality Commission Report (2014). Available at: www.workplacerelations.ie/en/cases/2014/November/DEC-E2014-078.html

SFI (2018) Annu*al report and accounts*, Science Foundation, Ireland. Available at: www.sfi.ie/research-news/publications/annual-reports/sfi-annual-report-2018/

TCD (2014) *Strategic plan 2009–2014*. Available at: www.tcd.ie/strategy/strategic-plan-201419.pdf

UCC (2017) *Strategic plan 2017–2022*. Available at: www.ucd.ie/president/t4media/UCD-Strategy2015-2020.pdf

Chapter 13

What does not happen

Interrogating a tool for building a gender-sensitive university

Liisa Husu

Introduction

Gender equality work in academia is often understood in terms of the enactment of positive actions and policies of making things happen. Gender equality promotion has traditionally focused on achieving gender equality through positive measures, on the one hand, and preventing gender-based discrimination on the other (Fogelberg *et al* 1999). The focus has initially been on women, but since the mid-1990s it has shifted towards changing academic organisations themselves. More recently the emphasis is on the integration of gender into knowledge production (Schiebinger 1999; Caprile *et al* 2012).

Thus, work towards a more gender-sensitive university frequently focuses positively on such issues as scrutinising and changing institutional structures, reviewing recruitment and evaluation systems, clarifying steps in career paths, integrating gender content into educational curricula and introducing gender-sensitive pedagogies, improving gender balance in decision-making, as well as the implementation of anti-discrimination policies. Promoting gender equality in academic careers has often meant implementing various interventions such as career training, capacity building, mentoring and coaching programmes, and structural change interventions that target diverse career obstacles and discriminatory regulations. Meanwhile, academic careers continue to be persistently gendered in Europe and beyond, especially in the professoriate where strong male domination prevails (European Commission 2019). This is despite a significant increase of women in the early phases of academic careers, as well as active gender equality policies adopted in academia in Europe and many parts of the world. Despite these active measures and development of anti-discrimination legislation over several decades to remove gender-related career obstacles, gender inequalities continue to persist in academic careers. The question of why gender equality development is so slow is still valid (Valian 1999).

Moreover, gender equality work is not only about more easily identifiable inequalities, such as the number of women at various levels in the academic hierarchy but also concerns less obvious and less easily addressed processes in academia. How can gender issues and concerns that are subtle and complex be included in discussions on gender inequalities and into gender-awareness training? It is a much more established process to focus on gender statistics, academic structures, procedures concerning career development and improving a more gender-equal representation in leadership positions and decision-making boards. How then to open up the everyday workings of academic cultures for critical discussion and reflection?

This chapter suggests that one approach towards building a more gender-sensitive university is, paradoxically, by interrogating and focusing systematically not only on what happens but on that which *does not happen*. This involves asking what does *not* happen in women's academic careers, interactions and academic work environments more generally and what impact these non-happenings have on aspirations, careers, the working environment and the processes of knowledge production.

Previous research demonstrates how historical gender discrimination and sexism have not vanished from academic settings even when gender discrimination has been legally outlawed and when gender equality is actively promoted. Rather, sexism, as well as racism, are adopting increasingly subtle and more covert forms (Caplan 1993; Husu 2001, 2005, 2013). These constitute the tangible deeds and actions that people experience as harmful, as documented in the testimonies of #MeToo, the UK Everyday Sexism Project (Bates 2016) and the Swedish *#prataomdet* [#talkaboutit]. These also chronicle what does *not* happen. The outcome can be that *nothing happens* in a career phase, academic arena or forum, or that what is supposed to, or should, happen *does not happen*. To make these phenomena visible they are called *non-events*.

It is necessary to clarify here that the use of *non-event* does not refer to its colloquial use, as when attending a party or celebration with great anticipation and finding it to be a let-down. Use of non-events draws from the meaning of events as occurrences or incidents that are happening in the flow of everyday life and also in organised events. In contrast to non-events in the colloquial sense, where the participant is actively disappointed about the event, the non-events discussed here refer to something that is often not initially apparent, or easily perceived by those involved. In this usage, the event, which then becomes a non-event, can either be an actual organised special occasion, like a conference or workshop, where somebody is not invited. It may also refer to a flow of everyday occurrences, for example, not being included in important informal research networks or collaborations which may become apparent very quickly in some cases, but years later in others. This approach can be seen as complementing rather than conflicting with conventional approaches to gender equality. The latter emphasise formal decision-making, policy and practice interventions and *what happens*, or what should happen. This complementary approach foregrounds informal decision-making, everyday interactions in academic contexts that are rarely regulated by policy or explicit practice and *what does not happen*. When it comes to more subtle forms of sexism, the conventional approaches to gender equality promotion and anti-discrimination policies often fall short. Specifically, many forms of subtle sexism, including non-events, easily fall out of sight or are difficult to capture in positive actions and anti-discrimination work.

The remainder of the chapter is structured into three sections. The first section discusses the conceptualisation of the phenomenon of non-event from different perspectives: from the 'creators', 'bystanders' and those affected by them. The second section links non-events to some key earlier theorising. Finally, the non-event approach is offered as an heuristic in furthering the gender-sensitive university.

The phenomenon of non-events

What is meant by non-events? Much of the empirical material used here is from a qualitative study for *Sexism, Support and Survival in Academia* (Husu 2001), conducted in a Finnish context. It was based on semi-structured interviews, as well as several workshops focusing on hidden and subtle forms of discrimination (Husu 2001, 2005) and written accounts by academic women, aged from 29 to 73 years, from 11 universities, at all career stages and from all the main disciplinary fields. It also included a small number of established academics who subsequently left academia. The interviews were conducted mainly in Finnish, transcribed, and analysed thematically. Written accounts captured the experience of gender discrimination. The total number of the informants was 102 (31 interviews; 71 written accounts). The study documented the diverse experiences of discriminatory treatment, acts and episodes that women academics described in interviews and their written accounts. It also drew upon things or actions that had *not* happened to them but they considered relevant or significant in their career development, career aspirations, or for their wellbeing at work. Furthermore, when the informants were asked what or who had supported their academic careers, many started to reflect on the lack of support they had experienced. This can also be seen as a form of non-event. Although this research was published almost 20 years ago, it is worth returning to it. Readers may recognise the subtle processes described and wonder how much it resonates with them, based on experience in their own institutions (Husu 2013). Over the last 20 years, the notion of non-events has been presented and discussed in numerous workshops and seminars, often activating a collective memory on the part of academic women. Through this, many women were able to talk and make narrative sense of earlier, sometimes mystifying, career experiences.

Non-events in academia can take various and sometimes very specific forms: silence, exclusion, being ignored or bypassed, reluctant support, lack of validation, invisibility, not receiving credit or being cited, not being listened to and not being invited along. Women academics *at the receiving end* of such non-events may have liminal consciousness of the process and its existence, barely perceiving what is taking place. They could perceive the non-events only fleetingly when they occur or with hindsight, sometimes many years later, when looking back over their careers. Such non-events are challenging for the women concerned to name, make sense of and respond to. As single events, they can often appear rather insignificant and not worthy of attention, but it is the impact of their accumulation in academia, over many years, that is of interest.

A female professor in natural sciences in her forties remembered several non-events from her career:

> *'Oh, my goodness, if I was a young man, I would be accepted in a quite different way, and I would have been pushed forwards. Some old professor would mentor me, would get me grants, take me to the sauna* [a traditional Finnish site of both leisure and work-related negotiations, especially for men] *and explain to me all the networks and so on . . . but I am outside all that'.*

A postdoctoral researcher in a human science field described how she struggled with making sense of something that, as a student, she had expected to happen but did not happen:

> *'I think I have received just treatment, in official matters, mostly. So, what has been an obstacle has been sort of unofficial. It really was like a revelation to me in adult age, because I am more from an upper class family, always been good in school, among the three best in class, I do not have any visible handicaps, I am quite quick in my speech and have good language skills, so I did not have any kind of social handicaps until adult age. I grew up believing that no one has any reason to presume that I would not be capable of something, because I was rather above the average on all these visible social attributes. But when I came to the university I had a couple of sort of shocks, when I wondered, that what is it . . . what was wrong with me, why couldn't I? And then I realized that oh dear, he* [the professor] *wants a boy. As if he was waiting until a suitable male student came along. And I realised that my credibility at the university is weakened by the fact that I happen to be a woman, and that was something I had never realised earlier, and I never on the whole realised that something could weaken my credibility socially'.*

The same interviewee described the general atmosphere in the department as depressing and distressing and went on to report that she had observed how the success of early career men was lauded while women's success was met by indifference:

> *'What I somehow cannot take is that those who should enjoy my success, are not doing so. So, I have always got unreasonably hurt and severely depressed, when I realise that the head of department is not terribly happy about some of my achievements. It feels that it is not always considered as relevant'.*

If nothing has happened, how can one know or claim to have become a target or experienced a non-event? This is the territory of hypotheticals and counterfactuals.

Women academics in the study could become aware of being potential targets for non-events when comparing their situation with their male peers. A young female scholar, who had not received the support and advice she would have needed to develop her academic career, simultaneously observed how her male peers were willingly advised and supported by their colleagues. A female professor was not invited or welcomed to a social event of the inner circle of her discipline but observed that her male colleagues were. 'Forgetting' or delaying the writing of recommendations, reviews and evaluations was another manifestation of non-events. A young interviewee in the human sciences related how she had asked her supervisor, a male professor, to write a recommendation to support her funding application. Although she had approached him weeks before the submission deadline, she found out, on the very day of the deadline, that he had 'forgotten' to write the recommendation. She also found out that, on the same submission round, the professor had remembered to write recommendations for his male protégés in accordance with the deadline (Husu 2001, 2005).

One persistent non-event practice, contributing to invisibility in the academic arena, is to 'forget' to invite women as keynote or panel speakers for conferences and seminars, unless specifically reminded, usually by female scholars. Ignoring gender perspectives in organising mainstream lecture series, conferences or seminars is another form of professional disrespect. This phenomenon has been recently tackled with humour by the Finnish political scientist, Sara Särmä, who in 2015 initiated the widely acclaimed website *Congrats, you have an all-male panel*. The website pools women's experience from academia and other domains, with photos https://allmalepanels.tumblr.com/ (see also Valian 2013 on all-male panels). This is an example of how social media platforms, established by women, can be used effectively to highlight and question sexism in different arenas.

Another example is the practice of including some women but granting more space and visibility to men. One informant, from a traditionally male-dominated human science discipline, described a research seminar organised by her discipline and university, in co-operation with a non-EU university. The programme was put together by a male professor from that university and the seminar took place in his home country. The informant observed how each female speaker in the seminar was given a half-hour of speaking time, whereas all male speakers where given an hour each. This led to some understandably critical discussion.

When interviewing academic women about the availability and sources of career support, their personal experiences of *not* receiving support were emphasised by several informants. Among these participants were some women who had left academia, some who were in the mid-career and women who were successful in attaining professorial chairs. An interviewee in natural sciences who had been highly motivated for an academic career, but later left for a successful career outside academia recalled:

> '*First when I read some reports on women and science, only then I started to think that really, it really is possible that you could get some support in your*

job from professors and others. And when I thought about it further, it seemed pretty normal that this should be the case. But somehow, all the time I was in the university, it was somehow so out of the question that I really did not have the faintest idea that you could get that kind of support – but only afterwards'.

The lack of professional support from mentors and female role models is significant for female academic career progression (Sonnert and Holton 1995) and can be defined within the non-event framework. A postdoctoral interviewee in her thirties, from a field in the human sciences, with a majority of female students but very few female professors, identified this lack of support as an issue. Asked whether men and women were treated similarly in the university, she said:

'Hmm . . . we all think that we are treated similarly and on paper it can be made to look like that . . . I think the most important thing is . . . sort of . . . if you lack identification objects [role models], *and the few women there are, they do not genuinely promote your development'.*

An interviewee who, in her school years, had dreamed of becoming a scholar had exited, despite two academic degrees with the highest grades, to make a successful career outside academia. Reflecting upon how she was treated whilst working as an assistant professor, she stated:

'I don't know, I have presumably very little experience directly of discrimination, but let's say [what was an obstacle] *that kind of general lack of support, that is lack of all kind of support. So, I got an impression that if I went on there* [at the department], *I would probably be very lonely later'.*

Not only do non-events impede women's early careers, they may also affect women in higher academic posts. Among the interviewees, several senior academic women in full professor or equivalent posts described attempts to subtly exclude them. For example, despite their formal high status, they were side-lined from departmental or organisational decision-making. Some senior academic women reported how their male colleagues did not bother to read or comment on their work; did not discuss with them or tell them about their own work; or their male colleagues rarely initiated collaborative research. In some cases, informants reported how female administrative staff willingly provided clerical assistance to male professors, whereas women professors were expected to handle these tasks themselves (see Chapter 4). These behaviours reported by senior women echoed the results from the MIT study on the status of women faculty, where senior women reported that they felt invisible, excluded from having a voice in their departments and from positions of any real power (MIT 1999).

Non-events also accumulate over time in academic environments so that they construct and shape both the informal and formal division of labour of specific academic settings in more persistent ways. For example, several informants, especially in highly male-dominated disciplines, had experienced a tendency on the part of male academics to try to use their female colleagues as 'agony aunts'. Women were expected to listen to the personal worries of their male colleagues, for example, about their marital or relationship problems, but the same women were then not invited, or made welcome, by their male colleagues to participate in informal professional discussions. More formally, in a study of 'doing gender' in a Finnish political science department, women doctoral students volunteered that they were not offered teaching assignments, considered meritorious for future career development in that male-dominated discipline, whereas their male counterparts were. These women doctoral students were not even aware that they could get such assignments (Kantola 2008). Non-events may appear fleeting, even insignificant, unknown and un-reflected upon, until many years later. Collectively they contribute quietly and invisibly to the background of so-called normal academic life.

Non-events as 'doing gender', homosociability and non-decision-making

Non-events can be seen as one way of 'doing gender' in academic organisations (West and Zimmerman 1987). Doing gender often takes place through overtly gendered actions but may also occur when people in certain key positions do not do certain important things and leave something undone, unacknowledged or excluded. Consciousness of this kind of 'not doing' is often only liminal, vague and difficult to quantify, as is often the case when doing gender (Yancey 2003). These actions contribute to persistent gendering in academic organisations, through gendering of academic careers, academic identities and academic culture and they demonstrate the slow pace of change towards a more the gender-sensitive university.

Non-events can also stem from or be related to non-decision-making processes (Bachrach and Baratz 1963; Lukes 1974). Non-decision-making can contribute or facilitate non-events. For example, sexual harassment before the #MeToo debate was an issue on which managerial avoidance and non-decision-making in academia was rather common even in the Nordic countries. This was evidenced, for example, by the Swedish academic collection of #MeToo testimonies: #akademiupror (see, for example, Salmonsson 2019). One such case, from a large Finnish university, concerned the sexual harassment behaviour of a senior male professor. Senior women scholars brought it to the attention of the highest university leaders. Yet no formal decision on intervention followed and the issue was buried in the vice-chancellor's private correspondence files, not recorded in the university's formal records and no action followed from within the university (Husu 2001, 253–260).

Many non-events are linked to homosocial behaviour of academic men that may appear to them as a normal or 'natural', non-intentional bypassing of or ignoring women. One way of understanding academic women's experiences of relative invisibility, lack of support or encouragement, feelings of exclusion from informal professional networks or communication is to see them as excluded by practices related to male bonding and male homosocial behaviour. Lipman-Blumen defined 'homosocial' as:

> *'seeking, enjoyment and/or preference for the company of the same sex'* and as the basic premise of her homosocial view of sex roles, suggested that *'men are attracted to, stimulated by, and interested in other men'*.
>
> (1976, 16)

The terms homosexual reproduction, homosocial behaviour, (male) homosociability, homosocial desire have all been used to refer to the phenomenon of male bonding in organisations (Hearn 1992; Roper 1996; Hammarén and Johansson 2014; and Chapter 8 of this book). Although homosocial behaviour has been discussed predominantly in organisational and management contexts, it appears to be a highly relevant conceptual framework for understanding the persistence of the gender order in academia. This concerns men's preference for other men in recruitment: universities are mainly led by men and there is continuing heavy male dominance in professorial appointments, as evidenced, for example, by European Commission (2019) *SHE figures 2018* and Chapter 3 of this book. Furthermore, men's preference for men in professional interaction, for example, excluding women from informal discipline or thematic networks or 'forgetting' to invite them, can be understood in homosocial terms.

Non-events also relate to women's relative invisibility or a 'visibility paradox' that women frequently encounter in academia, particularly in male-dominated fields such as engineering (Faulkner 2009; Van den Brink and Stobbe 2009). On the one hand, for male colleagues, women academics may be highly visible as women with male behaviours on a continuum of: women being complimented on their looks and clothes in academic and professional settings, to getting sexist comments or being targets of sexual harassment. On the other hand, academic women may remain relatively invisible to their male colleagues and managers as academic colleagues and peers: another form of non-event.

Non-events as a heuristic concept in gender training and research

From talks or workshops about sexism in academia conducted over two decades in the Nordic region, Europe and beyond, it is noticeable that women academics, from very different fields and different countries, readily grasp the concept of the non-event. It often acts as a trigger to remember, reflect and make sense of many less obvious gendered events in their own careers. Women start to remember and assess various seemingly 'small' unpleasant and ambiguous experiences in a new light. The concept of non-events can help to make sense of something that may have been difficult to pin down, name or articulate clearly but which had a negative, discouraging or damaging impact, both personally and professionally. Similar dynamics can be observed in the #MeToo movement, relating to the experience of sexual harassment and violence.

The concept of non-events can be used as an 'eye-opener' in the provision of gender equality training for management; career training; training for doctoral supervision; research leader training; and in general awareness-raising activities. Episodes of non-events can be developed into vignettes or case studies for use in gender training. Equally, participants' own experience and personal narratives can be used powerfully to 'break silence' about these pervasive acts and processes. Collective memory work is a fruitful way to highlight the issue of non-events in academic careers, through training, education and in research (Haug 1987; Widerberg 1998; Jansson *et al* 2008; Livholts and Tamboukou 2015).

Conclusion

Foregrounding non-events complements and deepens our understanding of the subtle dynamics of gendered academic institutions. Non-events impact on how gendered academic identities, academic careers, gendered academic cultures, gendered academic organisations and gendered knowledge production are constructed in the daily interactions in academic life. This occurs despite the norms, regulations and policies underlining equal treatment and gender equality. Non-events can be observed and understood from different perspectives: individual careers, disciplinary or departmental cultures and institution-wide. Even though many non-events may seem like minor, fleeting or one-off incidents, they are most often part of longer-term patterns and processes. What makes non-events challenging to respond to and deal with is that those who experience them may have only liminal consciousness of their existence. They may even perceive them only in hindsight. Finally, a non-event framework could be applied from an intersectional perspective, drawing, for example, from the dynamics of everyday racism and gendered ageism. Non-events can also be a methodological tool used for analysing and challenging inequalities more generally.

References

Bachrach, P. and Baratz, M. (1963) Decisions and nondecisions: An analytical framework, *American Political Science Review*, 57 (3), 632–642.

Bates, L. (2016) *Everyday sexism: The project that inspired a worldwide movement*, Palgrave Macmillan, London.

Caplan, P. (1993) *Lifting a ton of feathers: A woman's guide for surviving in the academic world*, University of Toronto Press, Toronto.

Caprile, M., Addis, E., Castaño, C., Klinge, I., Larios, M., Meulders, D., Müller, J., O'Dorchao, S., Palasik, M., Plasman, R. and Roivas, S. (2012) *Meta-analysis of gender and science research*, European Union Publications Office, Luxembourg.

European Commission (2019) *SHE figures 2018*, EU Publications Office, Luxembourg.

Faulkner, W. (2009) Doing gender in engineering workplace cultures II: Gender in/authenticity and the in/visibility paradox, *Engineering Studies*, 1 (3), 169–189.

Fogelberg, P., Hearn, J., Husu, L. and Mankkinen, T. (1999) *Hard work in the academy: Research and interventions on gender inequalities in higher education*, Helsinki University Press, Helsinki.

Hammarén, N. and Johansson, T. (2014) Homosociality: In between power and intimacy, *Sage Open*, January–March, 1–11.

Haug, F. (1987) *Female sexualization: A collective work of memory*, Verso, London.

Hearn, J. (1992) *Men in the public eye: The construction and deconstruction of public men and patriarchies*, Routledge, London.

Husu, L. (2001) *Sexism, support and survival in academia: Academic women and hidden discrimination in Finland*, Department of Social Psychology, University of Helsinki, Helsinki.

Husu, L. (2005) Women's work-related and family-related discrimination and support in academia, in M. Texler Segal and V. Demos (eds), *Gender realities: Local and global*, Vol. 9, Emerald Group, Bingley, 161–199.

Husu, L. (2013) Recognize hidden roadblocks, in L. Al-Gazali, V. Valian, B. Barres, L. Wu, E. Andrei, J. Handelsman, C. Moss-Racusin and L. Husu (eds), *Scientists of the world speak up for equality*, Nature, 495 (7439), 35–38.

Jansson, M., Wendt, M. and Åse, C. (2008) Memory work reconsidered, *NORA—Nordic Journal of Feminist and Gender Research*, 16 (4), 228–240.

Kantola, J. (2008) 'Why do all the women disappear?' Gendering processes in a political science department, *Gender, Work and Organization*, 15 (2), 202–225.

Lipman-Blumen, J. (1976) Toward a homosocial theory of sex roles: An explanation of the sex segregation of social institutions, *Signs: Journal of Women in Culture and Society*, 1 (3, Part 2), 15–31.

Livholts, M. and Tamboukou, M. (2015) *Discourse and narrative methods: Theoretical departures, analytical strategies and situated writings*, Sage, London.

Lukes, S. (1974) *Power: A radical view*, Palgrave Macmillan, London and New York.

MIT (Massachusetts Institute of Technology) (1999) *A study on the status of women faculty in science at MIT*, MIT Faculty Newsletter XI: 4, special edition. Available at: http://web.mit.edu/fnl/women/women.html

Roper, M. (1996) 'Seduction and succession': Circuits of homosocial desire in management, in D. Collinson and J. Hearn (eds), *Men as managers, managers as men: Critical perspectives on men, masculinities and managements*, Sage, London, 210–226.

Salmonsson, L. (2019) Is #akademiuppropet a kind of digital counter-public? *European Journal of Women's Studies*, November, doi:10.1177/1350506819885708

Schiebinger, L. (1999) *Has feminism changed science?* Harvard University Press, Cambridge, MA.

Sonnert, G. and Holton, G. (1995) *Who succeeds in science? The gender dimension*, Rutgers University Press, New Brunswick, NJ.

Valian, V. (1999) *Why so slow? The advancement of women*, MIT Press, Cambridge, MA.

Valian, V. (2013) Invite women to talk, in L. Al-Gazali, V. Valian, B. Barres, L. Wu, E. Andrei, J. Handelsman, C. Moss-Racusin and L. Husu (eds), *Scientists of the world speak up for equality*, Nature, 495 (7439), 35–38.

Van den Brink, M. and Stobbe, L. (2009) Doing gender in academic education: The paradox of visibility, *Gender, Work and Organization*, 16 (4), 451–470.

West, C. and Zimmerman, D. (1987) Doing gender, *Gender & Society*, 1 (2), 125–151.

Widerberg, K. (1998) Teaching gender through writing 'experience stories', *Women's Studies International Forum*, 21 (2), 193–198.

Yancey, M. (2003) 'Said and done' versus 'saying and doing': Gendering practices, practicing gender at work, *Gender & Society*, 17 (3), 342–366.

Chapter 14

Towards a gender-sensitive university

Rita Bencivenga and Eileen Drew

Introduction

One question underlies all the chapters of this book: Is the idea of a gender-sensitive university a contradiction in terms? That universities are gendered institutions is not in dispute. Contributors to this book have demonstrated where the main problems lie; what needs to be done; and provided examples of good practice and change processes that would support the alignment of universities with gender sensitivity.

Towards gender sensitivity: Identifying barriers, hurdles and glass ceilings in academia

The diversity of barriers and mechanisms of resistance to change are evident from the succession of studies and reports, policy initiatives and interventions across the EU to promote gender equality and diversity in universities (Chapter 1). The shift towards a greater degree of gender equality has to be viewed against a political climate that exhibits often contradictory phenomena such as the emergence of neoliberal movements and new constructions of patriarchy, designed to limit and counter feminist calls for the engagement of all genders in the promotion of gender equality in academia (Chapter 2).

Work by Nielsen (Chapter 3), shows how the assumption of 'selection on merit' (developed further in Chapter 9) is circumvented by more than unconscious bias on the part of individual selectors and panels in the recruitment process. Recruitment is underpinned by the prevalence of practices that undermine the excellence principle, where expediency, cloaked as rationality and pragmatism, leads to pre-selection in determining the appointment of candidates to academic and research entry posts and professorial chairs. Chapter 3 considers the social and organisational contexts in which gender dynamics play out in recruitment and selection, focusing on the interaction of the decoupling strategies used by decision-makers in recruitment and selection. Nielsen's study shows how cultural and institutional environments shape most hiring decisions in academia, as gender bias systematically assumes the form of homophily and social closure in the networks of academic recruiters.

Further evidence of the distortion of career progression on merit is posited in Chapter 4 by Kinahan, Dunne and Cahill, that illustrates the association of academic success with a male norm. Bias plays a role in assessment procedures involved in academic promotion, leading to a gendered perception of who is worthy of promotion and leadership. Workload allocation also contributes to the gender imbalance, allowing men to concentrate on their research and teaching, while female staff pick up the labour intensive administrative and pastoral work. As Pine testifies, from her personal and professorial experience:

> Women are judged when they are not likeable enough. But being likeable, for all its social desirability, held us back at work. We ended up so busy doing all the pastoral care, and all the boring paperwork, and all the millions of unwanted jobs, that we never seemed to have time to ask for recognition.
>
> (2018, 193)

Chapters 3 and 4 underline the lack of fairness between male and female aspiring academics, in terms of recruitment, promotion, pay, mentorship and uneven workload allocation. They demonstrate that isolated interventions, such as unconscious bias training for recruitment and promotion panels or overhauling HR practices are not enough to overcome the deep-seated and endemic sexist practices that prevail in academia.

Work-life (im)balance is another barrier that working mothers face in academia. The irregular and informal academic work regime can be an important attraction for men and women embarking on an academic career since it appears to offer flexibility and autonomy. However, universities have undergone restructuring and downsizing as a consequence of budgetary cuts, hence working excessive hours has become the norm (Drew and Marshall, Chapter 5). While entrants to academic institutions may have expectations of flexible working, which is perceived as more compatible with becoming a parent or carer and achieving work-life balance, they quickly discover that they are part of 'greedy institutions' in which the career ladder to academic success is based on the capacity of academic 'sprinters'. A number of factors contribute to this: citations and rankings (Chapters 3 and 8); applying for research grants (Chapter 2); gaining visibility and international exposure through the conference circuit (Chapters 8 and 13); being career mobile and what Pine calls 'putting your research out there' (2018, 190). As a result, the academic race can be a very lonely, individualistic and predominantly male activity and one that undervalues even fundamentally human attributes: 'the qualities I generally associate with motherhood—love and support, empathy and nurturing—are not those I associate with being successful at work [as an academic in an Irish university]' (Pine 2018, 193).

The #MeToo movement has served to lift the lid on what had previously been a closet topic of a spectrum of sexist behaviour including sexual harassment and violence. Pine (2018, 184) testifies to 'how often I encounter casual sexism, which for all its superficiality, can be bruising'. Sexual harassment and violence are now recognised as a critical barrier to gender equality in academia, particularly when the university campus presents itself as a physically dangerous setting to women. In Chapter 6, Paoletti, Quintin, Gray-Sadran and Squarcioni present the results of an institution-level initiative to identify the places on one French university campus where women felt unsafe and the actions, leading to remedies, that took place in response.

Towards gender sensitivity: Addressing gender inequality in academia

At a societal level, the pay gap between men and women is another barrier to gender equality in academia. In Chapter 7, Galligan, McMahon and Millar present the contexts of two universities: Trinity College, Dublin (TCD) and Queen's University, Belfast (QUB), prior to gender pay gap reporting, to compare the diverse results of a gender pay audit. The audit results demonstrate the impact of different national policies and sectoral employment conditions. In QUB, market conditions determine that there can be a wide variation between professorial salaries, starting at time of appointment. In TCD, a more structured and centralised approach to pay determination is the norm, allowing much less latitude for wage variance in the Irish higher education system. From the chapter's analysis, pay progression processes hold important lessons for the academic sector throughout Europe.

Obstacles and resistance to fairness in gender relations in academia are not only circumscribed to male and female academics; they also apply to the male category of gender itself. As any critical and intersectional approach would underline, men are not a monolithic group. Contending that gender equality in academia remains silent regarding men and masculinities, in Chapter 8, Hearn draws upon: contemporary critical theorising, research and debates on men and masculinities, as well as of the situation of gendered individuals, men's individual academic identities and men's gendered careers in academia. Hearn demonstrates the variety of masculinities which have been observed in society and that can be used by policymakers, even at institution level, to drive a broader inclusion taking into account gender variations and intersectionality.

Like other private and public sector organisations and in society, unconscious bias is one of the main barriers to equality in academia. By playing a role in recruitment, promotion and funding decisions, it challenges the prevailing meritocratic principles underpinning academia. Gvozdanović and Bailey, in Chapter 9, show that it is important to adopt a comprehensive approach in designing a university-level policy to tackle gender inequalities. While unconscious bias plays an instrumental role in academic procedures that impact decisions and career outcomes, it is important to note that bias is not the only factor at play in those assessment procedures.

Implementing structural change towards gender equality involves several components: allies within and outside the organisation, change agents committed to their vision and strong enough to have a pervasive influence, funding to cover the costs of the process, aligning gender equality with the institution's objectives, being familiar with the relevant contexts internal and external, to drive organisational change. The SAGE Change Management Model promoted by Bailey and Drew (Chapter 10) takes account of this and the fact that academic institutions have different starting points. However, the process is similar, as is the need to deal with potential resistance. Drawing upon the evidence, communicating the need for action through raising awareness of the concepts and highlighting successes, are fundamental to the process of change towards gender equality in academia.

Promoting different concepts of leadership, to counter the challenges to gender equality, is the focus of Chapter 11 (Power). Leadership style is another gendered aspect of academia, influenced by the leader's environment, their situation and/or their relationship with followers. The powerful role of academic leadership in mitigating the effects of unconscious bias is also emphasised in Chapter 9 (Gvozdanović and Bailey) and the SAGE Change Management Model further underlines the need for top-down buy-in on the part of leaders and senior managers. The under-representation of women in senior leadership positions cannot be overstated and is reinforced by Faniko *et al* who suggest that:

> the biggest challenge for diversity management may be to address the reluctance of women at the early stage of their career to value or express their own career commitment. Hence, efforts to enhance the representation of women in managerial positions should take into account the ambition-depressing effects for women of perpetuating a masculine organizational culture, especially at early career stages.
>
> (2016, 911)

This finding supports the views expressed by Kinahan, Dunne and Cahill in Chapter 4 and the message by Husu in Chapter 13, that junior women academics deserve more acknowledgement, recognition and career mentoring to be able to progress as potential academic leaders.

Drawing upon Irish experience, Chapter 12 highlights the importance of using research and university funding as a lever in driving gender equality. Doona shows that the entry of the Athena SWAN Charter, a flagship accreditation scheme, has provided an essential impetus for institutions to address the issue of gender inequality. However, it was the political intervention to link institutional funding and research to the attainment of Athena SWAN that has radically transformed the sector over a short period of time. As Doona shows, all the Irish funding agencies have insisted on institutions producing and implementing Gender Equality Plans making gender equality a strategic goal.

In Chapter 13 Husu sets out the 'invisible', but all too damaging, effects of 'non-events' that are encountered throughout women's careers. In themselves, they may not represent major hurdles but cumulatively, the evidence shows that they contribute to the chilly climate and put a break on women's academic career advancement. This analysis is particularly important in explaining the higher drop-out of women at doctoral and postdoctoral levels throughout the EU (Chapter 1). Apart from the intense personal loss that this represents to the individual researcher or academic it is a major leakage of talent from the EU academic pool and is not sustainable.

The role of GEPs in driving gender sensitivity

A recurrent theme in all the book chapters is that concerted action is necessary to achieve more gender-sensitive academic institutions. Fixing the numbers and fixing the women has made way for fixing the institutions and fixing the knowledge base. The refinement and tailoring of a template for Gender Equality Plans, in the context of each institution, is one example of success and is a key mechanism in propounding this. GEPs depend on contextual and institutional factors along with the assessment of needs. They cover a wide range of thematic areas: leadership and decision-making, organisational culture, work-life balance, recruitment and career progression, gender in research and education practice and harassment and assault. All of these areas are core to redressing gender inequality and opening up educational opportunities for all genders.

Conclusion

Numerous challenges counteract with progress towards gender sensitivity. Prevailing forces that pose obstacles to driving a gender-sensitive university include: the emergence of far-right movements that seek to dismantle the hard-won advances in gender equality; a resurgence of patriarchy in new forms; and neoliberal managerialism that promotes a market-driven climate in which performativity, competitiveness and commodification prevail. Changes supporting the process towards equality and diversity require the increased engagement of men and the shift towards fluidity in fields previously excluded, such as gender, race, ethnicity, gender identity and expression and body ability.

Gender equality and gender-sensitivity are not fixed concepts but depend on context, previous experience, cultural and social traditions. They are affected by many factors, including globalisation, technology and ideologies. Becoming a gender-sensitive university involves a profound transformation by pursuing a multilevel, paradigmatic cultural shift, requiring motivation and resources. This book shows how awareness about gender equality and gender sensitivity are progressing in contemporary academia, while acknowledging the difficulties and obstacles in reaching those goals, drawing upon international and national contexts. The concept of a gender-sensitive university will be constantly evolving in response to progress achieved and the outstanding needs of those working or studying in it. It will be engaged with knowledge acquisition, drawing upon gendered learning and contributing to it. Progress will require re-envisioning academia to reflect a more inclusive conceptualisation of gender and intersectionality.

Countervailing forces, that include globalisation, technological change and neoliberal ideologies, already impinge upon modern academic life, speeding up and intensifying work. These and other international and transnational trends are of growing importance in determining what is valued and who will progress to leadership positions in our institutions. Hence, gender equality constantly produces and reproduces backlash and resistance in ever more diverse forms. Heilman and Okimoto (2007) noted that it is women who face negative consequences, in traditional male domains, whether they act in a gender typical or atypical way, in conforming to, or rejecting, male norms of behaviour (Chapter 4).

As Hearn (in Chapter 8) and Drew and Marshall (in Chapter 5) point out, men, as well as women, may experience unconscious bias when they do not align with the requisites for the dominant work-centric-masculinist model. Gender-sensitive institutions must therefore promote new ways of organising and distributing fairly not only academic work but also responsibilities for family care and leadership. This will require changes in personal and collective behaviours; formal and informal norms, rules and behaviours. Academia will only be truly gender-sensitive if, learning from the past, it can avoid repeating the same mistakes, through the capability and the willingness to foresee and prevent new exclusions and new biases, implicit or otherwise. The future challenge will be to 'fix it forward' in all areas.

At a recent Irish Universities Association event, former Irish Minister of State for Higher Education Mitchell O'Connor (2019) shared a vision that encompasses the underlying message of this book:

> There is enormous potential . . . to partner with European counterparts to expand the horizons of knowledge, enhance collaboration across boundaries and foster cultural understanding and experiences . . . [to] promote common European values and a strengthened European identity by bringing together a new generation of Europeans, who are able to cooperate and work within different European and global cultures, in different languages, and across borders, sectors and academic disciplines. These alliances aim to act as models of good practice to progressively increase the quality, international competitiveness and attractiveness of European higher education.

References

Faniko, K., Ellemers, N. and Derks, B. (2016) Queen bees and alpha males: Are successful women more competitive than successful men? *European Journal of Social Psychology*, 46, 903–913.
Heilman, M. and Okimoto, T. (2007) Why are women penalized for success at male tasks? The implied communality deficit, *Journal of Applied Psychology*, 92 (1), 81–92.
Mitchell O'Connor, M. (2019) Speech at close of IUA Seminar on *Ireland's Place in a new European University System*, 29 January 2019, Dublin. Available at: https://www.education.ie/en/Press-Events/Press-Releases/2019-press-releases/PR19-01-29.html
Pine, E. (2018) *Notes to self*, Penguin, London.

Glossary

AS	Athena SWAN managed by AdvanceHE (UK)
AHSS	Faculty of Arts, Humanities and Social Sciences (TCD, Ireland)
ASSET	Athena Survey of Science, Engineering and Technology (UK)
AURORA	Developing future leaders for higher education
BME	Black and Minority Ethic
BRI	Bibliometric Research Indicator (Denmark)
CEDAW	Commission on the Elimination of Discrimination Against Women (UN)
CEO	Chief Executive Officer
CNRS	Centre national de la recherche scientifique (France)
CSMM	Critical Studies on Men and Masculinities
DIT	Dublin Institute of Technology (Ireland) (now the Technological University Dublin)
DoES	Department of Education and Skills (Ireland)
EDI	Equality Diversity and Inclusion
EGERA	Effective Gender Equality in Research and the Academia (FP7)
EIGE	European Institute for Gender Equality (Lithuania)
EQ-A	Enhancing Quality in the Arts
ERA	European Research Area
ERAC	European Research Area and Innovation Committee
ERC	European Research Council
ESSIMU	Enquête Sexualité, Sécurité et Intéractions en Milieu Universitaire
ETAN	European Technology Assessment Network
EU-28	European Union—28 member states
EU-Horizon 2020	Framework 8 Horizon 2020
EUA	European University Association
Eurofound	European Foundation for the Improvement of Living and Working Conditions

EWORA	European Women Rectors Association
FEMPI	Financial Emergency Measures in the Public Interest (Ireland)
FEMS	Faculty of Engineering, Mathematics and Science (TCD, Ireland)
FESTA	Female Empowerment in Science and Technology Academia (FP7)
FHS	Faculty of Health Sciences
FP6	EU 6th Framework Programme (2002–2006)
FP7	EU 7th Framework Programme (2007–2013)
GAP	Gender Action Plan (Athena SWAN)
GARCIA	Gendering the Academy and Research: Combating Career Instability and Asymmetries (FP7)
GENDER-NET	ERA-NET for promoting gender equality in research institutions and the integration of the gender dimension in research contents (FP7)
GenSET	COST Gender in Science Engineering Technology Project
GEP	Gender Equality Plan
GIA	Gender Impact Assessment
H2020	Horizon 2020 8th Framework Programme (2014–2020)
HEA	Higher Education Authority (Ireland)
HEI	Higher Education Institution
HR	Human Resources
HRB	Health Research Board (Ireland)
HS	Faculty of Health Sciences (TCD, Ireland)
IADT	Institute of Art, Design + Technology Dún Laoghaire (Ireland)
IE	Ireland
IGAR	Integrating Gender Analysis into Research (FP7)
INTEGER	INstitutional Transformation for Effecting Gender Equality in Research (FP7)
IoT	Institute(s) of Technology (Ireland)
IRC	Irish Research Council (Ireland)
IHREC	Irish Human Rights and Equality Commission
ISCTE-IUL	Instituto Universitário De Lisboa, Portugal
IUS	International University of Sarajevo, Bosnia and Herzegovina
KHAS	Kadir Has University, Istanbul (Turkey)
KPIs	Key Performance Indicators
KU Leuven	Katholieke Universiteit Leuven (Belgium)
LEAD	Living Equality and Diversity eLearning Programme (Ireland)
LERU	League of European Research Universities

LGBT*IQ+	Lesbian, Gay, Bisexual, Transgender, Intersex or Questioning
MBA	Master's in Business Administration
MIT	Massachusetts Institute of Technology
NHS	National Health Service (UK)
NPM	New Public Management
OECD	Organisation for Economic Co-operation and Development
PTG	Pessac, Talence and Gradignan campus, Bordeaux (France)
QUB	Queen's University Belfast (UK)
REF	Research Excellence Framework (UK)
RPO	Research Performing Organisation
SAGE	Systemic Action for Gender Equality (H2020)
SALI	Senior Academic Leadership Initiative (Ireland)
SAT	Self-Assessment Team
SciPo	Sciences Po Bordeaux (France)
SFI	Science Foundation Ireland
SSH	Social Sciences and Humanities
STEM	Science, Technology, Engineering and Mathematics
SwafS	Science with and for Society (EU)
SWG GRI	Standing Working Group on Gender in Research and Innovation (EU)
TCD	Trinity College, Dublin (Ireland)
TCGEL	Trinity Centre for Gender Equality and Leadership (TCD, Ireland)
TU Dublin	Technology University Dublin (formerly DIT) (Ireland)
UCC	University College Cork (Ireland)
UK	United Kingdom
UNIBS	Università degli Studi di Brescia (Italy)
UPGEM	Understanding Puzzles in the Gendered European Map
VIRAGE	VIolences et RApports de Genre (France)
WIRDEM	Women In Research Decision-Making
WiSER	Centre for Women in Science and Engineering Research (now TCGEL)
WITS	Women in Technology and Science (Ireland)

Index

Note: *Italicised* page numbers indicate a figure on the corresponding page. Page numbers in **bold** indicate a table on the corresponding page.

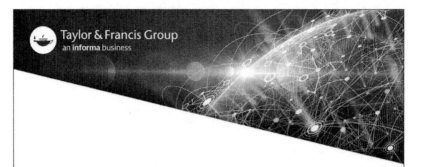

Printed in Great Britain
by Amazon

20910138R00120